THE PEOPLE OF THE SECRET

THE PEOPLE OF THE SECRET

by

Ernest Scott

Introduction by
Colin Wilson

THE OCTAGON PRESS
LONDON

Copyright © 1983 by The Octagon Press Ltd.
All Rights Reserved
No part of this publication may be reproduced or transmitted
in any form or by any means, electronic, mechanical or
photographic, by recording or any information storage or retrieval
system or method now known or to be invented or adapted,
without the prior permission obtained in writing from the publisher
The Octagon Press Limited
14, Baker Street, London W1M 1DA, England,
except by a reviewer quoting brief passages in a
review written for inclusion in a
journal, magazine, newspaper or broadcast.

ISBN 0 86304 027 6

Printed and bound in Great Britain at
The Camelot Press Ltd, Southampton

CONTENTS

	Page
Introduction	1

Chapter

1	The Hidden Tradition	15
2	A Secret Directorate?	39
3	The Inner Alliance: Rome, Christianity and Islam	53
4	The Vehicles: The Jewish Cabbala, the Tarot, Nostradamus	67
5	Love Courts, Troubadours and Round Tables	81
6	Alchemy: The Disguised Path	105
7	What Gold did They Make?	129
8	Gurdjieff and the Inner Circle of Humanity	155
9	Freemasons, Sufis, Initiatory Societies	173
10	Assassins, Kali-Worshippers, Dervishes	192
11	Sufi Discourses, Rituals, Initiation	219
12	Science Fiction and the Ancient Tradition	232
13	The Executive of the People of the Secret	250
Appendix A	Some Important Figures in the Sufi Tradition	254
Appendix B	The Khwajagan	260

INTRODUCTION

Colin Wilson

The notion of an "ancient wisdom", guarded by hidden custodians or Masters, is usually attributed to that remarkable and inventive old lady Madame Blavatsky – perhaps because her disciple Annie Besant wrote a book of that title. And when, more than thirty years after her death, the Theosophical Society decided to publish *The Mahatma Letters*[1] – purportedly written by two of these "Masters" to A. P. Sinnett – most critics seemed to feel that Sinnett must have been singularly gullible to be taken in by them. The modern view of the matter is stated in Richard Cavendish's *Encyclopaedia of the Unexplained*:[2] "Through the Theosophical Society the idea of an occult Master first became popular in the West. It was a glamorous simplification of the tradition common to both East and West from time immemorial, of the searching spirit who asked, 'Master, what shall I do to inherit eternal life?'" In short, the Masters are the product of wishful thinking.

The idea sounds eminently reasonable. What it fails to take into account is that the tradition is far more than a story about a "searching spirit" who wanted to be saved. It is a specific and widely held doctrine that can be traced throughout many centuries and many countries. And modern mythological science is inclined to believe that when a "legend" is as widespread as this – the Flood is another example – then it probably has at least *some* basis in reality.

There can be no doubt, of course, that according to the ordinary laws of common sense, the whole idea is preposterous. Human beings possess the highest intelligence on the surface of this earth; and the highest human beings – certain teachers, priests, philosophers – have exhibited an intelligence that goes

---

[1] *The Mahatma Letters to A. P. Sinnett*, Ed. A. T. Barker, Theosophical Publishing House, London, 1932.

[2] Richard Cavendish, *Encyclopaedia of the Unexplained: Magic, Occultism and Parapsychology*, Routledge, London, 1974.

far beyond that of "the mob" as the average human intelligence is beyond that of a chimpanzee or porpoise. The highest knowledge we possess is to be found in the works and sayings of these philosophers and teachers. A book like Whitehead's *Adventure of Ideas*[3] deals with the impact of these ideas on civilization; and it explains the history of civilization perfectly adequately in terms of ideas. The notion of "hidden masters" seems superfluous. Worse still, it seems indefensible. Anyone can see that we would all *like* to believe in the existence of superhuman intelligences, because it would provide us with a comforting sense of meaning and purpose. We can recognize this element of wishful thinking in a poet like W. B. Yeats. As a young man, he found the real world — of Victorian London — crude and unbearable; so he insisted on the real existence of fairies. He also quotes Shelley's lines about an old Jewish cabalist, hundreds of years old, who lives "in a sea cavern 'mid the Demonesi", and who

> May have attained to sovereignty and science
> Over those strong and secret things and thoughts
> Which others fear and know not . . .,

and admits that he was attracted to the Theosophists because they insisted on the real existence of the old Jew and his like.

Since this is so self-evident, how is it possible to defend the real existence of hidden masters — of the proposition that there exists "in some hidden centre, perhaps in the Highlands of Central Asia . . . a colony of men possessing exceptional powers", and that these men are "the secret government of the world"? For this is, in fact, the central thesis of the present book, and it is argued with an intelligence and persuasiveness that leave no doubt that its author — a lifelong student of the so-called "occult sciences" — is fully aware of all the obvious objections to his thesis. He argues for this secret tradition, not because he thinks it ought to exist, but because he thinks there is convincing evidence that it probably does.

Let me say at once that my own view on the matter is neutral. I found the book absorbing, and its erudition impressive. In my own book *Mysteries*[4] I have argued that alchemy cannot be dismissed as a crude form of chemistry, but needs to be

---

[3] A. N. Whitehead, *Adventure of Ideas*, C.U.P., Cambridge, 1933.
[4] Colin Wilson, *Mysteries*, Hodder and Stoughton, London, 1978.

understood as an attempt to express certain laws of the universe of which modern science is still largely ignorant. But while I am willing to keep an open mind about "the secret tradition", I am by no means wholly convinced that it has been kept alive by a hierarchy of "masters".

Still, even to accept the possibility of such "masters" may seem to place me in the same boat as theosophists, ufologists and various other modern "cults of unreason"; so it is incumbent on me to explain how I can do so while still regarding myself as a basically rational person.

In the Introduction to my book *The Occult*,[5] I discuss the theories of Dr David Foster, the cybernetician who wrote *The Intelligent Universe*.[6] Dr. Foster argues that he cannot wholly accept the Darwinian view of evolution, according to which living creatures are moulded solely by physical circumstances. He uses the simile of one of those plastic wafers that housewives use to programme their washing machines. An acorn, he says, contains a similar "programme" to make it grow into an oak tree. And, as a cybernetician, he finds it difficult to understand how this complex programming came about through "natural selection". In cybernetics, blue light can be used as a programme for red light, because it has higher energy; but red light cannot programme blue light. In the same way, the mind of a watchmaker needs to be more complex than any watch he is asked to repair, just as his fingers must be delicate enough to handle its mechanisms. If his mental powers were cruder than the watch movement, then his intervention would probably wreck it. And nature *is* a thoroughly crude and clumsy watchmaker. A Darwinian will reply: "Quite so; and it *has* wrecked 99 per cent of its watches; but the remaining 1 per cent survives..."

But this fails to explain how the watches came to exist in the first place. David Foster argues that, looking at things as a cybernetician, this suggests to him that there is an equivalent of "blue light" in the universe – some higher form of organization (or intelligence) which stamped its pattern on the acorn and the human gene....

Now this is, admittedly, an extreme view. Bernard Shaw was

[5] Colin Wilson, *The Occult*, Panther Books, London, 1979.
[6] David Blythe Foster, *A Monograph on the Theory of the Intelligent Universe* (the Author), Windlesham, 1964.

also a believer in creative evolution; but he only supposed that some obscure force of life, working on an *unconscious* level, has continued to struggle and wriggle until it has finally achieved its present position in the evolutionary scale. David Foster seems to be arguing that this Shavian life force would hardly be in a better postition than nature itself to create a Swiss watch.

I would suggest a kind of compromise: that there could exist some purposive form of intelligence on an unconscious level, working away in the dark (so to speak), yet with a definite sense of aims to be achieved. I can best illustrate this by citing the example of the *microstomum* worm, which I have discussed in *The Occult*. The *microstomum* seeks out a polyp called *hydra*, not for food, but for the sake of its stinging capsules. When the *hydra* has been digested, the stinging capsules are picked up in the lining of the flatworm's stomach, and passed to another set of cells which carry them to the flatworm's skin, where they are mounted like guns, ready to explode when predators attack. Once the flatworm has acquired enough "bombs", it ignores *hydras*; they are not its favourite food.

Now our own digestive processes are unconscious; but this highly purposive *and* unconscious activity seems to defy explanation in Darwinian terms. In Darwinian theory, nature is in the position of the weather, which can "sculpt" a rock to look like a face; but it is impossible to see how such a "wind" could bring about the complicated goings-on in a flatworm's insides. The same goes for a creature called the flattid bug, whose colonies disguise themselves in the shape of a coral flower – which does not exist in nature. It is preposterous to imagine that some colony once accidentally achieved such a disguise, which enabled it to survive, and that it somehow learned to repeat the trick from generation to generation . . . .

And where does that get us? Well, it suggests some deeper sense of purpose existing in nature, on a level below (or, if you like, above) our "daylight consciousness". And, moreover, that this unconscious purpose is in some ways *more intelligent* (or complex) than our conscious purposes. But then, we might ask, what is human intelligence? Is it not the ability to grasp and drag into the daylight of consciousness the knowledge that exists inside us on an intuitive level? This was the theory of knowledge that Plato expressed in the *Meno*, where Socrates leads a slave to work out a geometrical proposition simply by asking him questions, and then points out that the slave must already have "known" the answer before he became *conscious* that he knew it. So let us suppose that there have always been certain men who have been able to grasp this "unconscious purpose" whose existence I have postulated – that is, who were able to grasp that nature has its own hidden, complex purposes, and is not merely a combination of crude and destructive forces. Would they not make every attempt to preserve their knowledge and to pass it on to future generations? And would not such an attempt take the form of an esoteric school or "invisible college"?

I can see that this argument may strike some readers as plausible rather than convincing. Yet I think that it *will* be found convincing if we can go to the heart of the matter, and grasp that notion of an unconscious yet intelligent and complex purpose. If I look out of my window at the field around our house, I see various natural *forms* – trees, grass, flowers – that seem to grow as simply and automatically as one of those chemical gardens we used to make at school. But if I think of the behaviour of the bombs in the stomach of the *microstomum*, I confront a far more complex purpose. And if this nature around me is seething with such complex purpose, then my senses tell me very little about what is going on. When the mystic Jacob Boehme went out into the field, he felt that he could see into the heart of every tree and plant, and understand its inner purpose. If he had succeeded in turning that insight into words and ideas, then it would have become something very like the secret tradition that the author is discussing in this book.

I have another reason for finding his arguments more than half-convincing. For many years now, I have been fascinated by the teachings of that remarkable man of genius, George Ivanovich Gurdjieff (about whom Ernest Scott has written in the eighth chapter). Gurdjieff's ideas first reached the general public as late as 1949, in a book called *In Search of the Miraculous*,[7] by his one-time disciple Ouspensky. Gurdjieff was always a mystery man, and Ouspensky mentions stories to the effect that Gurdjieff spent many years searching in Central Asia

[7] P. D. Ouspensky, *In Search of the Miraculous*, Routledge, London, 1949.

for a Brotherhood who had preserved certain ancient teachings. In his autobiography *Meetings with Remarkable Men*,[8] Gurdjieff tells how he became obsessed with the idea of "secret teachings" in childhood, when he read about the discovery of certain inscribed tablets on an archaeological site, and realized that they told a story that he had heard from his father. This implied that ancient knowledge *could* be preserved in a fairly unchanged form. Later, according to Gurdjieff, he became a member of a group of "Seekers after Truth", many of whom met their death in attempts to penetrate remote parts of the world where such knowledge might be found.

Now I have always been inclined to regard this part of Gurdjieff's story as deliberate myth-making, like Madame Blavatsky's secret Mahatmas in Tibet. Yet in writing a short book on Gurdjieff – which necessitated reading everything that has so far been published about him – I found myself increasingly willing to believe that Gurdjieff has actually discovered some important sources of "hidden knowledge" in his search. Perhaps the most convincing and impressive of all these books is a recently published volume called *Secret Talks with Mr. G.*, issued anonymously in America.[9] Here Gurdjieff speaks of his search for the principles of "objective magic", and leaves no doubt that he is trying to explain himself as honestly and accurately as possible. There is no hint of leg-pulling. Gurdjieff explains that his interest in magical phenomena (also described in *Meetings with Remarkable Men*) led to the development of "psychic powers" in his early manhood. (It is known that he became a medium and "magician" in his mid-twenties.) He developed remarkable powers of telepathy, hypnosis and psychometry (the ability to "read" the history of objects).[10] In *Secret Talks with Mr. G.*, he describes how he became bored with this kind of "magic", and decided to try to discover the "objective use of his talent". In investigating "objective magic", he became convinced that "all mystical states, trances and mediumistic abilities . . . were no more than

---

[8] G. I. Gurdjieff, *Meetings with Remarkable Men*, Routledge, London, 1963.
[9] *Secret Talks with Mr G.*, Institution for the Development of Harmonious Human Beings Publishers, Nevada, 1968.
[10] He says: "The means for psychometrizing objects [had] appeared in me spontaneously several years earlier."

accidentally-induced hysteria . . ." – i.e., that they were purely subjective. Gurdjieff defined objective magic as the manifestation of laws of a higher cosmos in a lower cosmos (i.e., our own). And he concluded that most human "magic" – telepathy, mediumistic trances, etc. – involved only the laws of our own cosmos.

According to Gurdjieff, the means by which he obtained this knowledge of "objective magic" involved "psychometrizing" sacred objects – shrines, monuments and so on.

At this point, it may be desirable to explain that the word "psychometry" was invented in the 19th century by an American professor, Joseph Rodes Buchanan, who stumbled upon the idea when a bishop told him that he could always distinguish brass by touch, even in the dark, because it caused a bitter taste in his mouth. Buchanan found this to be true, and decided to find out whether his students could distinguish other chemicals by touch alone – wrapping them in thick brown paper. He soon found that many of them *could* accurately identify such chemicals. Then came the most interesting step – the discovery that these "sensitive" students could somehow "pick up" the contents of letters in sealed envelopes, sensing the state of mind of the writer, and whether it was a man or woman. Buchanan's brother-in-law, William Denton, tried his own students with geological specimens, and discovered that they could often describe accurately the history of bones, rocks, meteors and so on. Both Buchanan and Denton became convinced that all human beings possess this faculty, in a more-or-less latent form, and that it would, if developed, enable us to "read" the past history of our earth. Recently, a Soviet scientist, Genady Sergeyev, has announced his development of a machine that can psychometrize objects, picking up various emotions that have been associated with them, in the form of vibrations which can be transformed into electrical impulses. Sergeyev believes he is in process of developing a kind of "time machine". Gurdjieff also seems to have developed a similar power – he speaks, rather obscurely, of mastering skills "such as time and space travel in the sense of visiting through images".

So none of Gurdjieff's claims need be dismissed as inconsistent with science. And his notion of psychometrizing sacred buildings makes sense in the light of Buchanan's discoveries. But what precisely was he hoping to discover?

Rather than attempt to quote Gurdjieff's own words – which are often obscure, and would require commentary – let me try to state his basic insight in my own terminology.

We assume that our senses tell us roughly the truth about "the world". This, says Gurdjieff, is nonsense. Having succeeded in achieving a state of "objective consciousness", Gurdjieff recognized "during these times . . . that these experiences were real, and that the usual reality in which I lived from day to day was false . . . compared to that reality, ordinary reality is a dream". For except in circumstances of emergency or great effort, our senses are lazy; instead of focusing the world, they content themselves with a blurred image, analogous to the way a drunk "sees double". If I spend a long time without making any real effort – if, for example, I watch TV for too long – I seem to lose my sense of reality; life takes on an unreal quality. But if, when I am feeling lazy, I force myself to take a long walk in the wind and rain, some inner muscle tightens, and the world becomes more "real".

Under ordinary circumstances, my senses do not show me reality; on the contrary, they keep it out. Half the things I see are mere symbols – book, tree, motor car; they have as little character as one of those children's drawings of a matchstick man. But when some effort has tightened that "inner muscle", my senses begin to let in meaning. I look at a tree, and it has individuality; it is itself, not just a "tree".

This insight into meaning – of recognizing that meaning exists outside ourselves – is one of the most delightful that human beings can experience. For, oddly enough, we have an innate tendency to doubt it. A child feels that a Christmas party is the most marvellous thing in the world; but when he wakes up groaning and vomiting in the middle of the night, the very thought of trifle and fruit salad disgusts him. And since life holds many such experiences for every human being, we all come to suspect that life is far grimmer and duller than we would like to believe. That is why "beauty is in the eye of the beholder" has become a piece of the conventional wisdom.

Yet when a poet goes out on a spring morning, he is overwhelmed by the recognition that, on the contrary, the world is a far more rich and complex place than most human beings ever realize. The "meaning" rushes in through his senses, bringing a flood of sheer delight. And, if he gives any thought to the matter, he then comes to recognize that there is something seriously wrong with most human beings. We live in a narrow, subjective little world, like a man with a bad cold who cannot smell anything less powerful than an onion. We remain wrapped in our silly, subjective little meanings, and hardly even begin to suspect the vastness and multiplicity of this extraordinary universe in which we find ourselves. It is as if we were *hypnotized*, trapped in a world of dreams.

Now although poets *recognize* this interesting truth about the universe in their "moments of vision", they still fail to act upon it. The "light of common day" returns, and they accept it as inevitable, instead of cursing it for a liar and a swindler. Yet every time the "glimpse of meaning" returns, they recognize that something *can* be done about it. It *is* possible to wake ourselves up. How? First of all, by careful self-observation. So many of our responses are purely mechanical, and if we can learn to recognize these, and even resist them, we can begin that process of self-control which is synonymous with freedom. Second, by galvanizing ourselves to *effort*. We spend most of our time in a drifting, will-less state, like Tennyson's Lotos Eaters, but problems and crises seem to shake the mind awake. Many people unconsciously seek out crisis – drama – because it makes them feel more alive. Gurdjieff taught himself to seek it consciously, as a means of jarring himself into wakefulness. "I had to forgo any limits, emotional, perceptual or knowable, that I had formed in myself, or had accidentally been formed in me by previous experience. I quickly recognized that any objective shock to the system could be used, provided it were safe enough to stop short – in some cases just exactly short – of total disruption of the life force in the body." And the "method" he came to teach depended upon keeping his students in a more-or-less perpetual state of alertness. Sartre said he had never felt so free as when he was in the French Resistance and might be arrested and shot at any moment. Gurdjieff's method was based on a similar recognition: that we could achieve freedom if we could be kept in a permanent state of "crisis".

In short, Gurdjieff started from the recognition that the poet's – or saint's – vision of meaning is *real*, not an illusion. Meaning is "out there"; we have to learn to fling open the senses. The Earth Spirit tells Faust: "The spirit world shuts not its gates/Your heart is closed, your senses sleep." It follows that if we could discover the way of opening the closed gates, we would be able to contemplate meaning directly. As Gurdjieff learned to contemplate it by "psychometrizing" sacred monuments.

Through these experiences, Gurdjieff came to believe that he had grasped certain recurrent "meanings" in the form of laws – in particular the Law of Three and the Law of Seven. (Anyone who wants further information about these is recommended to read Ouspensky's *In Search of the Miraculous*.) He also recognized that "in the world there were forms which were 'Holders of Knowledge' which could be tapped intentionally, if only I knew how to release them. But I also knew that these were not remembered by modern civilizations, and that in order to locate them and read them it was necessary to somehow obtain a map of the ancient world which contained an accurate description and location of the anciently existing monuments and shrines."

In *Meetings with Remarkable Men*, Gurdjieff has described how he came to obtain such a map through an Armenian priest, and how he took it with him to Egypt. But he withholds further details. In *Secret Talks with Mr. G.*, he is more forthcoming:

"I could feel the specific moods of old objects in particular, and it was in this state that I encountered either accidentally or through intervention of higher – I hope higher – forces, an ancient monument. Through this monument which I accidentally tapped by the use of certain active substances in collaboration with a few words of antiquity, I learned the secret of relation of the two great cosmic laws."

For students of mysticism, the interesting thing about Gurdjieff's descriptions of his experiences of higher consciousness is that they are repeatedly confirmed by other mystics. The clearest thing to emerge is that our usual notion that consciousness is essentially *simple* is untrue. There are many forms and levels of consciousness. I will offer only one example – a description of an experience under nitrous oxide, taken from

R. H. Ward's *A Drug-Taker's Notes*.[11] Ward describes how, after inhaling the gas, "I passed ... directly into a state of consciousness already far more complete than the fullest degree of ordinary consciousness, and that I passed progressively upwards ... into finer and finer degrees of this heightened awareness." He noted with surprise that "I was not being made unconscious by the gas I was inhaling, but very much the reverse". After passing through a phase of emotional experience, "compounded of wonder, joy and a wholly peaceful *inevitableness* for which there is no name", Ward describes an intellectual realm, a realm of ideas. He passed through this region too quickly to grasp any of these ideas, but could recollect later the insight that "everything was one thing, that *real knowledge* was simultaneous knowledge of the universe and all it contains, oneself included."

Similarly, Gurdjieff speaks of "toying with the interchangeability of objective and subjective phenomena", and says: "The important point for my realization at that time was not the exact relation of one cosmos to another, but that I perceived directly now that everything in the universe was directly connected, and that moreover, these forms were all connected just because they were all one and the same, repeated to provide an illusion of complexity."

What emerges from the comparison of these two accounts (both too long to quote fully here) is that Gurdjieff and Ward both experienced clearly that consciousness is *not* a physical state – the opposite of sleep or unconsciousness, a mere reflection of the body's awareness – but a *self-sustaining* entity, a universe in itself. Consciousness is *not* a by-product of the body as heat is a by-product of fire. It somehow has its own independent existence.

This is a difficult thing to grasp – like the idea of infinity. But one implication is clear. If consciousness is not a by-product of the body, then its relation to the body must be analogous to the relation between a mirror and the light that falls on it. We could conceive the human race as millions of fragments of a broken mirror. But the light exists in its own right. Which again suggests that our chauvinistic view of ourselves as the only

[11] R. H. Ward, *A Drug-taker's Notes*, Gollancz, London, 1956.

highly conscious form of life in the universe – or at least, the solar system – is fundamentally mistaken. It is not simply a question of whether there are intelligent *beings* on other worlds; they would also be mirror-fragments. What is at issue is what is reflected in the mirror: consciousness, an intelligence far beyond anything we normally experience.

I submit that if we can accept this view of the universe – at least as a logical possibility – then we have accepted the position which is the starting point of this book. From the natural human standpoint, Madame Blavatsky's Mahatmas were probably pure fiction, and it would be sheer gullibility to accept the notion of higher beings, or higher forms of knowledge, without practical evidence. But if Gurdjieff and Ward – and hundreds of other mystics – are telling the truth, then this view is just a kind of parochialism. In fact, you would *logically* expect the universe to be peopled with higher beings, higher forms of intelligence, with meanings to which, in our narrowness, we are blind. You might also expect that, if some of the mystics were more successful than Ward in grasping the precise meanings of the "intellectual realm" of higher consciousness, they would have attempted to express these meanings, either in words or symbols, to be passed on to other explorers of the realms of consciousness. And this again is what Gurdjieff asserts. In *Meetings with Remarkable Men*, for example, he tells of a visit to a monastery in Turkestan, where he saw a peculiar apparatus whose purpose was to teach priestesses the postures of the sacred dances; it consisted of a column standing on a tripod, with seven arms projecting from the column; each arm was jointed in seven places. The dances, says Gurdjieff, expressed the Law of Three and the Law of Seven. Ritual dances based upon these laws became an important part of Gurdjieff's "method".

It is important, then, to recognize that the present book should not be classed with volumes on UFOs, spirit communications or occult phenomena. I am not now dismissing such works out of hand; only pointing out that they progress from the particular to the general, from observations and "sightings" to theories about "the unseen" or unknown. This book starts from a diametrically opposite position. It argues, like David Foster, that mechanical evolution cannot account for life on earth.

There is evidence, it says, that "order" is increasing, and that this suggests intelligent direction or "intervention". One of the most remarkable and sustained attempts to work out a cosmology based upon this assumption is to be found in J. G. Bennett's immense work *The Dramatic Universe*,[12] and this might be regarded as the starting point of our author's argument. Bennett goes, of course, an important step beyond David Foster. David Foster argues only that, to the eye of a cybernetician, evolution seems to suggest some intelligent intervention. Bennett chooses to call these agents of intelligent intervention "demiurges", speaking of them as "the instruments of the universal individuality whereby the evolution of life on earth has been aided and guided within the framework of natural laws". He elsewhere calls them "a class of cosmic essences that is responsible for maintaining the universal order..."

From this foundation, Ernest Scott ventures into fascinating realms of historical speculation. His method is imaginative and undogmatic. He asks, in effect: supposing the "interventionist" theory of history is true, where – in the history of the past two thousand years or so – could we find evidence for its operation? What follows then is an erudite and closely argued excursion into cultural history, with special reference to the Cabbala and to the Sufi tradition. I read the typescript of this book immediately after reading Arnold Toynbee's *War and Civilisation*,[13] and I found that their effect on me was very similar. Toynbee was once described by Professor Trevor-Roper as "a reader of tea-leaves", and it is arguable that the *Study of History*[14] is a magnificent piece of imaginative speculation rather than an essay in historical detection. But, for me, his vision not only excites and stimulates; it brings history to life – as, when I was a child, Conan Doyle's *Lost World*[15] brought pre-history to life. Reading here about King Arthur or the secrets of alchemy or the Freemasons or Assassins, I seldom

---

[12] J. G. Bennett, *The Dramatic Universe*, Vols. I-IV, Hodder and Stoughton, London, 1956–66.

[13] Arnold Toynbee, *War and Civilisation*, Royal Institute of International Affairs, London, 1950.

[14] Arnold Toynbee, *Study of History*, O.U.P., Oxford, 1935–61.

[15] A. Conan Doyle, *Lost World*, John Murray, London, 1979.

bothered to ask "Is this historically true?" I simply enjoyed the bold sweep of his speculation, much as I still enjoy the big dipper at the fair. Yet looking back on it afterwards, I found that there were very few individual points at which I felt inclined to quarrel with his conclusions.

Now, having read it twice, I still do not know whether I am "convinced". I only know that I count it a compelling intellectual adventure, as far above the general run of occult speculative literature as Winwood Reade's *Martyrdom of Man*[16] is above the general run of school history textbooks. If its author had been born a few centuries ago, he would have been burnt for heresy. But his real crime would not have been in expressing heterodox and dangerous ideas, but in expressing them so brilliantly and persuasively.

[16] W. Winwood Reade, *The Martyrdom of Man*, Watts, London, 1932.

Chapter One

THE HIDDEN TRADITION

A comet crosses the sky and it furrows the earth – and men's wits – with the energy of its passing.

Asteroids collide and scatter their substance across the heavens.

On earth, a continent sinks, an island re-emerges from the ocean. A desert becomes a new sea, a fertile land becomes a desert.

Nations, whole races, rise, decline and disappear: leaving only legend to mark their place and their passing.

All accident, all arbitrary thrust and collision of blind forces signifying nothing?

Or all purposeful, intentional, having reason and significance within some present moment vastly greater than we can imagine?

Until very recent times there was little doubt in men's minds about the answer. *Things happened by intent*. The intent might be benign at the level of human life or it might be hostile but at some level, on some scale, it was meaningful.

Even if the intent was implacable, the existence of intent was never doubted. "The Serpent has swallowed the Sun" and "The Lord giveth, the Lord taketh away" are observations separated by millennia but they represent the same unquestioning acceptance that Somebody or Something exerted Will and that by extension, Purpose, high arbiter, governed all.

So it was for untold generations of men.

Then across the space of a few brief centuries a new picture was forced upon us and the basic assumption that had supported man – consciously or instinctively – for perhaps 20,000 years went into the discard.

It so happened that Western science had chosen to investigate natural phenomena from a certain (it now appears arbitrary) standpoint and had discovered that it was possible to isolate the forces that produced phenomena. It discovered also that it was possible to invoke these forces, to duplicate the phenomena and to predict the outcome.

Suddenly there was no place for purpose in the universe. Phenomena in a purposeless vacuum worked perfectly and on the principle of Occam's razor – not to introduce, arbitrarily, elements not necessary to explain what has to be explained – the baby was thrown out, a little gleefully, with the bathwater.

The universe, it now seemed, was a mechanical system of pulls and pushes. There was no freewill because all was determined in advance. There was no contingency. Where mechanical laws were total, there was no place for either.

Given the co-ordinates of one even and sufficient information, all future events would be predictable. The universe would either run down or blow up. We did not yet have enough data to say which, but one or the other.

If enough monkeys danced long enough on enough typewriters, the complete works of Shakespeare would in the end type themselves. It was statistically inevitable.

All observed phenomena, including life, were – now *had* to be – accidental consequences of purposeless forces acting at random without the agency of anything whatever outside the ultimate mechanicalness which was the ground of nature. Life presented no problems either. "Higher" forms would evolve from "lower" forms because mechanisms inherent in earlier situations contained the inevitability of later situations.

Whether our superstitious ancestors liked it or not, this was how the universe was. Intellect had solved the ultimate secret by showing that there was in fact no ultimate secret. Demonstrably, there was no ghost in the machine.

With some reason, this release from previous assumptions was accompanied by euphoria. William of Ockham, of the 14th century, collaborating with the 20th century, had abolished God, and the scientists, brash in their new-found freedom, saw themselves as the founding fathers of a new future for humanity, a new world order: sane, rational, enlightened, unsuperstitious. All the untenable assumptions of the past were error and they had been swept away by what Wells, as late as the 1930s, could call the "brotherhood of efficiency, the Freemasonry of science".

With the hindsight of even three or four decades, this view now seems startlingly ingenuous but nevertheless the generations which produced it deserve praise for their honesty. They were being true to their lights and they had no reason to suspect that quite different lights would presently become uncomfortably visible.

Having concluded that mechanism was all there was, Western science began to notice that, at the extreme micro and macro ends of things, disquieting events could be observed which suggested that somehow mechanism – which undoubtedly existed – also existed side by side with something alarmingly like freewill.

Some experiments had shown that energy was a continuous stream. Others, equally convincing, suggested it was corpuscular and discontinuous.

One experiment suggested that a quantum of energy was concentrated enough to hit an individual atom: another showed that it was so large that it could divide itself between two slots cut in a gross metal plate.

Worse, energy seemed to know in advance whether there was one slot or two and to modify its performance accordingly!

At the other end of the scale of size, Einstein's work – for the layman's understanding at least – seemed to boil down to the discovery that two and two no longer made four – except perhaps in those (negligible) areas of ordinary sensory experience where the difference was unnoticeable.

In 1925 some of the world's top mathematicians had a look at the problems that had piled up in consequence of the work of Bohr, Planck, de Broglie and Einstein. They came to a very strange conclusion. All the anomalies inherent in the new data could be accommodated and handled quite well *if you used only equations*. You could not, under any circumstances, form a picture of what was going on.

Mass, length and time, the basic co-ordinates of a mechanical universe, were simply ineligible as units for dealing with the situation that had now emerged.

Which was intolerable. Things *must* be either here or there, not "maybe here" or "maybe there". Two and two *must* make four. In a universe whose basic laws (as uncovered by Western science) expressly excluded uncertainty, how could there be uncertainty?

In 1927, Heisenberg suggested the principle of Indeterminacy and, from that moment on, the push and pull universe was on a diminishing economy.

After a partial absence of only a few centuries and a more or less total absence of only a few years, the ghost was back in the machine.

It was ironic perhaps that the ghostly suspicion was first conjured into visible appearance in the sanctum of physics, the most materialistic of the sciences, and equally ironic that psychology, the most "idealist" of the sciences, should succeed for much longer in ignoring the ghost in its own machine (ESP and the like) and strive so doggedly to rehabilitate Lord Kelvin.

Here again, Western science to a certain extent was the victim of its own attempts to be honest. The behaviourists were being true to their lights. Human behaviour was demonstrably mechanical and a push on a chemical rod in the human engine produced a psychic effect, as causally and as certainly as the push of an iron rod produced a physical effect in a steam engine.

While physics had been driven screaming into a non-sensory continuum, psychology did not quite see how, even if it wanted to, it could follow suit. Although Jung had perhaps sketched the hazy outline of such a country, its terrain continued to be regarded as in some way preternaturally unscientific.

Like a Pavlov dog, Western science felt itself subjected to intolerably conflicting impulses which it could not resolve in action and predictably, perhaps, it became neurotic.

Could it be that the West's dilemma at all levels was caused by the same recurring mistake – that of artificially limiting the field of inquiry? This seems to be illustrated in at least one unlikely aspect.

In all Western scientific inquiry it had been tacitly assumed that data for the solution of its problems could arise only in the West. This is essentially an unscientific assumption, but one that was made imperiously at all times.

As it now begins to appear, data for resolving the West's scientific impasse *was available in the East* all along but the East's culture and philosophy, both ancient and modern, was consistently assumed to be either puerile or defective – or both.

The knowledge of the East was not tried and found wanting. It was assumed to be inferior and not tried.

The Hidden Tradition

Nor was the evidence of significant data in the East in any way hidden or difficult to come by. Some extremely significant pointers to certain branches of inquiry, *which had already been confirmed in the West*, were lying about inviting attention. Jalaluddin Rumi (13th century) was on record with a theory of the evolution of form, six hundred years before Darwin.[1] Suggestive pointers to very sophisticated psychological processes, like the mechanism of learning, were outlined in the traditions of the Coptic Church and the Suhrawardi Sufis.[2]

It is difficult to avoid noticing that this astigmatism in Western science confirms one of the axioms of the West's most heterodox philosopher Charles Fort.[3] What might with affection be called Fort's Theorem, declares that if you encounter data which lie outside an area which you have defined for yourself as containing the only possible data, you will either fail to see it altogether or else will plausibly discredit it in terms of your own prior assumptions.

In fact in 1927, when Heisenberg was giving form to the cat that had appeared among the pigeons, the solution to the West's scientific impasse was already circulating unobtrusively in Europe and America: an apparently fortuitous accident of Eastern origin. Perhaps aid to under-developed countries works at different levels.

This material did not take the form of a scientific paper and was unfamiliar in texture. It did not therefore have the impact which the West would normally accord to a revolutionary idea. It took the form of a very ancient teaching about the nature of man and few thinkers in the West noticed it at all. Fewer still saw that, behind its unfamiliar appearance, lay a method of reconciling the apparently insoluble conflicts of Western science.

Although this material was probably of universal application, it had one aspect of extreme pertinence for the dilemma of

[1] "Originally you were clay. From being mineral you became vegetable. From vegetable you became animal and from animal man. During these periods man did not know where he was going but he was being taken on a long journey nonetheless and you have to go through a thousand different worlds yet." (Mathnawi III Story XVII)

[2] See 'Tincture Technique', by Richard Drobutt in *New Research on Current Philosophical Systems*, Octagon Press, London, 1968.

[3] Charles Hoy Fort (1874–1932).

Western science in the first third of the 20th century. It implied that freewill and causality were not irreconcilable; both could be accommodated within a framework that possessed *different qualities of time*.

Causality in fact could be the field of operation for will at another level.

The West had been quite right in detecting both; quite wrong in its assumption that they could not exist together.

Remarkably enough, this idea already existed in the West but had taken root in certain unwarranted assumptions of "occultism" and, having no apparent justification, had been passed over.

By contrast, many of the corollaries of this teaching have had almost instinctive currency in huge populations in the East for several millennia.

There it takes the form of a legend that the affairs of humankind, the ebb and flow of history, are subject to purposive direction from a higher level of understanding; the process being manipulated by a hierarchy of intelligences – the lowest level of which makes physical contact with humanity.

This idea, at a simple level of exposition, was presented recently in a book review in a popular newspaper; the writer having apparently summarized material which is now more or less openly available in the West.

The writer said:[4]

> For many centuries there has been a strange legend in the East. It suggests that in some hidden centre, perhaps in the Highlands of Central Asia, there exists a colony of men possessing exceptional powers. This centre acts, in some respects at least, as the secret government of the world.
>
> Some aspects of this legend came to the West during the Crusades; the idea was renewed in Rosicrucian guise in 1614; it was restated with variations last century by Mme Blavatsky and the French diplomat Jacoliot; was suggested again by the English author Talbot Mundy and most recently by the Mongolian traveller Ossendowski in 1918.
>
> In the mysterious Shangri-la of this legend, certain men, evolved beyond the ordinary human situation, act as the regents of powers beyond the planet.

[4] *London Evening News*, February 10, 1969. 'Do these Supermen Exist?'

Through lower echelons – who mingle unsuspected in ordinary walks of life, both East and West – they act at critical stages of history, contriving results necessary to keep the whole evolution of the earth in step with events in the solar system.

If in the West this seems like a very tall tale indeed, it is one nevertheless that has engaged thinkers behind the European scene for centuries. In 1614 for example when a mysterious document called The Fama appeared in Europe, some of the best intellects of the day spent a generation chasing clues to its origin and trying to get itself enlisted. There is no historical record of anybody succeeding.

A hoax? Maybe. But in 1961 an article appeared in a small magazine[5] which to the ordinary reader seemed like a simple travel documentary.

To others who knew – or believed they knew – how such things are arranged, it produced much the same effect as did The Fama on their forebears 350 years ago; though attempts to enlist were not this time quite so disastrously negative. Since 1961, a further stream of hints seemingly connected with the same tradition have been appearing regularly

The writer then lists a number of recent publications,[6] deals with them briefly and goes on to conclude:

The tradition of which all this seems to be a part has been linked with such diverse phenomena as the restoration of culture after Jenghis Khan, Arabian poetry, the Troubadours, the joker in our playing cards, Freemasonry, the Templars, the Renaissance, the Saracen culture of Spain and the Franciscan Order of the Roman Church.

It has also been noted that some of the latest ideas in Freudian and Jungian psychology were outlined by members of this same tradition as long ago as the 11th Century, when there was no Western vocabulary capable of dealing with the ideas.

In view of the extent of the claims which are implicit in some of the literature now appearing in the West, it is remarkable that orthodox scholarship has not yet, apparently, responded with the interest which this material would seem to justify.

---

[5] *Blackwoods Magazine*, December, 1961, 290, pp. 481–595.
[6] *The Sufis* by Idries Shah (W. H. Allen), *The Teachers of Gurdjieff* (Gollancz), *Reflections* (Zenith Books), *Special Problems in the Study of Sufi Ideas* (Octagon Press), *Wisdom of the Idiots* (Octagon Press), *New Research on Current Philosophical Systems* (Octagon Press), and some of the writings of Robert Graves.

If we include the above quotation, our total material so far converges on three distinct, if startling, suggestions:

(1) That in the first quarter of the 20th century, Western science had not only reached a critical stage but an impasse and that, simultaneously, material possibly capable of resolving the situation appeared unobtrusively from the East.
(2) That this "intervention" derives from a source superior to, and qualitatively different from, ordinary intellect.
(3) That similar "intervention" occurs at critical points in human history and has done so in all cultures and all ages in a form appropriate to the moment.

Preposterous as these ideas appear in the context of Western thought, we shall examine them in turn.

There are reasons for believing that between 1920 and 1949 an influence of the kind suggested in (2) above operated in France, England and America. To avoid compromise with the sometimes fragmented language of occultism, we shall refer to the source of this influence simply as the Tradition.

Part of the intention behind the 1920–1950 operation appears to have been to reveal publicly, perhaps for the first time, the *mechanism of the Tradition's own operation*. It might be conjectured that human intellect had for the first time reached the capacity for processing the evolutionary ideas involved and had perhaps earned entitlement to this information.

Among those who were in contact with the Tradition during this period and whose subsequent life work reflected its aims were a London journalist, Rodney Collin, and the mathematician and philosopher, J. G. Bennett.

Rodney Collin wrote two significant books[7] in which he attempted to show that both biology and history functioned in a different kind of time from that experienced in events normally registered by the senses. These books were significant in many respect but perhaps chiefly so in that they suggested that the matters now being handled by Western science could not be dealt with by ordinary "linear" thinking.

This was the conclusion that had already been forced upon the mathematicians of the 1920s but they did not possess the key to

---

[7] *The Theory of Eternal Life*, Stourton Press, Cape Town, 1950, and *The Theory of Celestial Influence*, Vincent Stuart, London, 1954.

the radical solution which Rodney Collin now suggested might exist.

Rodney Collin also attempted an analysis of Western history in which the decisive operations of "schools" of the Tradition were suggested. In this survey, a great deal of Western history took on a startling and vivid new dimension. Events and sequences in history which, to even the most perceptive of historians, had appeared random and meaningless were shown to be purposive in terms of Will acting in a different kind of time. The mechanicalness of events and the automaticity of people were in fact the building material out of which Intelligences immediately above the level of man contrived an intentional structuring of events.

Behind the partial freedom from causality in which these Intelligences worked, there lay a larger aim: that of nurturing and tutoring the life of the earth so that it might remain harmoniously in step with the evolution of the solar system.

Collin attempted to give a progressive, logical development to his exposition – suggesting for example the consequences that might be deduced from the absence of a zero term in a geometrical progression – but in the main the impact of his work was an emotional one and it probably lacked the essential overlap into the orthodox field necessary to attract the attention of ordinary science.

This appeal to science, in terms which it might plausibly regard as its own, had to wait another twelve years for the work of J. G. Bennett.

Bennett had made contact with the Tradition soon after the 1918 Armistice and remained in contact with it until the operation was withdrawn about January 1949.

Bennett believed that the operation of the Tradition at this stage held decisive possibilities for mankind. Science was truly at a crossroads and if it took the wrong turning, or continued on the course it was following, it would inevitably involve into a prolific but sterile technology. He probably saw this in its fullest implications long before the same warning began to circulate from artists, poets and intuitive philosophers like Orwell. Bennett's tremendous work *The Dramatic Universe* was forty years in preparation, the last volume finally appearing in 1966.[8]

[8] *The Dramatic Universe*, Vol. IV, Hodder & Stoughton, London, 1966.

A man's life starts with a fertilized cell and his earliest life is worked in cellular time, perhaps 1,000 times faster than clock time. Multiplication of cells and the functions which unfold from them, are conducted at terrifying speed so that a whole phase of evolution is recapitulated in the foetus in a matter of days.

Compression is at its maximum at the start. Progressively, less and less happens as an organism achieves extension in time. Less and less inner process, that is, happens in each successive interval of clock time. Man, however, chooses to experience in clock and calendar time and it seems to him that time goes increasingly fast. His life accelerates from beginning to end. A period of 24 hours seems an age when we are toddlers; a whole week, a month goes by like a flash when we have grown old.

From this and other indications, it is deduced that to represent biological processes as they are, and not as we happen to experience them – against clocks and calendars – we should have to set out a human life on a logarithmic and not an arithmetical scale.

The period of man's gestation is 10 lunar months. The period of his childhood is 100 lunar months. The full span of his life averages 1,000 lunar months.

If these points, 10:100:1,000 are marked at equal intervals round a circle, we may have some representation of a complete life, together with milestone marks that show the rate at which inner events have occurred or will occur. Various "cosmologies" can be constructed on this scheme which do not concern us here.

The figure is, however, a starting point for obtaining an "organic" picture of history. We shall return to this in a moment.

If the basic proposition is accepted that history obeys the same laws as cellular life, an interesting series of analogies becomes available.

As cells perform different functions in the body of a man, so men perform different functions in the body of a culture.

Masons, engineers and architects maintain and replace the structure of a culture just as their corresponding cells maintain and repair a human body.

There are soldiers and policemen to defend a culture as

there are reserves in the adrenals to defend the human organism. There are scientists and thinkers to direct a culture as there are brain cells to direct a body. There are poets and artists and mystics who form the emotional life of a culture as there are nerve cells to conduct the emotional life of a man.

Analogies can be extended in many ways. For example, a human life may be based on the satisfaction of eating and drinking or on the excitement of movement and travel. It may be ruled by a passion for research or by some deep emotional drive. Similarly, a culture may be ruled by one functional group. Peasant states, merchant states, warrior states and monastic states come to mind.

A man who is balanced in his functions but who is led by a developed intellect is an advanced man. So a culture which is balanced in its functions but is led by a developed intelligentsia is an advanced culture.

The analogy between the body of a man and the body of a culture was glimpsed by the pathologist Virchow more than a century ago. It has since been noticed by many scientists but is generally held to be too fanciful for serious study. There may be reasons to suppose that it is not "fanciful" enough.

A sperm cell originates a new individual. Suppose a conscious man originates a new culture. Suppose that within life there are always a few men, unsuspected and hidden, who are able to process conscious energy and are therefore in touch with the pattern of conscious energy outside life. In J. G. Bennett's terminology this would correspond to the Demiurgic level. Such conscious men would be to a human culture as a sperm cell is to tissue cells in a human body.

A conscious man would inseminate a new culture as a sperm cell fertilizes a new individual. Not all sperm cells originate new men and not all conscious men would originate new cultures. Those that didn't, would nevertheless vivify a culture, as abundant sexual energy tones and vivifies a man.

Here may be glimpsed one aspect of a sexual – even an incestuous – analogy which permeates both myth and epic poetry and is, at surface level, always incomprehensible.

If a civilized culture has such a structure, it should be possible to represent any of its aspects from its cellular equivalent. Its time-scale, for example, would be some extension of the logarithmic scale which appears to apply to human life.

Rodney Collin suggests that the logarithmic terms of human life, 10: 100: 1,000 should be extrapolated into the series 100: 1,000: 10,000 (lunar months) which is roughly 8, 80 and 800 years.

If the analogy holds, eight years will be the period of gestation of a culture; eighty the period of its physical self-expression and 800 years the total of its life. At the end of 800 years it will die.

Some men die before they are 70 or 80. Some live to be over a hundred, but the intervals given by the 10: 100: 1,000 lunar months series will represent the human average and the periods 8, 80 and 800 years will represent the average for cultures.

During the eight years that a culture is in the womb, the Conscious Man who has impregnated it gathers round him a body of material, an inner circle of disciples. A Teaching is worked out. The teaching is the personality of the coming culture, it may take the form of artistic expression, or a new principle of science. Perhaps a book is composed or a code of principles. Some symbol is worked out which will be the signature of the culture till it dies. A culture's character, like a man's character, is formed in the womb and the whole of its life will be an expression of that character and no other.

Eighty years is the period of a culture's physical expression in the outside world, exemplified in the dazzling expansion of invention and creation which is so visible – and so inexplicable – at the beginning of each cultural period.

Perhaps the Dispersal, which J. G. Bennett related to the appearance of the four Root Languages, is the first glimpse we can hope for of this mechanism at work. This example may however be exceptional, since it involved not one but four simultaneous operations. On the other hand it may be less exceptional than it looks if we notice that the 6th century BC, which was the century of Pythagoras and the century when Europe was born, was also the century of Buddha in India and Confucius in China.

It is not without interest that the cyclic nature of culture, the birth, self-expression, decay and death sequence, has been partly deduced by ordinary intellectual means by men like

Toynbee and John Napier, though there may be reasons to suppose that the "inventor" of logarithms was in touch with a contemporary operation of the Tradition.

The analogy between cells and cultures may be extended further. A son does not wait for his father to die before he can be born himself. Similarly the generations of culture overlap. A new culture begins long before its parent dies – and perhaps while its relatives on another continent are still adolescent.

We may also suppose family strains in the body of civilization which is made up of all cultures, taken together. However different the men of Rome may seem to us, we have some sense of kinship with them. We and they are of the same family. We do not have the same feeling of consanguinity with cultures of, say, Africa or China, even when these are more recent than Greece or Rome.

The cell/culture analogy may even yield a method of rediscovering the past where this has left traces too faint to suggest an outline. Suppose cultures take their place in the long-body of humanity in the same sequence as the glandular functions emerge in a man. Also, that these functions lie on the logarithmic scale. The succession should lie therefore on the sequence Pancreas, Thyroid, Parathyroid, Adrenal, Posterior Pituitary and Anterior Pituitary.

Is any trace of such a sequence discernible? Such essence-nature as it may be possible to glimpse in past cultures, Rodney Collin suggests, do not appear to contradict this scheme. The traces of Aurignacian Man are heavy, lymphatic and lunar. Magdalenian Man is swift, decisive and thyroid-Mercurial. The vast stone-work of Egypt, Sumer and Ancient India suggest the poised, solid Parathyroid or Venusian nature. The Graeco-Roman and Persian periods are ages of iron, passionate, adrenal and Martian.

Early European, Medieval and Renaissance cultures till the near-present correspond to Posterior Pituitary function.

Plotted on the logarithmic time-scale it would seem that the six functions so far developed in the "long body" of humanity occupy places lasting 32,000: 16,000: 8,000: 4,000: 2,000 and 1,000 years respectively.

Earlier it was suggested that a culture is begotten by a conscious man. This may happen on the home ground, so to speak, or it may happen in a wholly new situation; just as a man may found a family in a distant land because he senses that the soil has become exhausted or the atmosphere vitiated in his homeland.

Rodney Collin's intuition leads him to pin-point Egypt as the source which sired Europe. The identity of the Individual can probably never be known, but certain key figures, half-legendary, like Solon, Thales and Pythagoras may suggest the "school" within which the birth was accomplished.

Plato's writing suggests that Solon *received something* from Sais in 590 BC and the Timaeus suggests that the Egyptians held Athens in special affection. Was this, Rodney Collin asks, the affection of parent for child?

It is significant that Solon, Thales and Pythagoras have a certain "extended" quality about them. They appear as men having not one skill beyond the human ordinary but a whole range of superlative achievements. Thales was a civil engineer, a politician, a mathematician and an astronomer. He is credited with the theory of a prime-source cosmic substance which was symbolized for external understanding as "water".

Pythagoras revealed a system of medicine (some unsuspected fragments of which appear to be embedded in the work of Cato the Censor[9]), a geometry which stated the laws of three-dimensional space and a musical octave which gave the key to harmony on many levels. He is credited with a theory of soul ascent and descent and also with access to his own reincarnative history. Into a lifetime of 80 or 90 years he packed, said Empedocles, "all things that are contained in ten, even twenty, generations of men".

Insights, two thousand years before their time, were in the very air. Xenophanes of Colophon is saying that the sun and stars have neither substance nor permanence. The stars are burned out at dawn and in the evening are recreated from *new exhalations*.

Arthur Koestler[10] thinks that this is an example of a rational account of the universe beginning to emerge in the only idiom available, that of superstition. Could it not equally be a glimpse

---

[9] *Cato the Censor on Farming*, Trs. Ernest Brehaut, Columbia University Press, New York, 1933.

[10] Arthur Koestler, *The Sleepwalkers*, Hutchinson, London, 1959.

of the modern idea of a re-creating universe? Or, if for "dawn" you wrote "Day of Brahm", an insight into the manvantaric idea?

Koestler makes much play of the fact that the Greek schools were contradictory, that their alleged insights cancelled each other out. "Every philosopher of the period", he says, "seems to have had his own theory regarding the nature of the Universe. To quote Professor Burnett, 'no sooner did an Ionian philosopher learn half a dozen geometrical propositions and hear that the phenomena of the heavens recurred in cycles than he set to work to look for law everywhere in nature and with an audacity amounting to *hybris*, to construct a system in the universe'."[11]

It may be that a very important point is being lost here. Access to a level of consciousness at which the laws of the universe may be *experienced* does not automatically provide the means whereby the knowledge can be verbalized or indeed rendered into "fact" at all. The implication "this is how things are, because I have been there and seen" is at the mercy of the intellectual and emotional instrument through which the translation has to be managed. It is not the divergence of the Greek schools that is remarkable, but the overlap of their insights.

Gestation over, the first-born of modern Europe was delivered into the light and air of Greece.

The picture of its expression, maturity and decline is wonderfully sketched by Rodney Collin.

> Within 80 years, on the shores of Greece and southern Italy, where only tile and timber had stood before, rose the most subtle temples ever built by man. To make possible this tremendous achievement, Pythagoras had already developed the inner laws of harmony and worked out their manifestations for a new architecture and a new music. Anaximander, a pupil of Thales, had invented the basic instruments of a new technology – the gnomon, the clock, the astronomical sphere. Unknown sculptors had woken Egyptian statuary from its age-old immobility and created the figure of the *kouros*, the wide-eyed man of the new age. Vase painters set a symbolic mythology of the relation between man and Gods in every home and the dramatic form of tragedy, created by Thespis,

[11] *The Sleepwalkers*, Chapter 1.

revealed the eternal clash between the wilfulness of man and the higher laws of the Universe. . . .

Yet behind this diversity we sense one informing source, some hidden centre of vitality which is suggested but never revealed by the strange role of the Eleusinian mysteries. . . .

It is interesting to observe the workings of the laws of scale. We saw how the human organism grows according to a definite curve from a single cell to many billions. So for a civilisation. Thus Greek culture, all its potentialities compressed at the beginning of the sixth century into one man and a handful of men, by mid-century had already absorbed some hundreds of the best and most creative individuals and by the end had organized into a new pattern of life thousands of citizens of Athens, Croton, Syracuse and a half-dozen other centres. This growth or incorporation of larger and larger numbers of human cells continued steadily. . . .

At the same time, in exact proportion to this "growth", the intensity of Hellenization diminishes and the last millions drawn into the Greek body politic tend rather to obscure its nature. No doubt they would have accomplished its destruction entirely had it not been for the more conscious men like Socrates, Plato, Aristotle and others who continue to be produced from the centre. . . .

Even so, the time comes when the inner life of the culture is insufficient to hold in check the decay which is always waiting to attack an over-ripe organism. . . .

The conquests fall away and the Greek world, like an old man, begins to shrink and stoop. When it is but four and a half centuries old it falls under the sway of the new Roman civilisation and thereafter lives a servile life teaching or pandering to its young master until, eight hundred years from its founding, the Greek homeland is overrun by Goths and the Hellenic civilisation finally dies as an independent organism.

It would be difficult to imagine a more vivid picture of the life and death of an historical organism seen from the insight of "biological time".

So the Greek cell in the body of human history lived its life, performed its function and died. It was sired from Egypt and its parent was one, perhaps the last, in a previous group whose cycle we do not know. It is possible that Egypt fertilized other ground than the Greek. In the 10th and 11th centuries AD we shall find an Eastern cousin with a remarkable role to play in the family affairs of Europe and we may suspect that its parent, too, was Egypt.

Beginning with Greece, Rodney Collin sees a chain of six cultures till the present. We shall continue to attempt a summary of his map of history.

While Greece was still only two centuries old, she transmitted, via the Epicureans and the Stoics, the energy of fertilization to Rome. Again a period of dazzling achievement seemingly from nowhere. As the signature of Greece was drama, music, philosophy and mathematics, that of Rome was a code of law and an Empire-wide chain of roads and public works.

At its height it served as the matrix for the third European organism – the Early Christian. Here there is open record of a Founder and his school and of a "signature", the New Testament, the sign manual of the whole organism-to-be. Yet astonishing and significant for the future as was this newest cell in the body of mankind, tremendous as was its scope, its external form followed the inevitable laws of birth, development and decline. It reached maturity with Constantine's edict of tolerance and then became subject to the progressive atrophy which no organism actualizing in time may evade. In Rodney Collin's phrase "eight centuries from its conception, the Papacy, its highest temporal expression was an object of commercial haggling on the Roman market".

So died the external form of the Early Christian culture. But long before, while it was still at its height, a new birth was planned.

In 529 Benedict founded Monte Cassino and conducted an operation which though it must certainly have had precedents in the cycles of antiquity has, till the present time, no parallel in Europe.

A conception was arranged but the birth had to be delayed.

If historical organisms have a relationship with the musical octave as well as with the logarithmic scale, and there are reasons to suppose that they do, there will not be a linear progression, a regular increase of frequency in an ascending scale. At two points there will be "intervals". Between Early Christian and Monastic Christendom there will be one such "gap" and the Dark Ages would certainly occupy such a place.

The withdrawal of the four Centres during the last Glaciation suggests a parallel on another scale.

Force had to be conserved till the time was right to leap the gap. Benedict's task was to encapsulate the gains of the past till a new ovum, existing but not yet actualized at the far end of the Dark Ages, was ready to be fertilized.

During the Dark Ages, the monasteries with their monks were self-sufficient (perhaps in the same way as the Centres, with their pilot populations, had to be in the Dark Ages of the Glaciation).

Outside there was disorder among events, confusion among men: processes without design, humanity without direction.

The gap lasted 500 years and the next cultural organism, the Medieval Christian, did not emerge till the 11th century. Its mother was a lonely valley in Burgundy; its father was the influence of Monte Cassino. Assisting at the birth somewhere in the shadows was the Comacine influence from Northern Italy.

The medieval Christian culture was two centuries in labour and in a sense it seems to have emerged from a single building, the Abbey Church of Cluny.

The Abbey was founded in 910 by twelve monks from Monte Cassino and from this peaceful retreat in strife-torn France an extraordinary influence spread. Within a century the Cluniacs had gained control of a thousand square miles of surrounding country and were establishing the rule of law and order where there had been little or none for five centuries. As with a human body whose crisis of illness is reached, infection is dispelled at a rate which seemed impossible only the day before. So with the Cluniac influence. By 1095 a great new building in a strange and wholly unfamiliar style was ready to be consecrated – the Abbey Church of Cluny. In it was encapsulated all the Gothic cathedrals to come. In each of these there was a suggestion of a whole unseen cosmology; each an encyclopaedia in stone, containing, for those who could read, so tradition has it, a summary of the Plan and Purpose of evolution.

Conceived in an ecclesiastical body, the Medieval Christian culture was nevertheless designed for a new and different kind of expression. Though conceived by conscious men who were deeply committed to a religious expression of the Great Work, the Medieval Christian culture depended for its execution on exponents who were not churchmen at all, but craftsmen.

The Hidden Tradition

As the zodiac seems to sweep the solar system with a predestined progression of influences, it might seem that in the 11th century the process of Conscious Direction was almost imperceptibly leaving the sign of religion and edging marginally into some secular modality that lay ahead.

An echo of this bi-valency seems to attach to the anonymous craftsmen who built the cathedrals – as it does to their descendants-in-theory, the modern Freemasons.

In passing, it might be noted that the period reflects another one in a different spiral when Universal Encyclopaedias in stone were also used to focus men's minds: the time of esoteric building in Islam.

As there were other schools beside that of Pythagoras in Greece, there were other neighbour schools to Cluny: Chartres for many studies, Rheims for music, Mont St. Michel for astronomy.

Now occurs an event whose significance seems to have been little considered.

A joint mission from Cluny and Chartres goes to Saracen Spain and is apparently received with fraternal regard. It sends back knowledge: logarithms, algebra, the Koran; perhaps one might guess, a technique of alchemy.

Here, apparently, a focus of intense Christianity is acquiring sustenance from a source which, *at ordinary level*, it could regard only as alien and indeed hostile.

Unless this visit was some extra-ecumenical whim of the Gothic school it suggests the existence of some hidden unity behind appearances. Could it be unity of a hidden Directorate of evolution *which subtends both Christianity AND Islam?* Constantine had an assistant at Cassino – Johannes the Saracen – who helped in translations.[12]

The idea of pilgrimage already existed but it is suddenly expanded by the Cluniacs. Northern Spain is cleared of the Saracens and Cluniac influence builds St. James of Compostela. The pilgrimage circuit now runs from Rome to Canterbury to Compostela. Could this idea have come from Saracen Spain as an instrument for broadening men's minds, for bringing new

---

[12] Constantine the Tunisian had already translated, at Monte Cassino, the Arabian El-Razi's alchemical book, the *Liber Experimentorum* (*Legacy of Islam*, p. 346).

currents into stagnant society? Perhaps the *Haj*, the Mecca pilgrimage, had proved its worth as a cultural instrument and was being used again.

So, on the one hand, the Cluniacs are going to a Moslem school. On the other hand, they are building cathedrals at the expense of Saracen territory.

This strange ambivalence is exemplified further. The Cluniacs greatly approved of the First Crusade. Perhaps at the level of political expediency it had many advantages. It drew off the looters and the freebooters from France and facilitated the Cluniac mission to extend local law and order. But it was directed, however obliquely, *against Islam*. On the one hand, collaboration: on the other, competition.

There is an incongruity here that has no obvious explanation, but if we consider the possibility that *at some level* both impulses are modalities of the same evolutionary directive, the problem disappears.

At the same time, the ways of the Hidden Directorate appear mysterious indeed to human judgment. Could it be that certain evolutionary gains may be obtained only within some environment of friction intentionally created?

Repugnant as this idea may be at the level of individual lives, it is not without support in the esotericism of Jewry.

Professor Norman Cohn has shown beyond any reasonable doubt that the famous *Protocols of the Elders of Zion* were deliberate invention.[13] But nobody seems to have examined the psychological basis on which the central theme of the Protocols could have arisen in the human mind. The suggestion, briefly, is that some hidden impulse at racial level continually arranges for the Jews to initiate such action as will ensure their own persecution *within which some result beneficial to Jewry can arise*.

If man is coaxed – all but coerced – along the optimum line of his own evolution by contrived situations which involve enormous suffering for individual men, the Hidden Directorate would appear to stand accused of a cynicism and despotism which individual men are to some extent already able to transcend. It is a problem which will press increasingly as further data emerges.

---

[13] *Warrant for Genocide*, Eyre and Spottiswoode, London, 1967.

But we must return to Rodney Collin's sequence of cultures. The Medieval Christian culture grew, its pilgrimages and its Crusades bringing cultural diffusion to Europe (as the Dispersal brought diffusion to the root races of the world). At its peak, the Cluniac influence spanned Europe from Portugal to Poland.

It delivered its possibilities, grew old and effete. Its adaptability became frozen. Its creativity became petrified in dogmatism. The Catholicity of the Universal Encyclopaedias became the monstrous tyranny of the Inquisition. The body of the culture lived on for a total of nine hundred years and was finally despatched by the French Revolution. Significantly, the Citizens razed the Abbey of Cluny in an act more symbolic than they knew.

But long before, a new impulse had been born out of the old. Round the Medicis had grown a new Idea, opposed to the dogmatism represented by the Pope and devoted to the best of the past.

The seed-bed this time was neither a philosophical school nor a monk's cell. It was the milieu of an intelligentsia. Cosimo Medici becomes the central magnet to which all that is new is attracted. He founds the first public library in Europe. The best of the past is salvaged from Constantinople. Florence becomes the epicentre of Europe. Everything seems to be in a process of remaking round a "court" of sensitive intellectuals. We see Donatello, Ghiberti, Botticelli, Mirandola and Alberti, each supremely qualified in his own sphere and a strange breed of hyper-specialists like Michelangelo and da Vinci, who are supremely qualified not in any one branch of human capacity but in nearly all. The glimpse is of the *uomo universal*, the *Weltmensch*. Pythagoras and Thales are re-echoed on a new turn of the spiral.

And how far, this time, the waves spread. Out of Florence come Queens, Cambridge, Magdalen, Oxford, Glasgow University, the voyages of Columbus, the conquest of Mexico, modern astronomy, the English Renaissance, the Encyclopaedias and finally, universal education.

The modern world was born into Florence about 1450; its signature: printing, painting and education.

The body of the Renaissance cell lives still. It may not die for another two hundred years. Its influence, even now, is seen as reactionary – as all lives must finally seem to their own offspring.

But though the Renaissance lives on to kindle or restrain in its declining years, it gave birth, just over a century ago, to its own successor, our all too familiar West of the present day. It is a lusty and perhaps wilful infant, this Synthetic Age of ours, and its imprint on the body of history is Electronics.

Its gestation lasted from 1859 (the Origin of Species) till 1865 (the unification of America).

It reached the peak of its development about 1935 with road and air transport and radio and the cinema established as its commonplace modalities. It is now on the path of maturity and gradual decline. Like all organisms it must suffer increasing rigidity, the onset of feebleness and eventual death. It may continue as a physical presence till the 27th century, but long before that, its successor, unseen and unsuspected, will have come to birth. If a culture sires its successor during its maturity, the latest cell in the body of history may even now be in gestation. If and when it is born it will have to make its mark in a world of increasing speed, tension and compression.

If we in the 1980s find the pace of evolution almost too much, we can hardly imagine the pressures which the human cells in the coming body of culture will have to accept as normal.

From Pythagoras to the Pentagon: twelve thousand generations of men, two thousand five hundred calendar years, six cells in the body of Western history.

Each cell overlaps its successor's time, sending influences forward, each successor influencing and being influenced by the presence of its ancestors.

Within each cell, smaller cells of influence, reinforcing the keynote of the whole, subject to the entropy of the whole.

Wave upon interlocking wave of influence, a living body of history.

And within and over all the inescapable signs of Purpose and Intent.

Rodney Collin's tremendous account need not stand or fall on "fact". Interpretation derived even from first-hand insight must inevitably be subject to the distortions of translation from one dimension to another. Even if the pattern is correctly "brought down", certain datum points from which cycles are seen to start may well be arbitrary. A scheme of history such as this must be judged in its wholeness and not by the seeming accuracy of its parts. It must be judged in P. D. Ouspensky's phrase "by the psychological method".

So judged, it must surely be felt to have an overall "rightness" which is invulnerable to a demonstration that this or that aspect must be "wrong".

There we must leave it.

Rodney Collin would certainly have condemned certain of our – unwarranted – intrusions into the broad sweep of his insights. He might not agree at all that the Withdrawal was an "interval" on a larger octave corresponding to the Dark Ages in the small cycle of Europe.

Almost certainly he would reject the suggestion that the Renaissance exhibited a zodiacal swing away from religion and towards a modality of Influence for which we do not even have a name.

Behind such a suggestion there is inevitably an implication: that religion is not *the* instrument of man's evolution, but only one of a number of similar modalities that apply in turn.

Nor would he, probably, agree with the suggestion that the Hidden Executive may achieve evolutionary gains by a process apparently indifferent to human life and suffering. Both suggestions would probably have been anathema to his Catholic beliefs.

We have not, however, introduced such ideas arbitrarily but because they are necessary to explain material which has only recently emerged: material which was certainly not available to Rodney Collin.

Standing on its own, each account presents overwhelming support for a single idea; that the life of man is subject to direction by Forces or Individuals above – but not infinitely above – the level of man himself.

Equally inescapable is the idea that such Direction is implemented at the level of life by human agents: that is, by exceptional men attuned to and partly identified with the level above.

Is the idea so very impossible? At each stage in evolution the universe expands to the human mind. The first limit of his horizon is nature. God is the trees and the seas and the wind. Then his consciousness expands one step and so does his universe. Now the planets represent divinity, and animism, once the good, is now the enemy of the better.

Again his mind opens. The sun is now seen as the Absolute, subtending and controlling the planets: gods serving God.

Later the sun is seen to be only one of many suns in a galaxy of suns and – faster and faster the horizon recedes – the galaxy is only one of innumerable galaxies in a greater whole. This lies at the end of a road where thought cannot reach at all.

At each stage man has to abandon the secure, the trusted, and – for his present moment – the ultimate. At each stage he has to struggle with the denying force of inertia. He has to surmount a mental obstacle as once he had to surmount biological obstacles. If he succeeds, he learns more, understands more, gets closer and closer to participating.

It may be that he is now required to confront – and accept – the mechanism of his own evolution. A new – yet old – concept may confront him: the presence of Men among mankind who are his teachers and his taskmasters on the evolutionary road.

He may now have to meet once again, after 30,000 years, but on a higher turn of the spiral of understanding, the presence of Secret People in his midst.

Who are they? Is it possible to glimpse them, first in the pages of history, then dimly at first, in the daily life of our own times?

Perhaps we may catch such a glimpse.

Chapter Two
A SECRET DIRECTORATE?

Over an immense period of time a process of life has been developed on earth and has culminated in man. The process has been achieved by making available on the planetary scene a succession of energies, each higher in frequency than the one before. Constructive, vital, automatic, sensitive, conscious and creative energies[1] have been "switched in" in turn and have given rise to the entire evolutionary progression from molecule to man.

The action of these energies – seen first in biology and then in history – suggests that each new, higher, frequency is applied while life is still struggling to come to terms with the one before. Here there may be an important pointer.

Man was capable of no more than minimal consciousness when he was confronted with creativity. Each new stage is switched in long before the organism is fully deploying the energy before. Tentatively some sort of general statement might be suggested: Energy X can be fully accommodated only in terms of a struggle to reach $X+1$.

In the natural progression, it can be assumed that at some stage man would have inherited unitive energy – the energy of love. By this is meant objective love and not its precognitive echo in sexual or polar love.

Seen against the progression of energies along the evolutionary process, it may be supposed that unitive energy would lie far in the evolutionary future. Man has not yet accommodated to consciousness, much less to creativity.

Yet it seems that in the appearance of Jesus on earth unitive energy *was* transmitted to man and we have to speculate that this happened before man was ready for it.

Because the fall of man was not in a decisive sense the fault of man, objective justice would require that he should not be obliged to carry more than his own share – probably marginal –

---

[1] J. G. Bennett's terminology.

of the consequences that flowed from it. Some operation of redemption must have been envisaged immediately the fall took place. An action would have to be taken in the planetary future in such a way as to short-circuit a fault in the planetary past.

As this required the removal of something already actualized in time, it could be accomplished only by an agency which was not only outside time but also outside existence. We must also suppose that there were compelling reasons why the operation should be attempted at the earliest possible point. It might be permissible to suppose that the Demiurgic level applied for help.

This call was answered; an Action was projected into mankind; a sacrifice was made; a lifeline was thrown.

It remained, however, for man to grasp the lifeline; and even before that, he had to be made to understand that such a lifeline existed.

Man was only marginally conscious and only a minute spark of the energy of creativity had crystallized in him. Yet he was now being asked to accommodate the second highest energy in the galaxy: the unitive energy of love.

If there is anything in our suggestion that a level of energy becomes incorporated in an organism only in terms of a struggle towards a higher level still, it will be seen that man was now in a doubly difficult situation.

He had been trying (with very little success) to incorporate x (consciousness) in terms of aspiration towards $x+1$ (creativity) *and was now required to include $x+2$ (unitive energy) as well.*

Man's difficulty was all but insuperable: and it may be surmised that the difficulty of the Demiurgic level, and through it the Hidden Directorate, was hardly less so.

The Event had enormous potentiality, but its potentialities could be actualised in full only within a catalytic action successfully performed by the Directorate.

We shall suggest that this catalysis was impeded and partly prevented by contingency at material level.

At that level, the Event was not understood. It was experienced in its entirety at Apostolic level by men and women who had been raised in consciousness by their proximity to the Event. At Pentecost they were raised further to the experience of union with unitive energy. The experience was so transcendent – perhaps obliterative – that they were no longer capable of comprehending the situation of those who had not experienced it: and who did not possess even the minimal basis (consciousness) upon which it could be experienced.

At the other end of the scale, ordinary men and women, using mind and emotion to confront the situation, could understand it only in temporal terms. If a man had faith he was already saved and would presently know it. Something had been done on his behalf and *it had already been done*. Ordinary mind could not grasp that the Promise was not to man in a temporal future but to Mankind in a non-temporal future. "My Kingdom is not of this World" may imply a regression far beyond the mere rejection of materiality.

In the legend of the Three Wise Men from the East there is a hint of the Directorate being involved in the Event from the very first and perhaps arranging the external details. In the early reaction of ordinary men and women and in the way the early church understood, there is more than a hint of the Directorate being baulked – at a moment of time which was absolutely critical – by the intransigence of human nature.

Such a situation is allowed for by the measure of freewill which man has and its consequences may not be annulled by *force majeure* from the Directorate, no matter how much is at stake. All that may perhaps be done is to contrive life situations which will provide increased opportunities for man to choose differently.

Perhaps the minimum basis on which the situation might have made a recovery would have been the acceptance of some idea that the universe consisted of a spectrum of Being. The idea did creep in, both in the concept of angels and in the communion of saints, but both carry a vague aura of apology, as though they were concessions to a superstition inferior to the canon as a whole.

The early church turned scornfully, indignantly, away from such an idea. In doing so, it turned away from one component of its total inheritance.

The four great Impulses of the past had been reduced to their essence and the Jews in their wanderings had made an amalgam of them all.[2] It was in this mixed and fertile soil that

---

[2] An idea developed by J. G. Bennett.

the Christian impulse was to take root. In the event, the early church rejected its birthright; it rejected the wisdom component *within which lay the techniques of developing consciousness.*

Perhaps the attitude of the Early Fathers is understandable. They reasoned that if man had now been given the ultimate energy, he had no longer any use for energies below the ultimate. Traditions concerned with levels below the ultimate were now obsolete, superseded – and by easy extension – anathema.

From the perspective of two thousand years it is clear that such an idea was wholly fallacious. The acquisition of a level of energy does not depose the level below it. On the contrary, the lower energy is made permanent and is incorporated.

The early church would have none of this. It turned away from all hints of a demiurgic tradition – and they were available in abundance from Egyptian, Greek and Jewish sources – and scornfully declared the interval between man and the Absolute to be sterile.

For some time – centuries perhaps – the situation might still have been redeemed and, in the theological teachings of some of the devout but heretical Fathers, one may suspect the attempts that were being made to redeem it.

The bid failed and it is interesting that an account has come down to us of a single afternoon when the matter seems finally to have been decided.

Perhaps the minimum basis on which the wisdom component could have found its legitimate place in Christianity would have been a creed which in some way suggested a spectrum of Being in the universe.

Something of the sort seems to be contained in the ideas of Arius, Presbyter of Alexandria, whose "Arian heresy" implied that the level of the Father was superior to the level of the Son.

In 325, Constantine, to lend Emperor's status to the affairs of his newly approved church, convened the Council of Nicaea.

The Council was doubly important in that it represented for the first time both church and state and its findings were to have the force of law – both spiritual and temporal.

On the ideas of Arius the Council could not agree and a compromise formula which sought to relate the Father and the Son as being "of the same substance" was suggested. To this, all but two Bishops finally agreed. The two dissenting Bishops continued to disagree.

Unanimity was essential if the inspiration of the Holy Spirit was to be claimed for the Council's conclusions. Both unanimity and the approval of deity were matters of personal concern to Constantine and he proceeded to ensure both by the simple expedient of having the two dissenting Bishops removed from the meeting.[3]

Thus the datum point of Christianity for the next 1,500 years seems to have been decided by nothing more than an overt act of political gamesmanship.

By deciding as it did about the nature of the Trinity, the Council of Nicaea removed any possibility that the concept of a hierarchy – and hence of kinetic element in the universe – could arise.

In return, the church secured for itself consistency, totality and exclusiveness. It got them – as other systems have – by excluding one element of the total situation. By virtue of its own definition the Christian church was now impregnable. It possessed all that could be possessed. No expansion of horizon could ever happen, because the ultimate horizon had already been attained.

This, of course, is not to say that Christianity failed, but if men have found within it the impulse to consciousness and hence through love to the unitive level, they may have been obliged to find the technique – in part at least – elsewhere. Even so, this may have happened on a scale which justifies the period of evolutionary time involved. But it is impossible to feel that the total promise of the Event has been fulfilled.

The situation which developed in the early Christian centuries was probably such as to frustrate effectively the Demiurgic catalysis which was both necessary and intended.

Yet Demiurgic responsibility for evolution remained. The Demiurges were still obligated to achieve evolutionary gains, in harmony with growth beyond the earth. Their agents, the Hidden Directorate on earth, were still required to contrive the social environment which would provide the necessary opportunities. The mandate of both is to raise the level of

[3] Condensed from the account in *Eastern Christianity* by Nicholas Zernov, Weidenfeld and Nicolson, London, 1961, p. 43.

consciousness of mankind in general and of suitable individuals exceptionally. Mankind in the West had subconsciously decided that this was no longer necessary.

The pupils believed that a complete textbook of Ultimate Mathematics had been thrown into the classroom. They insisted that it was, therefore, no longer necessary to learn arithmetic. The suggestion that higher mathematics needs a knowledge of arithmetic had no rationale in the Christian West because it had been excluded from the early formulation.

It is not surprising to see that all attempts to reintroduce the lost component and to place man in touch with a genuine technique whereby he might develop true consciousness (as opposed to the walking-dream consciousness which he does possess and which he mistakes for the other) have at all times and places been regarded as a deep and subtle attack on religion itself. This is as true of Islam as it is of Christianity.

For some two centuries after the Council of Nicaea it would seem that Directorate participation was either withdrawn or confined to a sort of holding operation.

Then, about AD 567, Mohammed was born. There seems to be nothing in his early life to suggest that an event of significance had happened, but presently the mark of higher activity begins to attach to circumstances. Mohammed spent periods during his youth with Bedouins in the desert and in conducting caravans from Mecca to Syria, southern Arabia and perhaps to Egypt. Arab religion at the time – "paganism" according to most authorities – was influenced in the north by Christianity and in the south by Jewish tradition. Legends suggest that before Mohammed, a number of individuals had left Arabia to try to find links with "the original religion of Abraham" and it may be that Mohammed made contact with this activity during his travels.

Perhaps a parallel exists here to the journeys from Greece to Egypt which resulted in the school of Pythagoras.

At any rate, some event took place which resulted in Mohammed deciding to retire to Mount Hira near Mecca. There, it would be seen, he made contact directly with a level of higher consciousness.

Soon afterwards he began to teach. His first audience consisted of his own family, his wife Khadija, his friend Abu

Bakr and his cousin Ali. Initial attempts to record Mohammed's teaching which he received in a state of trance were abandoned and his hearers began to memorize for oral transmission the material which he delivered.

The nucleus of a "school" was thus established for which additional human material was waiting on the periphery. After Mohammed's death in 632 a group of some 90 men and women came together and through them the further development of the impulse was realized. Such descriptions of them as exist suggest that they included people who already knew that the possibility of higher consciousness existed and were searching for an Operation through which it could be exemplified.

One such was Salman the Persian, originally a Zoroastrian who had gone from one Christian teacher to another and been passed along through a series of testing trials and tribulations which culminated in his being sold into slavery.

It was this event, apparently disastrous for his search, which in fact brought him to the Companions.

This inner group of 90 took an oath of fidelity and are said to have adopted the name Sufi. Many derivations of this word have been suggested, including that of Suf – meaning wool – from the fact that the group adopted a rough woollen cloak as their garb. Ain Sof, the Cabbala term for the Unknowable, has also been suggested as has Sophos, wisdom. Idries Shah[4] has said that a certain effect on human mentation is associated with a sound which might be written as S-OOOOF and it does not seem that the derivation of the word Sufi need be sought further.

Does this mean that Sufism derives from the school that formed round Mohammed? There are reasons to suppose not. Uways el Qarni, who died in 657, was regarded as a Sufi master but he never met Mohammed.

Five hundred years later another Sufi master, Hakim Jami, implicitly denied the formal Islamic origin of Sufism by declaring that Plato, Hippocrates, Pythagoras and Hermes were on an unbroken line of Sufic transmission.

Within our suggested mechanism of history there is no problem. When Demiurgic levels first incarnated on earth to

[4] Idries Shah, *The Way of the Sufi*, W. H. Allen, London, 1964, p. 16. Arabic documentation of the term, however, begins only after AD 815.

achieve closer control of evolutionary trends, certain ordinary men were initiated by them: that is, ordinary men were given access to a technique whereby their minds could become able to process conscious energy and hence to achieve contact with the Demiurgic intention.

A certain number of such Initiates have been maintained within the ordinary life of men in all places and at all times. Sometimes they are known or suspected. Usually they are quite unknown.

Such men have been given different names in different ages. It is clear that certain of the Old Testament Prophets and the Priest-Initiates of Egypt were of this order. The Sufis are the exemplars of this unbroken Tradition in recent historical times. The term has been adopted within recent years by groups imitating such outward form of Sufi practice as they have been able to discern and the word has to some extent been debased during the 20th century in both East and West.

We are concerned only with the original and generally invisible Tradition and to conclude that Sufism is the esoteric aspect of Islam only is clearly unwarranted on the evidence.

The line, by whatever name it is known, is the line of esotericism in all religions. It is also the line of esotericism in many other modalities of evolution whose existence is generally unsuspected.

There may be reason to suppose, however, that enhanced techniques of "soul-making", relevant to the present stage of mankind's development, were made available by the Demiurgic level, through its Directorate on earth, at the time of Mohammed. Put bluntly, these techniques constitute the trade secrets of Sufism.

The Sufic influence was certainly exercised within the framework of Islam as it has been exercised within the framework of all religions without being identified with any.

We shall see that it was employed within Medieval Christianity in an effort to restore the wisdom component which had been excluded by the formulations of the early Church.

Here it might be permissible to venture a speculation in general terms. So long as a religion develops according to its evolutionary potential, Sufic activity will coincide with its orthodox expression. As a religion becomes formalized in dogma – that is, when it begins to desert its evolutionary possibilities – the Sufic influence separates and is then seen by orthodoxy as a heresy. At a certain stage of divergence, when nothing more can be salvaged, the kinetic component withdraws entirely, at which point the religion becomes subject to the law of diminishing returns and finally extinguishes itself.

There is certainly no indication that the development of Islam was any less free of contingency at material level than Christianity was. It may be that in the matter of contingency Prophets and Messengers are sometimes faced with cruel alternatives. Rejecting all compromise with events as they develop may mean that the Message with which they are charged will be denied actualisation altogether. They may choose to some extent to compromise with contingency and thereby ensure that the Message is actualized at least partially.

Something of the sort has been suggested, in that Mohammed's original insistence on an exclusive monotheism was altered marginally as the price of securing the survival of his Companions and hence of his Message.

Certainly the early promise that a genuine theocracy would arise with spiritual authority subtending a stable structure at all levels was not fulfilled.

To begin with, there was the familiar explosive expansion along almost every line of human activity which we have seen associated with the birth of every new cell in the body of history. Mohammed's successor, Abu Bakr, sent armies into the Sassanian and Byzantine empires and was welcomed as a liberator. Before he was assassinated, Syria, Egypt, Upper Mesopotamia, Armenia, Persia and Cyrenaica had all fallen to the mounting wave of Islam. But, as always, the impulse channelled through a genuine prophet had to be actualised in terms of human instruments congenitally contaminated with pride and jealousy and all the permutations of egoism in human behaviour.

Islam in no way avoided its share of human shortcomings. On the one hand, there was a sublime reverence for man's highest aspirations. There was just law-giving, a surging expression of art and architecture. On the other hand, there was egoism, conflict and hatred in many of those who sought to serve the new ideas.

Umar, the second Caliph, was murdered. Uthman, the third Caliph, and a Meccan aristocrat, aroused widespread opposition by apparently favouring his own family and he, too, died by assassination.

Ali, the fourth Caliph, was Mohammed's cousin and the husband of his daughter Fatima. Ali was opposed by Mu'awiya, a relative of the murdered Uthman. In 661 Ali, too, was murdered and at this point arose the schism within Islam which has never been bridged to this day.

The successors of Ali drew together as a separate sect (the Shi'ites), while the supporters of Mu'awiya and his line of Umayyad caliphs regarded themselves and their Sunnite tradition as the true succession of the Prophet.

At some point in its development, a religion begins to diverge from the impulse from which it derives; a departure which appears to be in the nature of things. It is as though space itself were curved and an unfolding event must actualize in a sequence diverging from the straight line of its own noumenon. At this point a religion elaborates dogma and ritual; it becomes obsessed with the letter and not the spirit of its own inner nature. Its outward expression becomes formalized, rigid and autocratic. We have suggested that this is the point at which the kinetic component appears to separate and is thereafter seen as a newly-arisen heresy.

From the external viewpoint it seems fair to say that the social and political body of Islam was showing advanced entropy within thirty years.

The Umayyad Caliphate, deriving from Mu'awiya, retained temporal control and continued the external expansion of Islam.

Damascus was chosen as the capital, Arabic chosen as the language of Empire. Laws were made, a uniform coinage established and toleration extended to Jews, Christians and Zoroastrians.

As the eighth century opened, a second wave of conquest began in North Africa. The Moslem war machine drove west and finally occupied Morocco. There the Saracen general Tariq is said to have ridden his horse into the breakers, waved his sword aloft and declared "O Allah, in thy name, if there be land beyond this sea, I shall conquer it, bearing witness to thy unity and omnipotence". There was land across the sea as it turned out: Spain, a land so torn by the chaos left by departing Romans and contending Visigoth rulers that it was ripe and ready for invasion.

In 711 Tariq crossed the Straits with an army. The word Gibraltar (Jebel-Tariq, Mount Tariq) marks the event. Within months he was in Córdoba and Moslem armies, Arab, Syrian and Berber, were pouring through Spain and mustering to cross the Pyrenees.

Legend has it that the Saracen captains looked down on the lush lands of France and called out "On, on, to the conquest of the world for Islam". One general is said to have had misgivings: "No. We shall remain in Spain. France is too green and my men would degenerate in that soft land." His misgivings – according to Moslem legend – gave Charles Martel time to gather his forces and the westward flood tide of Islam finally broke on the battlefield of Poitiers in 732.

So the Saracens settled for Spain. Visigoth landowners made terms with the invaders and the cities and monasteries followed suit. Settlement was facilitated by a number of widely contrasting factors. The serfs were still tied to a Roman slave system but could now obtain at least nominal freedom by embracing Islam. There was no lack of fervent converts.

The Jews regarded the occupation as a merciful deliverance from Christian persecution and welcomed the Saracens with open arms. They remained a powerful component of "Moorish Spain" for 700 years.

Yet another, almost a theoretical factor, helped. The Council of Nicaea had declared against Arius but the Arian heresy remained, for the Visigoths, orthodox Christianity. Not surprisingly, the Neo-Platonic ideas in Islam found an answering echo among Spanish Christians.

But there was little of a unified nature about the Moslem conquest of Spain. Within the occupying forces there was conflict and hatred. Arabs denigrated Syrians and both were contemptuous of the Berbers. The latter were so badly treated by their brothers in Islam that generation by generation they drifted back to their African homeland.

Dissension at Spanish colonial level was matched by dissension at the heart of Islam. The Umayyad rulers had

Islamized Persia but the Persian aristocrats had contrived to retain positions of an executive nature, from which, it is said, they hoped to keep alive Zoroastrian ideas.

Finally, in protest against taxation, they rebelled and in 749 defeated the forces of the Caliph and proclaimed the first of a new line of caliphs, the Abbasid, choosing a descendant of Abbas, the uncle of Mohammed. The centre of government was then moved to Mesopotamia where the second caliph of the new line laid the foundations of Baghdad in 763. Here a stable Caliphate was to continue for nearly a century.

Concurrently Córdoba had crystallized as the centre of the Umayyad regime. It was to become a showpiece of Islamic rule. At its peak it contained 700 mosques, three public baths, a Palace with 400 rooms and a city library with 400,000 books.

At this stage it is difficult to resist the temptation to speculate, from a human standpoint, upon the experience of the Hidden Directorate. It must surely have been compounded of a mixture of alarm, disappointment and qualified satisfaction.

The Directorate had vested high hopes in Islam as the vehicle of a major evolutionary gain. It had seen much of the intrinsic promise destroyed by the intransigence of human nature. Yet two stable centres now existed, 3,000 miles apart, serving, at least in name, a spiritual reality.

If we think of Córdoba and Baghdad as magnetic poles we can see that the whole of Europe lay in the field which they subtended. Within this field much might yet be achieved. Within it, a required, a fore-ordered, rise in the specific gravity of human nature could still be contrived. Humanitarianism, science, art and a technique of man's individual as well as corporate evolution might be induced.

A wholly new basis of human life was called for, utterly beyond the wildest imagination of the men of AD 1000. Step by step, trend by trend, man and his institutions would be impelled or restrained along a predestined road. Over and over again man would step aside and be guided back; or would step off the road and be halted and impelled to retrace.

Institutions once regarded as fundamental verities of human experience would melt away. Monarchy would yield to the social management of man by himself. The concept of nation would change to the concept of continent, and from continent to the conception of the entire world as one.

Man would be offered a glimpse of an expanding universe and his mind, which measured in leagues, would strain to measure in light-years.

Within the millennium which lay ahead of the year 1,000, the specific gravity of human soul-stuff would be required to rise *by an amount greater than had been achieved in all the eras that had gone before.*

Within the force-field that was moulding him, man would understand little and co-operate hardly at all. From the viewpoint of his own present moment in any of the unfolding centuries, he would see only change without pattern; quixotic ebb and flow; disruption, chaos, order restored and chaos once again. Sacred standards would be cast down and strange, seemingly arbitrary, new standards created.

From the present moment of a lifetime of seventy years, all would seem the whim of chance and accident, all without purpose or meaning.

Yet from the present moment of Intelligence able to contain the whole history of mankind as a single perception, all would be true end-gaining, deliberate, law-conforming and almost – but never quite – inevitable.

If not quite inevitable then certainly necessary; for a great event lay ahead in man's temporal future. It existed already in eternity and was required to be actualized in time.

The event is a mutation in man's evolutionary nature involving a new modality of experience, a new organ of perception. Though latent, perhaps, since man emerged from his primate ancestry, it is an organ of experience that has only intermittently been active in certain exceptional individuals. Man is due to inherit it one day as part of his total experience.

For this event man had to be prepared. Certain promising races of pre-men were inexplicably extinguished and it has been conjectured that this happened because they were unable to come to terms with intellect – for them an incomprehensible and unmanageable experience.

By analogy, a function giving access to a four-dimensional world might be equally disastrous to intellect-based Modern Man. A certain minimum standard of soul, a certain minimum psychic specific gravity is necessary before such a radical new modality may be risked.

Preparation for this – in our view – was begun as a deliberate operation of Higher Intelligence 1,000 years ago.

The first steps involved a certain social tolerance, a certain expansion of intellect, a certain instinctive humanitarianism. These had to be established before the first tentative switching on of the new organ could be regarded as viable.

How mankind was prepared within the ferment of the last thousand years, we shall hope to glimpse in succeeding chapters.

Once we have the key we shall see that the ebb and flow of history itself illustrates the goals that were required to be gained. Here and there it may be possible to see the agents of the process at work – the Secret People serving, perhaps members of, the Hidden Directorate.

But for the most part, their presence, like their purpose, will be obscured from the view of the men and women among whom they walked.

Chapter Three

THE INNER ALLIANCE: ROME, CHRISTIANITY AND ISLAM

Before we look at the impulses which radiated from three points in the Moslem world and led to the awakening of Europe, it will be useful to look briefly at the state of European knowledge as the Moslem conquest was developing.

The Roman Empire in the West had officially come to an end in 476 when Romulus Augustulus was deposed, but for a century before this, Rome had been a capital in name only. Shortly before the Council of Nicaea in 325, Constantine had moved his seat to the Greek city of Byzantium, taking many of the treasures of Rome with him. Even at that time Rome was only a shadow of its former glory: Athens already housed the chief schools of philosophy, Beirut the schools of law. Science was studied in Egypt and Syria, Alexandria had the great library.

Though the official language of the Empire was Latin, the cultural language was Greek and it was Greek, not Latin, that became the official language of the new Byzantine Empire. Thus knowledge resided in Greek, a language which almost nobody in Western Europe could speak. Only the monks preserved Greek and only the monasteries had, therefore, the key to pre-Christian learning.

But the monasteries were almost invariably sited in inaccessible spots remote from the battlefields and remote, therefore, from contacts which might have served to inject a revival of learning into the stream of ordinary life. Helping further to keep Europe at the level of warring tribes was the Church's deep suspicion about almost everything that derived from the pre-Christian past.

There seems to have been one exception to this – the Celtic Church. The spread of Christianity throughout the Roman Empire had thrown a few isolated Christians among the Druidic Celts of Ireland and it was to extend this nucleus that the Church sent Palladius to Ireland in 431. Though he built several churches, his mission largely failed and the conversion of Ireland had to wait for St. Patrick.

Patrick was a Romano-Briton who had been sold into slavery in Ireland. He escaped to Gaul, crossed the Channel to England and returned home. Later, as he rose in the church hierarchy, his knowledge of Ireland and the Irish language made him an obvious choice for a missionary effort to succeed Palladius.

Patrick was well received, and Celtic Christianity was probably born at the meeting between Patrick and King Logaire at Tara. The Irish reacted to the impulse of Christianity as no other nation did. They reverenced religion but they loved life. They also respected learning. They already possessed a wisdom tradition from their own Eastern ancestry and it had been carefully preserved in their initiate system. Their *ollamhs*, or bards, were also healers, whose methods and training are astonishingly paralleled by Sufic methods in use at the present time.[1]

When the Irish accepted Christianity they did so on their own terms – which was to deny any conflict between the love of learning and the love of God. They must, one feels, have been a sore trial to Patrick.

In the work of Rodney Collin we saw that a new cell may be born into the body of human history by the action of a conscious man – or men – on a carefully selected site. We also saw that a cell of history in decline may be reborn from a "shock" administered from outside the line of its own actualization. In the conversion of the Irish we may suspect the rebirth of Celtic culture by a "shock" from Christianity.

Once again there was a period of incubation, then an explosive expansion ... By the 6th century, Irish learning was famous and scholars were being drawn to Ireland from the fringes of Europe. Mostly they came by the old trade route from the Loire to Cork, but some came through Britain and across the Irish Sea to Bangor. Some indication of the extent of the traffic may be gathered from the fact that in 550, an entire ship was chartered to bring scholars from Gaul to Cork.

[1] Robert Graves, in his introduction to *The Sufis*, by Idries Shah, W. H. Allen, London, 1964.

Officially, Celtic Christianity had no independent existence, but its spirit and its methods were wholly different from those of Rome. It saw no reason to reject a heritage from the past, whereas Rome could find little good to say of anything that preceded Jesus.

The Irish Church preserved pagan literature because it valued knowledge. It read pagan poetry side by side with the Christian Gospels. When it copied the Gospels, its monks were inspired by more than devotion and skill or even love of the message they were transcribing. In the Book of Kells, from a monastery in Ireland, and in the Lindisfarne Gospels, from a monastery off the Northumbrian coast, there seems to be illumination at more than manuscript level. The work suggests inner illumination – both light and joy.

The Celtic Church acted as a magnet to minds that sensed something defective in the official presentation of Christianity and the magnet caused a two-way flux from Europe to Ireland and from Ireland back to Europe.

With St. Columba (521–597) and his pupil Columbanus, the missionary stream outwards began. Columba established Iona in the Western Isles of Scotland as a place whose energies are so palpable even today that they impress Roman Catholics, atheists and drop-outs alike with a sense of the sublime.

Columbanus founded more than one hundred monasteries on the continent of Europe, an immense achievement which, for some reason, seems little noticed by either Rome or secular history.

His foundations included Luxeuil, Bobbio, St. Gall, St. Bertin, Kumieges, St. Riquier and Remiremont – monasteries that reflected piety and wisdom in combination.

Rome can hardly have been unaware of events – and the possible danger of a spread of learning not altogether under its control. Perhaps in the mission of Augustine to Britain in 597 there may have been a secondary briefing.

When he met Celtic church leaders from Wales, Augustine invited them to co-operate in converting the Anglo-Saxons *under the auspices of Rome*. The Celts refused, and the conflict of essential natures which manifested openly at this time was never resolved.

It may be that from its own initiate tradition, the Celtic Church knew the significance of certain dates and held them as a matter of conscience and not of convenience. Rome insisted on her version and at the Synod of Whitby in 664 imposed Roman orthodoxy on the Celtic Church. The independence of the Celtic Church, and perhaps the contribution it might have made to a future wholly different from the one we know, was terminated.

A glimpse of the Celtic Church's activity – and perhaps its methods – a century later, may be gleaned from the writing of a monk of St. Gall. He tells how two graduates of the Irish schools accompanied merchants on a trading mission to France. Mingling with the merchants at a fair, they stood calling their wares like other traders. But what they called out was "We have wisdom to sell." "For," says the monk of St. Gall, "they knew that if men get anything for nothing they think little of it."

The incident came to the ears of Charlemagne, who sought out the merchant monks and asked them the price of their wisdom. "Proper places and noble souls and such things as we cannot travel without, food and wherewith to be clothed", they told him. Charlemagne installed them at his own court where a school was presently established in which *"rich and poor sat together"*.

Rodney Collin, tracing the sequence of cultures, describes the fate of the Celtic Church in a single sentence. *It was murdered.* It did not, however, die at once. That a true developmental influence lingered on within it for another two centuries may be deduced from the fact that Sufic-Celtic traces are discernible in the 9th century.

A well-known Celtic cross of the period, now in the British Museum, incorporates the Arabic formula *Bismillah er Rahman, er Rahim*, suggesting that the Celts were once again in touch with an influence from a genuine psychokinetic source.[2]

We suggest that because they had retained a knowledge of genuine psychokinetic technique from their Druidic inheritance, the Celts came close to reintroducing the missing wisdom component into Christianity. The effort failed, and a second attempt had to wait for other centuries and other sites – the events which followed the expansion of the Moslem Empires.

[2] T. W. Arnold and A. Guillaume, Eds., *The Legacy of Islam*, O.U.P., London, 1968, p. 114.

The Inner Alliance: Rome, Christianty and Islam

We shall now make two suggestions, different in their degree of plausibility. The first is that Initiates of high degree accompanied the Saracen armies into Spain. The second is that a large proportion of the world of today derives – largely unsuspected – from the activities of these schools of Initiates which began to operate from Córdoba and Toledo in the early years of the ninth century.

These schools were supported by immense efforts both of human industry and of spiritual force channelled into Spain from the East.

The Moslem conquests had overrun in part or in whole, the cultural areas of Byzantium, Persia, Greece and Egypt and almost at once Arab scholars and their collaborators proceeded to collate, analyse and reissue the corpus of human knowledge which derived from all these sources. From an esoteric standpoint, "the beads of Mercury had been reunited". It was an immense task, and one to which Western scholarship has given scant credit, except in highly specialized works.

Helped by Nestorian Christians in Syria, the work began with the translation of ancient texts. Simultaneously, with these texts as a basis, Arab pragmatism gave rise to new and significant syntheses.

One of the earliest of the great "Arab" scholars was Al Razi (865–925), a man who has been rated by modern German scholars as being comparable in intellect to Galileo. Like the other medical authors of the time, he was Arab in language, Persian in origin.

Razi had a greater degree of freedom from prior assumption than orthodox Moslems, and this was echoed in his work. His medical insights were great and his mind versatile. He studied the symptoms of measles and smallpox and interspersed treatises on gynaecology and ophthalmology with books on the theory of music. He founded a hospital and in his investigation of alchemy, provided, at exoteric level, the basis of much modern chemistry. Some of his medical works were required reading in European universties as late as the 17th Century.[3] His portrait adorns the great hall of the School of Medicine at the University of Paris.

---

[3] E. J. Holmyard, *Alchemy*, Penguin, London, 1957.

A little later, Avicenna (a Persian whose family came from Balkh) wrote a hundred books, one of them over one million words long. He classified 760 drugs, including opium and cannabis. He produced treatises on heat, energy and gravity and suggested, a thousand years before his time, the limiting velocity of light.

Razi and Avicenna – both Persians – are only two of an enormous number of Arab scholars who provided the raw material required for the coming injection of intellect into Europe, yet many of them are virtually unknown to the European science and philosophy which they sired. Some of their work remains untranslated to this day.

Yet these scholars of the East represented only the external corpus, almost the manual workers, of the operation, which was directed from an altogether different level.

That Arabic influence was leaping into Europe by the early 800s is shown by the remarks of one Paulus Albarus of Córdoba. He is on record as complaining that among his fellow Christian churchmen few of them knew their own tongue, i.e., Latin, well enough to write so much as a letter of greeting to a brother, but that "herds of them could learnedly expound the Arab pomps of language".[4]

It is difficult enough to follow the ordinary, external shifts and trends of history. To trace in detail impulses which, by their very nature, are invisible at the time of their origin and which may only be suspected from their effects, is altogether impossible.

All we can hope to do, in respect of the secret aspects of the events which entered Europe at this time, is to try to note certain key individuals and certain key events, more or less at random, and then see whether a common thread can be found connecting them.

We shall hope to show that a common thread does connect the whole history of Europe and that the threads lead back to Spain on the one hand and to the Middle East on the other.

For a brief period, a third thread runs south and east to Sicily.

[4] Helen Waddell in *The Wandering Scholars*, Constable, London, 1927. She notes that the later fashion for Arab poetry emanating from the Sicilian school of Frederic II was thus anticipated by 400 years.

As Córdoba became stabilized as a showpiece of colonial Islam, several schools of Initiates formed within it, using the external form of Islam as their "cover". Some such camouflage was necessary, for the work they had to do was as incomprehensible to the zealots of Islam as it was to what was now accepted Christianity. Such agents of the Great Work as became partly visible were viewed with equal incomprehension – and hostility – by both. As the price of even relative freedom to work, the Sufic Initiates generally conformed to the letter of Mohammmedan orthodoxy. Occasionally, however, the work they had to do could be done only by crossing into open defiance of official dogma. For this reason there were Sufi martyrs to Islam, as later there were Western martyrs to the Inquisition.

One such was Mansur el Hallaj (858–922) who emphasized the importance of Jesus as a member of the chain of Initiates. He spoke the Sufi secret ("I am the truth"), and for his heresy against orthodoxy he was dismembered alive by the Moslem Inquisition (Caliphate of el Muqtadir). As he died, he prayed for mercy for his murderers.

It would seem that the very first aim of the Iberian Operation was the injection of an intellectual component into the soul-stuff of Europe – an action which is reverberating in waves of increasing amplitude to this day.

The second was the injection of a modality for which there is no generic term in English at all. "Secular religion" might be the closest suggestive description.

The twin vehicles of this were what would now be called "Freemasonry" and "Illuminism" – impulses which at their seventh harmonic were to encompass the French Revolution.

The third aim was to introduce a new and subtler shade to the concept of love.

The fourth was to provide a psychokinetic technique whereby certain individuals, working perhaps in pairs, could increase their level of conscious energy. The fifth was an action to obtain an immediate development in respect of a few exceptional individuals who would serve as transmitters.

To increase intellectual and philosophical speculation the chief instrument was probably mathematics. Another was the open publication of the Cabbala.

"Illuminism" was injected into the European consciousness from the school of Ibn Masarra (883–931) in Córdoba, traced by Professor Asín.[5] From the experiences to which Masarra's pupils were given access they were able to glimpse the heights to which human consciousness *could* aspire. Ripples from this school were to coalesce in the allegories of Dante, the work of the Augustinian scholastics, the theology of Duns Scotus, the science of Roger Bacon and the reluctant ecclesiastic recognition of the Blessed Raymond Lully.

The love theme, which was to soften and enhance the harshness of European life for centuries to come, was introduced through the Troubadour movement. Though the primary intention here was probably to restore a defective feminine element which had been lost in Pauline Christianity, it produced the curious tangential effect of creating the Cult of the Virgin Mary which today is usually assumed to be Christian from its beginnings. But memories are short; the dogma of Mary's Immaculate Conception, for instance, was only proclaimed an article of faith (by Pope Pius IX) in 1854.

To provide a technique which would enable individual men who were ordinary (or almost so) to work towards achieving a decisive rise in the level of their own conscious energy, Alchemy was given out.

And to provide quickly men able to serve as transmitters, a few exceptional individuals were developed rapidly in the Córdoba and Toledo schools and sent out into the social, political and religious streams of Europe.

One undoubted example of the latter category was Gerbert d'Aurillac, born in Auvergne in 940. Gerbert was a forceful character in his early days, if there is anything veridical at all in the account given of him by William of Malmesbury in the *Gesta Regum Angelorum*. According to William, Gerbert was a fugitive monk of Fleury, by whom the ordinary arts, arithmetic, music and astronomy were lapped up as inferior to his genius.

He fled to Spain, stole a codex "conscious of the whole art" from under his master's pillow (with help, apparently, from the

---

[5] Miguel Asín Palacios, *The Mystical Philosophy of Ibn Masarra and his Followers* (translation of *Abenmasarra y su escuela: Origines de la filosofía hispano-musulmana:* Madrid, 1914), tr. by E. H. Douglas and H. W. Yoder, Leiden, 1978.

The Inner Alliance: Rome, Christianity and Islam

master's daughter), fled and was pursued. The direction of his flight, according to William, was "betrayed by the stars", so Gerbert hung himself under a bridge between earth, air and water, thus putting the stars out of their reckoning.

Gerbert then invoked the Devil and was assisted by him across the Bay of Biscay. He returned to France and became scholasticus of Rheims, where Otto, the future Emperor of Germany, Robert Capet, soon to be king of France, and Fulbert, the future Bishop of Chartres were his pupils.

Gerbert constructed a water organ and a clock as well as a brazen head which solved mathematical problems for him. Otto made him Bishop of Ravenna and afterwards Pope. "So did he urge his fortunes, the Devil aiding him, that nothing which ever he planned was left imperfect."

What does seem to be known about Gerbert, outside William of Malmesbury's imagination, is that he secretly withdrew from his monastery of Fleury in Burgundy and spent some years in a Sufi School at Córdoba or Toledo. He emerged speaking Arabic and in some way transformed.

If there is any doubt about the source from which Gerbert received his teaching, the following story would seem to give a very clear pointer.

According to William again, the treasure of the Caesars lay buried in the Campus Martius beneath a statue with an outstretched arm that said *Percute hic* ("strike here"). Many men struck the arm and went away disbelieving. Gerbert, however, watched and noted where the shadow of the outstretched finger fell at noon. He marked the place and came back at night alone with his chamberlain and a lantern and pick. Where he struck, the earth opened and they went down into a great hall where a king and queen of gold sat feasting with golden servitors. Light streamed from an enormous gem in the roof of the cavern and in a corner Gerbert saw a boy with a bow and arrow ready to shoot. Gerbert forbore to touch anything, but his chamberlain, overcome with greed, picked up a golden knife. In an instant the golden boy shot his arrow, broken the gem and destroyed the light. With masonry toppling all round them, Gerbert seized the knife from the chamberlain, threw it back into the cavern and the pair made their escape.

Apart from some elaboration about the nature of the treasures, this story related about Gerbert is familiar from another source. In its simpler version it says, briefly: "For centuries an ancient Egyptian statue which was reputed to indicate the position of a hidden treasure baffled all attempts to find it. It was the figure of a man with one hand and finger outstretched.

"All seekers, except one, tried to find the hoard in the direction in which the finger pointed. The one dug at the spot where the shadow of the finger rested at mid-day. He found the treasure."[6]

Where does *this* story come from? It is traditionally attributed to Abulfaiz Dhu'l Nun, who died in 860. And who was Dhu'l Nun? He was a Sufi teacher, third in succession after David of Tai (died 781) and Maaruf Karkhi (died 815) of the Sufi school of The Builders. In modern Freemasonry, the celebrated masonic word Boaz is said to be Al Buazz, a corruption of Dhu'l Nun's first name Abulfaiz.[7]

The Sufic origin of Gerbert's course of instruction could hardly be more clearly indicated. The Sufic origin of Freemasonry is also strongly suggested.

Every legend about Gerbert has one idea in common: *He was not an ordinary man*. The invention of machines of one kind or another is in line with the exceptional mechanical talents of the *Weltmensch* from Pythagoras to Leonardo. But the legend of the brass head which could answer questions is another matter altogether. Perhaps because one French church history took William of Malmesbury too literally, this head of brass has been taken as an actual mechanical contrivance, and it has been seized upon by modern computer engineers in search of their own ancestors.

More than one modern cybernetic expert has suggested that Gerbert (or Sylvester II as he became when elected Pope) invented the world's first binary computer.

In *Computers and Automation*, 1954,[8] the following appears: "We must suppose that he (Sylvester) possessed an extraordi-

---

[6] *New Research on Current Philosophical Systems*, Octagon Press, London, 1968.

[7] Idries Shah, *The Sufis*, W. H. Allen, London, 1964.

[8] Quoted in *Dawn of Magic*, by Pauwels and Bergier, Gibbs and Phillips, London, 1963.

nary knowledge and the most remarkable skill and inventiveness. This speaking head must have been fashioned under a certain conjunction of stars occurring at the exact moment when all the planets were starting on their course . . . ."

In fact Sylvester is by no means the only medieval figure to have had this kind of binary computer. Robert of Lincoln (Robert Grosseteste) had one. So had Albertus Magnus. Albert took thirty years to make his.

In *Valentine and Orson,* an old French romance connected with the Alexander cycle, there is another legend of a brazen head. This one told all who consulted it everything they sought to know. It was kept in a castle in Portugal and was the property of a giant named Terragno. "Giant" is one of these key words like "brass", "gold", and "light", which we shall find cropping up over and over again. Like the other words, "giant" may have a meaning vastly different from its apparent one.

The Templars also were supposed to have a head which was all-wise and in consequence they, like Gerbert-Sylvester, were linked with the Devil.

In modern times, C. S. Lewis has contributed a story of remarkable power in which the "head" idea is the central theme. Here, however, the head is probably at its lowest level of understanding in all literature. It is the severed head of a criminal which has been revitalised so that it makes contact with extraterrestrial evil, symbolised as "macrobes" – roughly equivalent to the ultimate evil which endlessly obsessed H. P. Lovecraft.

Looked at from a slightly less material level, the gradations of heads in esoteric legend (they are of different metals) are strangely similar to the gradations through which the Philosopher's Stone is purified in alchemy. There may also be similarity with the gradations of colour in a Red Indian chief's head-dress.

Could it be that Sylvester's "head of brass" refers to a non-material "head" that Sylvester *had made by his own efforts?* This head was able to answer infallibly because the substance of which it was made was coextensive with an energy level containing the answers to all questions which can arise in time.

There might be support for such an idea in very recent times. The Indonesian mystic Pak Subuh has more than once referred to the fact that at a certain level of development a man need not store knowledge at all – in the ordinary intellectual sense. He implies that it is possible to have access to a level at which answer and question exist together *as a one-to-one correspondence*. Here there is a clear link with the binary computer idea which has so fascinated cybernetic historians looking for their own origins in an early but exceptionally talented Pope.

It is certainly not without relevance that the methodology of Subud (the cult which regards Pak Subuh as its leader) has been identified with a Sufic (Nakshbandi) origin.

Of possible further relevance is the statement of a modern Sufi master, Ahmad Mustafa Sarmouni, to a Western investigator. "Faced with two possibilities you spend time and effort to decide which to accept. You review the whole spectrum of political, emotional, social, physical, psychological and physiological conditioning before coming up with the answer, which more often than not, does not satisfy you even then. Do you know, can you comprehend, what freedom it gives you if you have no choice? The choice that you make, your decision, is based upon such positive knowledge that the second alternative may as well not exist."

We suggest that the brazen head of Sylvester, like all the other heads that have worried people from the early Middle Ages till the present time, was a head of a symbolic kind, the nature of which has been suggested in the foregoing paragraphs.

Yet if Gerbert did possess some higher faculty it does not seem that he fulfilled his potential. With his rise to the Papacy a very great possibility surely existed: that the Directorate would be able to work within the Christian Church from the top down to restore the elements which had been lost – or discarded – in the involution of the first millennium.

It may be that Gerbert failed some high hope that had been vested in him. Certainly it would seem that after him, the Directorate had to begin a long process of infiltrating developmental trends into the Church from the bottom up instead of from the Papal throne down.

Let us suppose for a moment that the "head of brass" symbolizes the regeneration of man to a certain level.[9] Suppose

---

[9] In Arabic *nahas*, brass, also means "unlucky, ill-omened". This is the word used in Saracen tradition for the alleged brazen heads, indicating the perils of developing will without knowledge and love.

that it means regeneration in terms of will at the level of the individual (and therefore impure) Self. Above this there would be another level, based on supra-Self, for which a "head of gold" might be the symbol.

Perhaps the process of opening a man to consciousness is one of the most perilous that can occur in nature. A very deep insight in this direction has been offered by a writer of the 19th Century[10]

> If you seek a finite end first, i.e., before you seek the universal, the Kingdom of God, which you are ordered to do, you have to give up (the finite ends) at every stage .... All sorts of gifts are offered. You may stop in any of them, but if you do, you commit idolatry .... If the human will creates itself into an entity, there is the second death: a miserable existence is created and made permanent. We were made mortal in order to save us from that .... If the immortality is made in the self-will it is contrary to the universal will and the result is a wrathful biting life.

An almost identical insight is conveyed in the system of the First, Second and Third Degree Hasnamuss Individuals described by G. I. Gurdjieff.[11]

If Gerbert did not submit his Head of Brass to the alchemical process which transforms it to the Head of Gold, but used the level he had obtained for the gratification of his self-will, then he betrayed the Directorate – and, incidentally, condemned himself to an infra-immortality which is the substance of every legend of Hell. Such a situation, if sensed by Gerbert's contemporaries, would be described in the only symbolism available at the time: he had sold his soul to the Devil.

It may be significant that the school which derived from Sylvester produced Benedict IX, noted for his profligacy, Laurence Archbishop of Malfi, John XX and Gregory IV, all reputed to be sorcerers.

In none of these men does it seem possible to catch even a glimpse of the spiritual radiance which surrounds the smallest action of the Sufi masters and it may be that in general the Directorate has not been justified of her European children.

---

[10] Maria Attwood in *The Suggestive Inquiry*, Trelawny Saunders, London, 1850.
[11] G. I. Gurdjieff, *All and Everything*, Routledge, London, 1950.

At the same time, it is wholly wrong to attempt to evaluate such matters from their externals.

It may be that certain of the later *adeptus* transformations can be achieved only against the friction set up by the deliberate creation of an environment of opprobrium and abuse. It is interesting in this connection to note that Gerbert was connected with the school of Dhu'l Nun. Dhu'l Nun was the founder of the order of the Malamati, which is also known as *the order of the blameworthy*. Incurring blame and opprobrium can be required of a man as part of a developmental process.

The smallest activity of the Directorate can be likened to an iceberg: only one-ninth – perhaps one ninety-ninth – is ever visible. All the rest is unseen and, over many centuries of history, quite unsuspected.

Chapter Four

THE VEHICLES: THE JEWISH CABBALA, THE TAROT, NOSTRADAMUS

Much that took place unnoticed in the 10th century became visible in the 11th, and has probably recurred ever since in harmonics through the centuries to the present time.

Perhaps events which first take place in association with conscious energies are compressed like a micro-dot. Projected into time, the image covers larger and larger areas with less and less definition. One occult tradition believes that all the violence in 2,000 years of Christianity is the working out of a single act – the wounding of Malchus by Simon Peter – which abrogated the conscious script of the drama. Attempts have been made to show that the "harmonics" of this can be predicted when plotted on certain esoteric symbols.

In something of the same way, the prophecies of Michel de Nostradame up to the year 7000 are said to be necessarily non-specific because they have to serve for recurring cycles of events which, though generically identical, take the colour and the form of the various environments in which they will be actualized. In other words, if one turn of the spiral is covered, all are covered, given that the same events take different forms in different ages.

Whether or not this analogy breaks down if pushed too far, it does seem possible to detect later harmonics of the events which took place in Spain in the 10th century.

One such event was an attempt to classify in a coherent form all existing knowledge of the time. A secret group in Basra, who were either Sufis or scholars working directly under a Sufi master, was charged in the early 900s with bringing all existing knowledge into one coherent system.

The group, known as Ikhwan El Safa (the Faithful Brethren, or the Brethren of Sincerity), completed the "encyclopaedia" in 980 with the last of 52 treatises.

Perhaps a first harmonic of this impulse can be seen in the 1250s with the *Novum Organum* of Roger Bacon; again in the mid-18th century in the work of the French encyclopaedists; and again today when science is making repeated and ever more despairing efforts to bring the whole of human knowledge into one unified system.

The Cabbala was introduced into Europe around the year 1000 and has probably been behind recurring events of a certain kind, century after century.

The last was as recent as the beginning of the First World War when Cabbalistic societies like Ordo Templi Orientis, Licht Liebe Leben and their English counterpart, The Golden Dawn, exercised an important though wholly masked effect on literature, science and politics. The privately printed *Vision*[1] of W. B. Yeats leaves little doubt that the Cabbala was still a practical instrument for trembling the veil well into the age of the aeroplane.

Another example of the stone in the pool of ether which sends ripples through time may be the Troubadours of the 12th century. Their relationship to the hippies of the 20th is obvious. Both are involved in a wandering existence. Both strum their stringed instruments. Both sing a strange version of the love theme. Both are associated with some strange hint of non-sensory experience. And both are at odds with the orthodoxy of the day.

The *Encyclopaedia of the Brethren of Sincerity* was brought to Spain from Basra in the first half of the 11th century either by a Sufi known as The Madridian (El Majriti), whose speciality was astronomy, or by his pupil El Karmani.

Although, from its origins, the encyclopaedia material was certainly concerned with the inner development of man, the initial concern of those who commissioned it and arranged the work was probably to provide raw material on which natural science could develop in Europe.

In the next century, El Majriti's work based on the *Encyclopaedia* material was translated into Latin by Adelard of

---

[1] *A Vision:* an explanation of life founded on the writings of Giraldus and on certain doctrines attributed to Kusta ben Luka, Wm. Butler Yeats, T. Werner Laurie, London, 1925.

Bath, regarded as Europe's first Arabist and the precursor of Roger Bacon.

Adelard was one of a number of native Europeans of exceptional quality who performed the second stage of injecting learning into the West. This group, known as the Translators, may be seen as a second stage of the original School. At this second degree, the members probably know a great deal. They may know the nature of the original operation in the Great Work, and feel an overwhelming sense of duty and devotion to carry it on.

Probably they do not know the secrets of the original group and the practical work of inner development may now be shading into the theoretical. This increasing "mechanicalness" is probably inevitable in the nature of time and it may even be used by the conscious men of the original School as an instrument which ensures inevitable – though increasingly dilute – transmission.

Such transmission is probably subject to an inverse law and at the tenth or hundredth harmonic may manifest simply as a blind urgency to propagate without reference to purpose at all. Something of this sort may obtain in the door-to-door canvassers of Christianity at the present time.

The Translators formed round the person of Raymond I (died 1151) in association with the Christian Jew Dominico Gundesalvo, Archdeacon of Segovia.

It is interesting that although Spain was being reconquered from the Moslems and Toledo itself had been retaken in 1085, the atmosphere of art, learning and religion associated with the Moslem occupation was so intense that work like that of the Translators' School could continue in spite of a total inversion of the religious and political externals. Arabs, Jews and Christians could apparently live and work side by side.

At the Translators' School the whole Aristotelian corpus was translated from Arabic into Latin, followed by translations of the Islamic and Jewish philosophers El Kindi, El Farabi, El Battani, Avicenna, Ben Gabirol and El Ghazali. Farabi is the "Neo-Platonist" whose *Treatise on Music* contains the germ of the idea of logarithms.

Outstanding at the Translators' School was Adelard of Bath (died 1142). He had studied at Tours and Laon and had then been drawn in a circuitous route, which is a familiar pattern in such affairs, to Sicily, Syria and Palestine. In Spain he rendered into Latin the work of El Majriti and the astronomical tables of Khwarizimi of Central Asia which included values for trigonometrical sines and tangents.

It is salutary to realize that the bases of Space Age rocket trajectories were being laid in Toledo eight hundred years ago by men whose names are barely known to the scientists of today.

Adelard gave a mathematical proof that total vacuum was impossible. He published a "dialogue" of 76 chapters, each treating of one aspect of the natural sciences, and he was probably responsible for a large number of scientific papers under the pseudonym of Magister A.

The fact that learning was becoming available in Europe's common second language drew more and more scholars to Toledo and Córdoba. They came to learn, to assist and to disseminate.

The English contingent, apart from Adelard, included Robert of Chester, credited with releasing alchemy into Europe in 1144, and Daniel Morley, who described his journey as "going to the wiser masters of the world".

Although ignored or ridiculed by materialist science today, the importance of alchemy is probably very great, not only in its external – and perhaps almost accidental – effect of siring experimental chemistry, but in another aspect as a reservoir of spiritual force wholly unsuspected in external judgment.

From Italy, Plato of Tivoli, John Brassica and Gerard of Cremona came to Toledo, studied and either stayed to help or went home with learning to distribute.

Gerard, who came to seek Ptolemy's Almagest, first translated by Al-Hajjaj in 829–30, never returned home. He died in Toledo in 1187, having made 71 major translations.

Others who made the pilgrimage and contributed to the scatter of learning were Henry Bate, Rudolph of Bruges and Hermann of Carinthia, who took Arab astronomy to the Balkans.

Other notables included emissaries from the School of Chartres and Peter the Venerable, Abbot of Cluny, who commissioned a translation of the Koran from Robert of Ketton.

Arab medicine was studied at Salerno which had been a medical school since the 10th century, when Constantine the African had translated Greek and Arab texts. It was founded under the Saracens by "four Masters, a Latin, a Greek, a Jew and a Saracen".[2]

Montpelier in the south of France was another centre where East was meeting West. Like Toledo it had a mixed population of Arabs, Jews and Christians. Here, as at Salerno, medicine was the chief speciality.

About the year 1000 the Cabbala became available in the West. There is no occult school, no mystic, no magician who has not been influenced by the Cabbala. It is the backdrop to every secret tradition in Europe. Its theory has influenced Western philosophy and its practice has been responsible for a whole range of mysterious people who flit in and out of history and folklore, all defying classification, but all causing a strange disturbing echo in the European subconscious.

It is almost always assumed today that the Cabbala is uniquely Jewish, the secret signature of the Jewish race. Though, as a partly written, partly oral, transmission it is likely to be distorted, it is regarded as an altogether exceptional survival from the past and the essential expression of the Jewish spirit.

It is believed that the Jews obtained it from some secret source which had preserved objective knowledge and that the survival of the Jews, their influence on the world and the extent to which they are supposed to be "different" all derive from their mysterious inheritance of the Cabbala.

Modern Cabbalistic legend asserts that Abraham acquired a corpus of mysticism and magic from Chaldea. When he arrived in Egypt he found that a similar but separate corpus already existed there, this deriving from the Egyptian archetype Hermes. Abraham's arrival in Egypt meant the reuniting of two separate elements in an originally integral system of mysticism and magic.

Moses is held to have been an Initiate of an Egyptian school which combined both traditions, and the first man to take the combined corpus into the world.

[2] P. Hitti, *History of the Arabs*, Macmillan, London, 1949, p. 579.

Later, Moses committed to writing the relatively open and exoteric part of the combined lore. This is the Pentateuch, Genesis being the most arcane of the five "open" books.

The truly secret part, concerned with the nature of the universe and the practical techniques of individual evolution, remained a wholly oral tradition confined to seventy elders. Perhaps because this part includes material on the ultimate nature of matter and energy, security had to be absolute, and the elders who were admitted to the knowledge were bound by the most terrible oaths.

When Jewry was subjected to further dispersion and the cohesion of the people in a simply physical sense became increasingly difficult, the elders were faced with a grave dilemma.

They realized that the body of real knowledge of which they were the custodians was in danger of being lost; the dilution and dispersal of the people preventing continued transmission in any ordered fashion.

Yet to commit to writing such dangerous secrets as were contained in the combined inheritance from Chaldea and Egypt was unthinkable.

This fear of objective knowledge "leaking" is reflected also in some texts of Chinese alchemy, where phrases occur like "Guard that there is not even a fly upon the wall while you work. For woe unto the world should the military learn the secrets of the Art."

In general, success in preserving actual techniques of ancient wisdom from the profane appears to be extraordinarily high. Apart from a modern Rosicrucian legend that the supra-mental force, which Bulwer Lytton called Vril, was used at the siege of Breda in the 17th century, post-classical history seems free of hints that ultimate secrets have been misapplied on any significant scale. The worst fears in this direction have already been realized. The "military" have now obtained a high order of control over the forces of nature by the back door. Nuclear energy has been obtained by pragmatic science without the agency of even a fly on an alchemist's wall.

Incidentally, it is believed in some quarters that the last surviving initiate of the old Chinese order of transmission made the decision to entrust part of his knowledge to Richard

Wilhelm. Jungian psychology is said to have diverted from sterile Freudianism as the result of Wilhelm's transmission to Jung. Significant passages occur in Jung's work which refer to a Chinese component in his system.

It might not be too fanciful to see Wilhelm as a "harmonic" of Abraham. The Chaldean cell is in decline and an attempt is made to fertilize a new cell far away by passing on an infinitely compressed micro-dot of objective knowledge to a suitable individual (Abraham).

The Chinese cell is dying and a similar operation is attempted. In circumstances of extreme difficulty and stress Lao Nai Hsuan opens Wilhelm's mind to the I Ching.

If some version of Jungian psychology were ever by a twist of fate to become the religion of some Post-Admass Culture it would perhaps contain the legend of how St. Wilhelm brought the Id-Child out of the East, confounding the Philistine Freuds on the way.

At any rate, according to modern Cabbalistic legend, the Jewish elders very reluctantly decided to commit their most treasured inheritance to writing, but to do so in such a way as to ensure, as far as was humanly possible, that it would remain unintelligible to the profane. Even this was done in three degrees of secrecy which have come down to the present time as the Sepher Yetzirah, the Sepher ha Zohar and the Clavicles of Solomon.

And what are these Clavicles of Solomon? According to the French Cabbalist Enel,[3] the Clavicles of Solomon are to be identified with the trumps of the Tarot pack. He says, "Count de Gebelin has found in the 22 major arcana, the symbolism of the Egyptian mysteries and he attributes their composition to Hermes. Certainly on the monuments of ancient Egypt it is possible to find depicted in hieroglyphs, most of the plates of the major arcana, which justifies the opinion of Gebelin."

Elsewhere Enel says, "The occult sense of the Cabbala is expressed in the keys or clavicles of Solomon, also called the Keys of the Tarot. Tarot or Rota is an ancient Egyptian word which refers to the celestial wheels which constitute the

---

[3] *Trilogie de la Rota* by "Enel", Cabasson, Toulon, 1931.

mechanism of nature. These rotas correspond to the Ophanim of the ancient Hebrews and the Cherubim of the Christians."

From this it would appear that the Clavicles of Solomon, the most secret section of Cabbalistic lore, would have to wait for their appearance till the publication of the Tarot. The Cabbala was being studied in Europe, however, from the 11th century and the Tarot is historically dated as having entered Spain and Italy in 1379.[4]

If the Clavicles and the Tarot had a common ancestry independent of both, there is no difficulty, and we shall see presently that this is probably the case. In passing, it might be noted that the word Tarot is no more likely to have been derived from the word Rota (which does not exist in Egyptian dictionaries) than from the Arabic *turuq* which means "ways" and has a very definite affinity with the *use* of the Tarot pack.

Such concepts do not strike the Western scientific mind felicitously. What *is* the Cabbala in understandable modern terms?

Some of its aspects and attributes have been defined by Crowley:[5]

> An instrument for interpreting symbols whose meaning has become obscure, forgotten or misunderstood, by establishing a necessary connection between the essence of forms, sounds, simple ideas (such as numbers), and their spiritual, moral or intellectual equivalents. . . .
> An instrument for proceeding from the known to the unknown on principles similar to those of mathematics. . . .
> A system of criteria by which the truth of correspondences may be tested with a view to criticizing new discoveries in the light of their coherence with the whole body of truth. . . .

Perhaps the Cabbala could most crudely be regarded as a cross-sectional plan of the Universe from the Absolute (Ain Soph) down to – and perhaps sideways from – the level of man.

Or as a cross-section of the Body of God, showing energy flows within it and the connections which exist – or may be made – between various terminals.

The Cabbala sees the "matter" of the Absolute as filling

---

[4] Annotation to *The Sufis* by Idries Shah.
[5] Aleister Crowley, "777", Neptune Press, London, 1955.

the universe, and the Absolute for his own reasons projecting this universe from his own noumenal nature.

The first such projection or emanation contains a number of others within it. Each of these in turn emanates from the one before and includes subsequent emanations within itself, thus giving rise to all the principles or gradations of energy in the manifested universe.

These rays or Sephiroth are connected to each other by paths annotated by the letters of the Hebrew alphabet. The trumps of the Tarot pack also identify these paths.

Given a knowledge of these energy levels and their lateral connections, a man may, beginning from his own level, ascend the whole diagram, identifying with, and *acquiring the properties of each*, so retracing the road along which he was projected from the Ain Soph.

Since the Cabbala became available in the West, an immense amount of intellectual effort – and spiritual aspiration – has gone into understanding and applying its principles. About most of it there is, however, a suggestion that something is not quite right. Either some key is missing, or the corpus has been corrupted in transmission. Much Cabbalistic writing and interpretation suggests improvisation. Conclusions are reserved and tentative. Although writers sense the perfection of the whole philosophical machine, they are aware that square pegs, here and there, obstinately decline to fit round holes.

Is the Cabbalistic corpus known to the West in some way corrupt? If this were so, it would not be a theoretical matter. Something like spiritual nuclear energy is probably involved in higher manipulations of the Cabbala, and it is obvious that if operations are based on an imperfect circuit diagram, errors may be disastrous. In the literature of the subject there is more than a hint that some operations have been disastrous – and though not visible as such, disastrous nevertheless.

Is there any evidence that the Cabbala of the West is corrupt? We have seen that the Cabbalistic tradition itself attributes the Cabbala's origins to an amalgam. Two separate though similar expressions of an ancient objective science came together, in a wholly oral transmission, later reluctantly written down in cypher. The version of this known to the West appeared mysteriously around AD 1000. Where did it come from? Incredibly it would appear that it did not originate in a Jewish source at all, but in a Sufic one. The accepted modern authority on Jewry, *The Jewish Encyclopaedia*, declares that it came from Basra, as one of the treatises composing the *Encyclopaedia of the Faithful Brethren* published in 980!

The statement seems unequivocal. "...The Faithful Brothers of Basra originated the eight elements which form God..." Then perhaps comes the clue to all the square pegs and round holes that have followed: "... *changed by a Jewish philosopher in the middle of the 11th century into ten*".

A present-day Sufi sheikh is even more explicit: "The Cabbala came from the region of the Faithful Brothers to two places, Italy and Spain. Its system of word manipulation may be derived from parallel and ancient Jewish teaching, but it is founded upon Arabic grammar ... there is no doubt that the Arab study of grammar and the meaning of words is at the base of the usage of words in the Cabbala for mystical purposes. . . . The Sufis and the Brethren had produced what they considered to be the most ancient teaching, the secret lore of fulfilment and power and handed it to the Arabized Jews. The Jewish Cabbalists adapted this teaching to contemporary Jewish thinking and the Cabbala of the Arabs became the Cabbala of the Jews and later of the Christians. . . . But the mystical schools of Sufism which never regarded organized book knowledge as a sufficient source, continued to ally practice of the Sufic Rites with the essentials of the old Cabbala teaching. . . ."

And elsewhere: "The alteration of basic Cabbalism (from eight elements to ten) deprived the Western development of the system of a great deal of its meaning and usefulness. Hebrew and Christian Cabbala literature later than the 12th century is therefore only of partial meaning. This includes all aspects of the Cabbala of ten elements as distinct from the 'Eight Cabbala'."[6]

In this matter of the relation between forces and sounds as represented by alphabets and grammar, the observations of the learned Cabbalist Enel are interesting.

The Cabbalists, he says, teach that the signs of sacred alphabets are the images of the creative forces of the Cosmos. Wattan, the Adamic language, was based on this principle. This

---

[6] Idries Shah, *The Sufis*, W. H. Allen, London, 1964.

The Vehicles : The Jewish Cabbala, the Tarot, Nostradamus

language has, of course, been lost, but Enel considers that it survives in principle in Aramaic "which is in complete harmony with the laws governing the universe". Parts of the Old Testament and the Talmud were written in Aramaic and the language in its Eastern and Syriac branches was largely superseded by Arabic. The link between an original language preserving correspondence with natural forces and both the Semitic and Arab later transmissions is therefore indicated.

If, then, a knowledgeable resynthesis of this ancient wisdom was made by the Basra encyclopaedists in 980, and fed into Europe through El Majriti and Solomon ben Gabirol ("Avicebron"), how did this become altered within a century so that it was "deprived of a great deal of its meaning and usefulness"?

Who altered it, and why? Did it happen because somebody thought he knew better? Or did it arise by accident in endless transcriptions? Or did someone fear that too much had been given out and strive to contain the danger by deliberate falsification?

The nature of the alteration was the addition of two elements to the original. This hardly looks like an error in transcription. Yet the nature of the alteration was such as to prevent the "machine" being employed in its entirety.

Examples of post-publication panic are not unknown in the literature of alchemy, and it would seem likely that a Jewish source, perhaps from a partial understanding as well as a sense of security, invented the Cabbala of ten elements as a "blind" to draw attention away from the potentialities of the "Eight".

The falsification may involve four Trumps of the Tarot, Nos. 14, 15, 16 and 20. Idries Shah says No. 14 "has been wrongly portrayed and interpreted". Enel notes that in the Egyptian, No. 14 is the Solar Genius. In the Medieval it is Temperance. No. 15, according to Shah, has also been wrongly portrayed and interpreted. Enel notes that No. 15 in the Egyptian is Typhon and The Devil in the Medieval version. No. 16, according to Shah, is a classic example of a word being misunderstood. Enel, however, has no misgivings about this, and gives the Tower struck by Lightning for both the Egyptian and the Medieval. No. 20, according to Shah, is "wrongly emphasized". Enel notes that this trump in the Egyptian is the Awakening of the Dead. In the Medieval Tarot it is Judgment.

Astronomy, trigonometry, music, chemistry, alchemy and the Cabbala, all, it would seem, dripped into the veins of a Europe still almost completely unconscious after the sleep of the Dark Ages. The transfusion took place in Spain from Saracen sources in the 11th and 12th centuries.

Our submission is that this was not by chance. It was not an accidental drift, concentration and redistribution of random material from the past: but a purposeful operation planned at a hidden level and executed at a lower level to produce a calculated effect – the awakening of Europe.

It would seem that the agents were of many degrees of awareness. They ranged from conscious men of an original School, through initiates of lesser degree, down to men chiefly impelled by the hunger for scholarship – but having nevertheless some knowledge of the Great Work.

At the outermost perimeter there were scribes and copyists performing their role mechanically; but all, whatever their degree of awareness, serving a purpose whether they glimpsed it or not.

At ordinary historical level the contribution of the Arabs to the awakening of Europe is undoubted, and it is now increasingly exciting scholars: but the attribution of the whole operation to schools of men possessing some kind of consciousness in advance of the ordinary human kind is regarded as either unproved or as pure fantasy.

The idealistic interpretation cannot of course be proved. Proof depends on fact and facts define themselves as the only admissible data. If some variety of data beyond fact is postulated, this can never be shown in terms of fact. Yet the analogy of this ring-pass-not of fact and supra-fact is freely admitted in human experience. The effect of Beethoven's Fifth is admitted to be a reality though it cannot be demonstrated with a thermometer.

In the absence of some subjective experience which validates the noumenal as a reality, the only support for a supra-causal theory of history must lie in analogy. Support for the analogy may be possible if it can be shown that "fact" is *consistently* amenable – and most plausibly amenable – to a hypothesis of higher causation. This is something like the "psychological method" of P. D. Ouspensky.[7] It is as far as "fact" can be pushed towards transcending itself.

Suppose, for example, that consciousness is two-dimensional and can record only what takes place on the surface of a sheet of paper. Within this "flat-land" universe, certain phenomena are regularly recorded. To begin with, a point suddenly appears. This point changes to a circle whose diameter gradually increases up to a certain limit. This activity, whatever it may be, now rests. The circle remains the same, but its colour changes, apparently arbitrarily. If these phenomena occur regularly and are carefully enough recorded, flat-land observers will be able to predict the whole sequence as a series of facts occurring in time. One of the predictions will be that the mysterious circle, after a time, grows smaller and finally becomes a point and vanishes. In terms of flat-land consciousness, there is no more to explain. "Fact" is wholly incapable of rising to the noumenal level which, in this case, would be *a coloured pencil pushing through the paper.*

Developmental "schools" are pencils piercing the pages of history. Their existence cannot be shown in terms of pages. It can only be experienced in terms of pencils.

But if it is seen that the idea of pencil gives consistently a more satisfactory explanation of the holes that keep appearing in pages, even flat-land consciousness may begin to feel that the hypothesis moves from possibility to probability.

And this, perhaps, is as far as any proof of a higher motivation of the historical process can be taken. The reader can only be shown the series of holes which appear in pages and left to consider whether they are not most plausibly explained by pencils.

Even those amenable to this sort of approach have objected to the identification of the "one-up" dimension with Schools of the Sufic tradition. They point out that much of the Iberian population is in any case concerned with material which is not specifically Sufic at all, being largely Greek and Egyptian.

---

[7] P. D. Ouspensky, *A New Model of the Universe*, Routledge, London, 1951.

To this it can only be replied that much Greek, Egyptian and Neo-Platonic material is held by Sufi schools to be in true alignment with the developmental needs of mankind.

Sufic Schools of the Directorate will use material from any source – artistic, scientific, religious or secular – which lies on the optimum line of man's possible evolution; an idea which is conveyed in the Sufic teaching aphorism: "Pears do not grow only in Samarkand."

CHAPTER FIVE

LOVE COURTS, TROUBADOURS AND ROUND TABLES

Between 1100 and 1300 the Wandering Minstrel declaimed his poems and sang his haunting songs of love round the Ducal courts of Provence. His apprentice or *joglar* played the viol, and the music they made and the ideas they spread abroad have been reverberating through Europe ever since, crystallizing in psychological ideas and literary forms unrecognizably remote from the origins.

There would seem to be no possible connection between the songs of Guillem, Count of Poitiers, in the 12th century, and modern university-sponsored excavations at Cadbury and Glastonbury in 1970, but we hope to show that there *is* a connection; for the legends of Arthur and the 20th century search for his origins alike connect back to a "something" which manifested historically as the Troubadour phenomenon.

The Troubadours were a mystery, even in their own day. The movement apparently sprang from nowhere, without seeming ancestry, and when it appeared it was ready-made in its final form. Superficially, it was an entirely local and somewhat aberrated conceit among minor princelings and effete aristocrats who, like Jack Point, "sighed for the love of a ladye".

Though seemingly the concern of the wealthy and the leisured, it nevertheless had scullions and kitchen maids in its ranks. But whatever the rank of the lady fair, the subtending idea was the same: she was unattainable and her suitor's love was hopeless.

Significantly, the lady was unobtainable, even at ordinary level, for she was not a maid, but a married woman. Strangely enough, her husband did not seem to regard the suitor as an enemy or even a rival.

Something of this strange and unnatural situation is to be found implicit in Arthurian material where the reader finds it impossible to discover where his allegiance is supposed to lie.

Lancelot is Guinevere's lover. She is Arthur's dutiful queen. Arthur is a hero-king. In the circumstances, the reader feels that Lancelot *ought* to be presented as worthy of the reader's moral disapproval. Instead *all three elements are presented as equally worthy*.

In such a typically Troubadour *ménage à trois*, much of significance is symbolized. The alchemical content is suggested in relation to King Mark, Tristan and Isolde by the alchemist Fulcanelli thus:

> Let us note that the queen is the wife both of the old man and of the young hero. This is in accordance with the hermetic tradition which makes the king, the queen and the lover combine to form the mineral triad of The Great Work.[1]

How did such an idea originate, and where did it come from?

In the light of documents which emerged in Spain after the Second World War, and of some hints released more recently from the East, there seems little doubt that the Troubadours were one more social experiment of the Sufi Schools operating from Spain.

Like most Sufi experiments its derivation is carefully obscured. Like most such experiments it was concerned to operate by manipulating environment so as to effect a change in a small selected section of a population.

Over the century and a half during which it was active, the Troubadour movement achieved a refinement of life and a standard of culture which probably went unequalled for 500 years.

When the operation withdrew, Provençal culture reverted to a level which historians do not hesitate to describe as barbarism.

It seems possible to detect a number of aims behind the Troubadour movement. The first was to suggest by a subtle symbolism the existence of a kind of love which could not be realized in human terms.

"The Sufis believe that within mankind there is an element activated by love which provides the means of attaining to true reality."[2]

[1] Fulcanelli, *Le Mystère des Cathédrales*, Paris, 1965; trs. M. Sworder, Spearman, London, 1971.
[2] Idries Shah, *The Sufis*, p. 165.

Secondly, perhaps, the reinstatement of a passive, recessive feminine element into the stream of European life. This element was primary in the Great Mother impulse and has probably been defective in the entire history of the West.

Whether the ingrafting of the Cult of the Virgin into Christianity was part of the intention or whether this crept into dogma by osmosis from the Troubadour impulse, it is impossible to say. Most likely the cult of the Virgin was adopted into Christianity on the well known principle "if you cannot beat them, join them".

It is certainly remarkable, as Robert Graves has pointed out, that "her greatest veneration today is in those parts of Europe that fell strongly under Sufic influence".[3]

The theory of the Sufic origin of the Troubadours has been strengthened in academic circles by the discovery in Spain of bilingual Troubadour songs in Arabic and Catalan,[4] and Roger Loomis[5] points to similarities between Moorish poetry in Spain and Troubadour poetry in Provence, such as the curious custom of addressing the worshipful Mistress as "My Lord" (Provençal: "Midon").

Loomis also refers to the work of Ibn Hazm, *The Dove's Neck Ring* which, he says might be regarded as a textbook on the courtly love of the Troubadours.

In Ibn Hazm's book the influence of love is described as "making a stingy one generous, a gloomy one bright-faced, a coward brave, a curmudgeon gay and an ignoramus clever".

It seems clear that the Provençal love poetry originated in Moorish Spain and was brought to Provence by Spaniards speaking both Arabic and the Catalan dialect. This was almost identical with Provençal, the "langue d'oc" of Southern France.

The word Troubadour is usually held to derive from the Provençal verb *trobar*, to find or invent, but Idries Shah has

---

[3] Robert Graves, Introduction to *The Sufis*.
[4] Friedrich Heer, *The Medieval World*, Weidenfeld and Nicolson, London, 1961.
[5] Loomis, *The Development of Arthurian Romance*, Hutchinson, London, 1963. The Orientalist, J. B. Trend, among many others, agrees that "the words 'troubadour' and 'trobar' are almost certainly of Arabic origin: from *tarraba*, to sing or make music" (in *Legacy of Islam*, 1968 edition, p. 17).

shown that the derivation is from the Arabic root TRB with the agental suffix *ador* added.[6]

This TRB root involves a play on words characteristic of Sufic thinking. The range of words that can be built on this consonantal root includes a meeting place of friends, a master, playing the viol and the idealization of women.

Sufi schools mounting an operation choose their terminology – and their codes – with great care, selecting a title whose root consonants will permutate to suggest words covering as many of their proposed activities as possible.

It can hardly be denied that the TRB permutations cover the known attributes and activities of the Troubadours.

The most characteristic feature of the Troubadour love poetry – on which the whole concept of courtly love and later of chivalry rested – was the idealization of woman. She was the poet's ideal mistress whom he worshipped from afar, without, however, any hope of obtaining her favour. Or so it would seem, viewed externally. Much of it, between the lines, was thinly disguised metaphysics, with unattainable Princesses used to symbolize a spiritual quality to which man might feel drawn, but which was essentially unattainable in his ordinary state.

The songs followed a set pattern of statement and refrain, the result giving a monotony which is the subject of much literary criticism. Lewis Spence[7] comments on the "monotonous repetition of amatory sentiment for the expression of which the same conceptions and even the same phrases are compelled again and again to do duty".

This is certainly a defect, if judgment is on aesthetic grounds, but the matter may take on another appearance if we suspect that the Troubadours, after the pattern of the Sufic schools of Spain, were communities meeting under a master for a specific purpose and choosing to operate through the medium of "poetry readings" accompanied by the viol and lute.

If there is a secondary meaning to the poetry – if it was in fact in code – the monotony may not be an inadvertent defect at all.

The first historical Troubadour of the West was Guillem, 7th Count of Poitiers and 9th Duke of Aquitaine (1071–1127). He

[6] Idries Shah, *The Sufis*, p. 318.
[7] L. Spence, *Legends and Romances of Spain*, Farrar and Rhinehart, New York, 1931, p. 17.

was the grandfather of Eleanor of Aquitaine, a lady of unusual talents and a marked capacity for survival, whose influence on later events, historical, cultural and literary, is quite astonishing.

Guillem had been a Crusader in the East. He had also fought in Andalusia where, presumably, he made contact with the Troubadour operation at its inception.

He was soon in conflict with the Church because his songs were held to be overtly – and therefore scandalously – sexual. Friedrich Heer, however, senses the concealed mysticism. "In Guillem's love songs, the vocabulary and emotional fervour hitherto used to express man's love for God are transferred to the liturgical worship of women."[8] One is tempted to add "and vice versa".

Guillem provided the talent initially, but it was left to his granddaughter Eleanor to build up what might be called the theatrical circuit. She created a network of minor courts round which the Troubadours circulated and within which the highly stylized concepts of courtly love and chivalry rapidly developed.

Eleanor was the richest heiress in Europe, with lands stretching from the Loire to the Pyrenees, from the Auvergne to the Atlantic. At the core was Provence, where she spent her childhood. With such possessions, she was thought a fitting match for Louis VII of France, whom she married in 1137.

Louis had never expected to be king, and had been educated as a monk: but the death of his elder brother put him unexpectedly on the throne of France. Temperamentally, he was excessively unsuited to the mercurial and passionate Eleanor. "I thought", said Eleanor later, "to have married a King, but find I am wed to a monk."

In 1146 Louis went off on the Second Crusade, taking his wife with him. Contrary to the Papal Bull on the subject, she insisted on taking her Troubadours with her.

The Crusaders, when they reached Syria, halted at Antioch and there Eleanor found an environment truly suited to her temperament. Antioch at the time was one of these princeling states which had grown up after a local conquest by the

[8] Friedrich Heer, *The Medieval World*.

Crusaders, who instead of returning home, preferred to settle in the exotic surroundings of their conquest. The ruler of Antioch was Raymond, who was Eleanor's uncle. His court, over which he presided in great style, included Christians, Moslems and Greeks. Some of the original Crusader-conquerors had married Saracen women, and the second generation were more than half Moslem in their ways.

The exotic atmosphere and the luxury in Raymond's court appealed greatly to Eleanor, who may well have known a family tradition in such matters from her grandfather, who had obviously had Arabic, if not Sufic, contacts in Syria or Spain.

Indifferent to the scandal, Eleanor decided to remain in Antioch with her uncle and let her husband go back to France alone. Louis, in spite of his scholarly temperament, was made of sterner stuff – and promptly set off for home taking his wife with him by force.

This was an action which had far-reaching effects indeed, leading as it did to the transmission of certain influences like the orders of chivalry into England.

Indignant perhaps at her husband's treatment of her, Eleanor on her return to France proceeded to have her marriage dissolved. This formality completed, she married Henry, son of Geoffrey of Anjou, who was shortly to become King of England.

The early years of her second marriage were spent at Angers, which rapidly became a resort of Troubadours and an academy of the cult of courtly love. Here Bernard de Ventadour wrote his love poetry in her honour.

In 1154 Henry and Eleanor were crowned King and Queen of England, but it quickly became apparent that neither her second husband nor the English climate was agreeable to Eleanor. When Henry, who was twelve years her junior, took as his mistress Rosamond Clifford (subject of the "Ballad of Fair Rosamond") Eleanor withdrew to Poitiers where she devoted her entire resources to developing the Love Court in its final form.

Poitiers became a university of courtesy, Troubadour poetry and chivalry; an academy of the courtly arts to which the nobility from far and near came for instruction. Several future kings and queens and many future dukes and duchesses were educated in Eleanor's campus and returned home to model their own courts on hers.

Thus the courtly ideal and the lyrical love poetry were distributed over Europe – together with whatever was secretly contained in these forms.

At Poitiers, courtiers were "tried" to decide whether they had kept the 31 articles of the Code of Love laid down in the *De Arte Honeste Amandi* compiled by Andreas Capellanus. One of the chief judges was Marie, Countess of Champagne, Eleanor's daughter.

In all this apparently weird activity, a subversive element was undoubted. Love Court judgments were always subtly subversive of the social order. Troubadour songs were openly subversive of the Papal authority.

The Troubadours and the Love Courtiers, like the jesters of the time (who were undoubted Sufi figures), claimed licence to criticize matters which were by common consent regarded as taboo.

Obviously something was going on. It would be tempting to equate or at least associate this something with the Albigensian heresy, but it would probably be wrong to do so. A study of such Sufic interventions as can be suspected from their outward effects, suggests that a Sufic operation is frequently in existence simultaneously with an "official heresy", but is never part of it. It may be significant, however, that the Troubadour and Love Court phenomenon almost exactly spans the period of the Albigensian heresy.

The Troubadour movement was greatly reduced by the siege of Toulouse in 1218 and the Treaty of Paris in 1299. It was virtually extinguished by the expanding powers of the Inquisition in the early 1300s.

Catharism (the "Albigensian Heresy") came from the East and was apparently rooted in Greek Gnosticism and 4th century Persian Manichaeism. It first appeared in Western Europe about 1140, and in two years gained a hold in the region between the Rhine and the Pyrenees. It had a widespread organization, with its own clergy, bishops and international councils. The most important bishopric was at Albi in Southern France, which gave the movement its name "Albigensian". In Languedoc and Provence it flourished alongside the court culture of the Troubadours.

Catharism enjoyed much aristocratic patronage especially that of Raymond VI, Count of Toulouse. It had a great appeal for women and numbered many nuns of noble birth among its supporters. The appeal was perhaps from the fact that women as well as men could become Cathars or "pure ones". Its appeal among ordinary people may have sprung from the fact that they could participate, Cathar literature being in the vernacular.

The Albigensian mystery is largely unresolved to this day. The Cathar massacres were so complete that almost nothing of their beliefs survived. What little is known comes from their enemies. They were certainly remorselessly hostile to the Church of Rome, which they believed had succumbed to the lust of gold and power at the time of Constantine and had ruled in unholy alliance with the princes of the world ever since.

The Cathars were said to believe that Satan had created the human race. He was a son of God, but was essentially hostile to man. Another son of God now had the task of redeeming the situation. Against the rigid dogma of the 11th and 12th centuries this was seen as a transparent attempt to elevate the status of Satan.

The belief seems strangely like the expression of some racial memory concerned with the events which we have interpreted in terms of the Demiurgic revolt.

In many respects Cathar ritual reflected the practices of the early pre-Constantine Church. There might also be a link with a common ancestor of Freemasonry in that the Cathar candidate was addressed as "a living stone in the temple of God".

Catharism was clearly a threat to Rome, and when various missionary attempts were repulsed, Innocent III appealed to the faithful to stamp out the abomination.

A Crusade was preached by the Cistercians and an inflammable situation rapidly turned into a French civil war between North and South. The war ended officially with the surrender of Raymond VII, which meant the defeat of the entire south. As soon as the Albigensians were crushed in the field, the Inquisition was set up at Toulouse and the last heretics were burned at the stake in 1324. At Monségur 200 men, women and children were burned alive in a single day.

Love Courts, Troubadours and Round Tables

The Cathars survived in Germany – in Cologne, Strasbourg, Erfurt and Goslar, for some time to come. Another stream of refugees went to Italy, where there were sympathizers in Florence. Others went to Liguria and Sicily.

The Troubadours as such were not persecuted; but with the collapse of the ducal courts in the South of France, the environment in which they worked was destroyed. The last of the Troubadours is said to have been Guiraut Riquier, a native of Narbonne, who lived until 1294 as a refugee at the court of Alfonso X in Spain.

It seems that a Sufic operation designed to inject a developmental impulse into a certain population at a certain time may run parallel to, but always separate from, an official religion. The same "mistletoe-relationship" may apply to an official heresy.

If the Troubadour and courtly-love medium was a local and minor instrument of the Directorate, it may be presumed that European events for a century and a half would fall well within the "present moment" of those directly responsible.

If so, the destruction of the Albigensians – the oak beside which the mistletoe grew – would certainly be foreseen.

Such operations as we are suggesting are characterized by a certain finality. They operate on a selected group for a particular purpose and for a certain time only. The impulse is then wholly withdrawn.

So penetrating is the energy involved, however, that harmonics of the original excitation may continue for centuries. For the most part it is only such echoes that are detectable and it is these that are investigated historically.

In the matter of the Troubadours, it is possible that the original operation, which was extremely local, was transferred to a larger octave so as to encompass the whole of Europe. It is at any rate clear that the courtly love and chivalric ideal, which had produced such marked refinement in human conduct, did not expire with the destruction of the Albigenses.

It might almost seem that when the Albigensian persecution was imminent, the impulse was transferred to a new carrier-wave, this time accented on a combined military and astrological theme, the Arthurian legend.

We suggest that the Arthurian legend was deliberately developed for this purpose.

But to glimpse this, we must return to Eleanor and her many activities.

Evidence of initiatory influences in her family has recently been given by Idries Shah.[9]

Eleanor's favourite son, Richard, was the famous Coeur de Lion. In Arabic, Coeur de Lion would be *Qalb el Nimr*. This contains two Sufic initiatory words. *Qalb*, "heart", comes from the QLB root, which "spreads" to give "essence" or "vital portion". "Lion" has a secondary significance as "man of the way", a familiar term for a Sufic aspirant on the way to higher development. Richard's nickname is thus an announcement to those who understand that he has been initiated. Since phraseology of this kind must also make sense at the literal as well as the esoteric level, he is also the lion-hearted, the bold and fearless warrior of the Crusades.

The whole Plantagenet dynasty was deeply involved in hidden activity, and some of this echoes today in modern chivalric orders.

Geoffrey of Anjou, Richard's grandfather, had a shield showing golden lions on a field of blue, a combination which would be recognized even by a modern alchemist as a statement to a certain effect. Geoffrey's father, Falk V, was "King of Jerusalem" and a great friend of the Saracen Regent of Damascus. Geoffrey "made a pilgrimage to the Holy Land" and visited his father, and it seems likely that his initiation took place at this time. Geoffrey adopted as his family emblem, the broom plant (*planta genista*), hence the Plantagenets.

The French for broom is *genet*, which has almost the same sound as *genette* (the civet cat). Among relatively modern secret societies in Europe, one had the title Knights of the Genet (Chevaliers de la Genette), and the 20th-century alchemist Fulcanelli regards it as one having genuine initiatory knowledge.

According to the *Oxford Dictionary* and other dictionaries, civet is derived from the Arabic *zabad*, "civet cat".

---

[9] Idries Shah, *The Sufis*, p. 393.

Did a similar sound shift serve to render *zabad* as *az-zabat* ("forceful occasion" in Arabic), and hence Sabbat? A closely associated word is *zida*, quintessence, main point, substance.

Thus the broom plant, the Plantagenets, a modern Hermetic society, the Witches' broom and the Sabbat may all have derived from a single event, the initiation of Geoffrey of Anjou, father-in-law of Eleanor of Aquitaine and grandfather of Richard Coeur de Lion.

Richard's mother, Eleanor, outlived her husband (after spending fifteen years as his prisoner in Salisbury), and emerged to take over the government of England while Richard went off to the Third Crusade.

There we find Coeur de Lion in a situation which makes little sense by ordinary standards, but is consistent with his hidden role: "Things outwardly opposed may inwardly be working together" (Rumi).

He is fighting Saladin, his Saracen foe, but is at the same time on the best of terms with him. Saladin sends his personal physician to attend Richard when he is ill, and Richard is reported to have offered his own sister as a bride for Saladin's brother.

Later, on his way home, he is imprisoned and passes his time composing Troubadour poetry!

It seems unlikely that Richard was the only member of the family with access to non-ordinary knowledge. His half-sister, Marie, Countess of Champagne, Eleanor's daughter, was almost certainly knowledgable and it was probably through her that the move was made to translate the chivalric ideal from its local situation into a pan-European one.

Material which is to be manipulated in a certain way for developmental effect is almost always constructed round actual people and actual events. In this case the central figure was the Romano-British chieftain Arthur. Historians now grant the historicity of Arthur. He is held to have been a battle leader of Celtic tribes who, in the *Götterdämmerung* of the Roman departure from Britain, rallied the Celts and inflicted a major defeat on the invading Saxons at the battle of Mount Badon somewhere between Kent and Wiltshire.

This battle is described by St. Gildas, writing 40 years after the event; but he does not mention Arthur. Arthur is first mentioned by name in the *Historia Britonum* of Nennius, a Welsh cleric writing about the year 800.

A colourful version of the Arthurian story was set down by Geoffrey of Monmouth in his *Historia Regum Britanniae*, written about 1135; and this was paraphrased in couplets by the French poet Wace in 1155. However, the legend had already reached the Continent in advance of Geoffrey's version from the Breton minstrels and from the recitations of Bleheris, an emigré Welshman who seems to have brought it independently to Poitiers.

The temptation should perhaps be resisted to link the wandering Breton minstrels with their contemporaries the Troubadours – or with the 10th-century Abu-Ishak Chisti, the Syrian founder of the Chisti order of Sufis whose followers were the origin of the medieval Court Jesters of Europe – and we should regard the Breton minstrels rather as the descendants of the Irish Ollamhs or the Welsh bards. Professor Sir Hamilton Gibb notes that "the author of one version of the Grail-saga even mentions an Arabic book as his source".[10]

Yet even if we do not establish a direct Sufic influence, we cannot ignore the possibility of a stream parallel to the Sufic coming down from antiquity through the Celts, who, as we have seen in the case of the Celtic Church, preserved the imaginative and poetic side of the old tradition when it was in danger of dying out in the rest of Europe.

It is perhaps because the Celts, through their comparative isolation from the rest of Europe, were still to some extent in touch with the old tradition that their legends were suitable for use as the basis of the new courtly romances by the Sufic element. Through the influence of Eleanor and her associates these were diffused through northern France and into Britain.

Friedrich Heer, whose insights in these matters are remarkable, says in *The Medieval World*: "In the great images of the *romans courtois*, two currents merged in a powerful confluence: the stream of material flowing into Western Europe *from outside* (our italics) during the 12th century, and the suppressed native springs of the Celtic and even more primitive cultures."

[10] H. A. R. Gibb, *Literature*, in *Legacy of Islam*, London, 1968, p. 193.

As we have seen, the Arthurian material – or raw material – already existed at Poitiers from the penetration of the Breton minstrels, from the travels of Bleheris and from Geoffrey of Monmouth's British "history".

The process of upgrading it to a world myth which would last for a thousand years was ready to begin. The architect, it would seem, was Chrétien de Troyes who was a courtier at Poitiers and a protégé of Eleanor's daughter Marie.

Chrétien used the Arthurian material, but he also cashed in on the popularity of a current verse form. This was the verse romance dealing with what today would be called the French national spirit, but was then called "the Matter of France". These verse romances, the most famous of which was the Chanson de Roland, commemorated the spirit of Charlemagne and the deeds of the Paladins in their fight against the Moors. Popular in tone, these verse romances were recited by pilgrims or Crusaders on the march.

Chrétien turned the Arthur material into a "Matter of Britain".

The suggestion that more than mere composition was involved here is made by Roger Sherman Loomis:[11]

> A perusal ... leads inevitably to the conclusion that some powerful forces had been at work between the 11th and 13th centuries to transform Arthur from an insular into an international figure.[12]

Chrétien de Troyes, who began his literary career about 1170, wrote five Arthurian Romances: Erec, Cliges, Lancelot, Ivain and Perceval.

A distinct suggestion that Chrétien was working under orders is contained in Chrétien's own comment on Lancelot, which deals with the love of the Knight Lancelot for Guinevere, Arthur's wife. He declares that he was given the "sen" (the controlling idea) from Marie of Champagne: thus

---

[11] *The Development of Arthurian Romance*, Hutchinson, London, 1963.
[12] Significant indications of the influences operating within the Arthurian legend can be detected in many proper names, e.g., Camelot which has baffled historians looking for a geographical location. Camelot may be a play on associated ideas. Camelot = *khamlet* (camlet in English), woollen cloth. (The Sufis are sometimes said to be named after the woollen cloaks they wore, from Suf = wool.) Also *kamilat* = completion or perfection as in *Insan-i-Kamil*, the Perfected Man.

showing the deliberate injection of the Provençal love-theme of the Troubadours into the Arthurian medium.

The basic plot of the fifth romance, Perceval, was given to Chrétien by Philip of Flanders, who was Marie's second husband. This again suggests a policy move; for in Perceval for the first time the story of the Grail is introduced.

Perceval is at the castle of the lame Fisher King and is attending a banquet. Before each course a procession passes through the hall, including a squire bearing a lance to which a drop of blood clings, and a maiden bearing a jewel-studded grail or bowl. Perceval fails to ask the correct question: "Whom does one serve with the Grail?", and next morning finds the castle deserted. He then sets out in quest of the Grail.

Chrétien apparently died before completing Perceval, and the Grail mystery is therefore unsolved. Jessie Weston[13] suggests that the grail and the lance were sexual symbols, and the ritual in the castle was an initiation rite.

After Chrétien's death, the theme was taken up by other poets. Four different sequels to Perceval appeared, in one of which it is clear that a Christianizing process had already begun.

Here the bleeding lance is identified with the Spear of Longinus, which is said to have pierced the side of the crucified Christ, and the Grail is identified with the vessel in which Joseph of Arimathaea caught drops of blood.

The Arthurian legend proceeded to spread like a self-multiplying organism. Versions of Chrétien's romances were made in Middle English, Middle High German, Dutch and Old Norse. Between 1210 and 1230 three long French prose romances, the *Prose Lancelot*, the *Quest of the Holy Grail* and the *Mort Artur* were written, probably by monks, and combined in a "Vulgate Cycle", so called on account of the great popularity which the contents enjoyed with the common people. It seems clear that the value of the Arthur material – and the energy it contained – were sensed by the Church. While the idealistic love theme is more or less intact in Lancelot in the Vulgate Cycle, the other two are already being "adapted" to validate the celibate ideal which the Church could endorse. The

---

[13] J. Weston, *From Ritual to Romance*, Doubleday, New York, 1957.

Vulgate Cycle was the main source of Sir Thomas Malory's *Le Morte d'Arthur* (printed by Caxton in 1485) and the *Morte d'Arthur* in its turn was the main source for Tennyson's *Idylls of the King*.

As the original Chrétien de Troyes romances were spreading over Europe a very remarkable "coincidence" can be observed in Britain.

We have suggested that when certain legends are to be used to operate on human psychology in a certain way, historical figures and historical incidents are chosen as a basis. We may also suspect that validation of the historical facts is sometimes arranged. By a very strange coincidence, the bones of the historic Arthur just happened to come to light as Chrétien's Arthur was catching the European imagination. A present-day journalist would recognize this event as precisely what was needed to "keep the story going".

Henry II is travelling in Wales and just happens to meet the one monk who knows where Arthur's grave is. It is at Glastonbury Abbey. Henry II, it will be recalled, was the husband of Eleanor, who has something like a family interest in translating the Troubadour mystique into a new medium.

The monks at Glastonbury start digging at the indicated spot and seven feet down come upon a stone slab and a lead cross with the inscription: "*Hic jacet sepultus inclytus rex Arturus in insula avallonia.*" Below, in a coffin made of a hollow log, is the skeleton of a very large man indeed. The medieval world accepted these relics as authentic, but the find has been regarded as a little too fortuitous by modern scholars, who recall that "genuine" relics were the stock-in-trade of any medieval monastery which hoped to attract pilgrims and hence funds.

Against this is one awkward fact. Hollow coffin burial is now known to correspond to a certain period; but it is thought that the Glastonbury monks would have had no way of knowing this in 1190. If they had been bent on faking a relic discovery for the greater glory of the Abbey, they would much more probably have "discovered" Arthur in a container of stone.

Against all customary usage, they discovered him in a hollowed-out log.

One possible explanation has not so far been considered. Glastonbury is associated with an esoteric tradition. In the 10th century, St. Dunstan, who was born near Glastonbury, was educated by the Irish monks there, before entering the household of King Athelstan. Athelstan through his nephew and his sisters was connected with both the Frankish Court and the Emperor Otto I. Sufic influences are known to have entered England at this time, and it is not at all improbable that Dunstan made contact with these influences. He was at any rate turned out of Athelstan's court "for practising the black arts".

Dunstan then became a monk and lived as a hermit till recalled to court by Athelstan's successor, Edmund. In 943, Dunstan was made Abbot of Glastonbury, and under him the monastery became a famous school with a high reputation for both music and geometry – subjects which had a particularly Arabic flavour at that time. Further, Dunstan is the patron saint of goldsmiths, which is a strange association unless gold has a secondary meaning. He is also reputed to have "tweaked the Devil's nose" with his goldsmith's tongs.

The matters associated with Dunstan's name have an inescapable flavour of alchemy, and legend says that the wonders performed by Dee and Kelly at the court of Elizabeth 600 years later were based on a quantity of "Philosopher's Stone" made by St. Dunstan, secreted in a hollow stone and recovered by Kelly's clairvoyance.

It may be that a secret Sufic school operated at Glastonbury behind the cover of an orthodox monastery. If so, it is possible that the discovery of the mortal Arthur at Glastonbury and the creation of the psychological Arthur at Poitiers were two sides of the same operation.

Sufic operations are notoriously economic, each component serving several purposes. Glastonbury Abbey had been burned down in 1184. Were Arthur's bones disinterred to attract pilgrim money for a rebuilding programme: and at the same time to endorse the Arthurian legend abroad, currently becoming a vehicle of Sufic psychology?

Love-poetry and the Arthurian Romances flourished in Germany at the end of the 12th and the beginning of the 13th centuries. Provençal poets had been received at the court of Frederic Barbarossa, and from 1180 onwards the German *Minnesänger* took up the medium – on the Provençal model – in Middle High German. These German poets were all members of the minor nobility, attached to the courts of rich patrons, the most famous of whom was the Landgraf Hermann of Thuringia.

Among the most famous of the Minnesänger were Heinrich von Veldeke, Friederich von Hausen (who died on the Third Crusade), Heinrich von Morungen (who journeyed to India), Rainmar von Hagenau, Hartman von Aue and, the father of German lyrical poetry, Walther von der Vogelweide.

The Arthurian romance also appeared in new forms. Hartmann von Aue wrote a German version of Chrétien's *Erec and Ivain*, and between 1200 and 1210 Wolfram von Eschenbach wrote his masterpiece, *Parzival*.[14] Here the Grail appears, not as a vessel, but as a "stone".[15]

Permutations of the Arthurian legend continue into the 20th century. One of the most penetrating allegories in modern fiction, C. S. Lewis's *That Hideous Strength*,[16] is based on it. In this, an esoteric order of chivalry has continued to the present day, able to call on Principalities and Powers to further its support for "the true West" over which Arthur in some mysterious way still rules. "For Arthur did not die: but our Lord took him to be in the body till the end, with Enoch and Elias and Moses and Melchizedek the King. Melchizedek is he in whose hall the steep-stoned ring sparkles on the forefinger of the Pendragon."

So compelling are the energies that surround Arthur that they can hypnotize Sir Winston Churchill into one of the most extraordinary statements ever made by an historian.

Investigating the historic origins of the story, Sir Winston says: "If we could see *exactly what happened*, we should find ourselves in the presence of a theme as well founded, as inspired and as inalienable from the inheritance of mankind

---

[14] Wolfram says that his source was one Kiot, a Provençal, "who learned the heathen letters [presumably Arabic] in order to read a book he found in Toledo".

[15] It is conjectured that Grail (Graal) derives from Persian *Gohr* meaning precious stone (figuratively "the Essence") with the (Arabic) definite article transposed to the end. *Gohr al* thus became Graal, hence Grail. Identical process produced the English word Admiral from Arabic *Amir al (Bahr)* = Commander of the (Sea), hence Admiral.

[16] Bodley Head, London, 1945.

as the Odyssey or the Old Testament. It is all true, *or it ought to be*" (our italics).

Perhaps the most penetrating summary of the whole subject comes from Friedrich Heer: "There can no longer be any doubt that the theme of the great romantic epics (in France extending from the work of Chrétien de Troyes to that of Renard de Beaujeu, in Germany from Hartmann von Aue to Wolfram von Eschenbach) is initiation, dedication, metamorphosis and absorption into a higher and fuller life at once more human and more divine.... All Arthurian romances of the first rank were attempts at expounding the process of man's interior development.... Through his relationship with the woman, the man gains access to his own soul."[17]

Some four years before this present book was written, a group of five people of different nationalities came together because of a common interest in esoteric subjects. Each had a speciality interest in one branch of occult lore. All of them had been convinced for some time that behind the various aspects of esotericism which they had studied piecemeal, there was some overall unity which eluded them.

They began to suspect, from hints that had become increasingly explicit from the early nineteen fifties, that the word "Sufi" pointed to the overall organization which they suspected but had not been able to identify.

This group decided to pool resources and see if they could take this idea further.

The group of five succeeded in making contact initially with one contemporary Sufic group and were allowed facilities for further investigation. The conditions under which they were allowed to investigate and the discoveries they made will be discussed later, but it is appropriate at this stage to look at one study which they originated.

They approached a sociologist, whose interest was European history, and asked him to consider, purely as a theoretical exercise, the idea that certain movements in history were not fortuitous but directed. In effect, the idea of The Secret People was presented to him as a purely hypothetical concept and he was asked to try to analyse a number of historical incidents

---

[17] Friedrich Heer, *The Medieval World*, p. 144.

"as though such an organization existed". The several historical occasions he was asked to study were in fact Sufic operations.

His analysis is now given, and we have added in italics after some of his conclusions a possible relevance, taken either from the Troubadour/Arthurian complex or from alchemy and associated subjects.

His report was as follows:

In all the periods studied, the incidents or events under review take place against similar backgrounds. A prevailing order claims, explicitly or implicitly, to have a monopoly of truth. In the past such systems were either religious or national, but, whatever the apparent form, the essential structure of such ideologies is essentially the same as that of modern totalitarian régimes.

All such systems seek to indoctrinate their communities with a given set of beliefs and the concept of heresy is a means of involving the population in the control apparatus. Each individual becomes the supervisor of his neighbour "for the good of all". The good so served is, in fact, the good of the control apparatus itself.

Assuming the existence of individuals and organizations concerned with breaking the monopoly of such rigid systems by conveying new knowledge into them (the given hypothesis), there would appear to be two main means possible.

(1) The use of some advanced capacity (perhaps related to ESP) to communicate directly with selected members of the community. Even if such capacities exist, their employment would be difficult or impossible to identify in operation and little more can be said about such a possibility.

(2) A direct approach from within the community itself through some centre which was
   (a) hidden and therefore unsuspected by the organization in power;
   (b) operating openly but seemingly engaged in an activity wholly innocuous to the official régime.
   (c) apparently part of the official régime itself.

The suggested historical groupings which fall under suspicion as being the subjects of such intervention exhibit certain characteristics in common and it may therefore be possible tentatively to suggest the general procedures possibly employed by some (postulated) individuals and groups conducting such intervention.

Characteristics of such interventions are:

(1) *They are said to be teachings.*
(Freemasonry's rationale is supposed to be a teaching transmitted from ancient times.)

(2) *They have a leadership.*
(The Rosicrucians regard Christian Rosenkreuz as their spiritual head. The Grand Master was spiritual and temporal head of the Templars. St. Francis was the head of the Franciscans.)

(3) *They use symbols or a language of their own.*
(The Troubadour codes. The ciphers of alchemy. The strange medieval figures who spoke no Western language but held up symbols. The "tools" of Freemasonry. The symbol language of heraldry.)

(4) *They are said to be for the benefit of mankind.*
(The Knights Templars were to protect pilgrims.

In recent times there have been suggestions of an influence, not explainable in terms of expediency or of either personal or national advantage, connected with the origins of the Red Cross.

Baden Powell's life attitude may have been decisively affected by his contact with the Regiment of Guides in the Second Afghan War. Much of the Scout and Wolf Cub symbology has a trans-personal and trans-national significance if investigated below its apparent surface triviality.)

(5) *They stress secret knowledge or development by stages or degrees.*
(Freemason and Rosicrucian secret societies are based on a degree structure allegedly marking, or at least symbolizing, advances in inner development.)

(6) *They cross the ordinary boundaries of nation, race and religion.*
(Both the real and the ostensible activities of Raymond Lully exemplify this. Alchemy was international and alchemists understood each other in spite of differences in race or language.

Eleanor of Aquitaine's courts were attended by the young nobility of Europe.

The Translators converged on Spain from many countries and returned to distribute their material.)

(7) *They are said to have come from outside or are connected with strangers or foreigners.*
(The mystique of Freemasonry.

The mystique of the gypsies. Historians continue to try

and trace some motivation behind the diaspora of the gypsies in the 15th century but find that what they are seeking eludes them. The possible simultaneous appearance of the Tarot pack in Europe has however been noted: as has the phrase "the affairs of Egypt".

The choice of a Syrian as the Patron Saint of England.)

(8) *They have powerful sponsorship from important figures in the host community.*

(Raymond of Toulouse for the Cathars. The family of Aquitaine for the Troubadours. The British Royal Families for the Orders of Chivalry. Royal patronage for cathedral builders.)

(9) *They require tests and practices for their operation.*

(The signs and passwords of the Freemasons. The trade practices of workers in traditional crafts and the rituals to which apprentices are subjected on obtaining the grade of Journeyman. The word Journeyman is almost overt in suggesting participation on a Path. The trade test of an apprentice cooper to the present day has thinly veiled initiatory elements.)

(10) *They have a myth or symbolical story or stories whose parallels are believed to be worked out in the life of the community or group.*

(The symbolology of Hiram Abif. The symbolology of the English Coronation rite. The symbolology of Morris Dancing. The order of knighthood based on Arthurian (chivalric) symbolism.)

(11) *They have unexpected links with each other not explained by saying that heretics are attracted to one another – which is not in any case true.*

(There is reason to suspect that much activity ordinarily assigned to well known individuals is in fact the result of influences emanating from groups with which the individuals were associated. The tales of Wolfram von Eschenbach and Chrétien de Troyes, the poetry of Dante, Spenser, Blake and Goethe: the Orders of Chivalry, Zen Buddhism and judo; the medicine of Paracelsus and the psychology of Mesmer: the devotional system of St. Francis and the disciplines of the Jesuits may all be variations of weft upon a single unsuspected woof.)

(12) *These links are sometimes tenaciously clung to, even at the expense of general goodwill in the community.*

(Local nobles continued support for the Cathars even when such action became anti-survival. The "fraternal links" of modern Freemasons are said to be supra-national even when the host communities are at war.)

(13) *The dogma, ritual or myth does not provide a true historical link with the origin of the movement.*
(The historicity of Christian Rosenkreuz is regarded as untenable. Arthur of the Round Table in incompatible with any historical Arthur. The belief that the Gypsies came from Egypt is untenable. Legends of historical incidents in which alchemical gold-making occurred are at one level veridical; at another, the historicity goes "soft" at the critical point.)

(14) *There are distinct signs of actual or former mental and physical practices such as exercises.*
(The dancing of the witches; the whirling of some dervishes; the Freemason memorising the "work"; a witch riding a broomstick; the psychological exercises of the Jesuits; Maypole dancing; working through a maze at the end of a pilgrimage.)

(15) *There is a connection with religion but it is never "official" religion.*
(The Arthurian literature is aspirational and devotional but the precise nature of the religious content cannot be pinned down.

Master Builders of the cathedrals seem to have worked independently of official Church policy, e.g., gargoyles and the symbolism of the great Cathedrals.)

(16) *There is always a connection with non-religious behaviour to such an extent that religious or mystical investigators become confused in trying to locate the association. Elements of art, science, literature, chemistry, commerce, military affairs intrude but cannot be accommodated in formal labelling.*
(The sexual components of the Love Courts. The sexual ambivalence of the Arthurian saga. The Baphomet legend in the Templar Order. The strains of science, chemistry and religion in alchemy. The martial elements in the Orders of Chivalry. The Hermetic Fair when a "Papal" enthronement was played as "Black Comedy" actually within the Cathedral of Notre Dame. The Christian "Feast of Fools" and the "Feast of the Donkey" – all seemingly religious activity with a non-religious or anti-religious component that defies analysis.)

(17) *It would appear that some force prevents, certainly at the time of their maximum operation, the coherent investigation of their location, operation and other attributes which would make it possible to mount effective opposition.*
(Witch covens and their procedures are endlessly reconstructed from testimony extracted from witches under

torture but coven meetings do not seem to have been raided in session.)

(18) *They are always studied piecemeal and an apparently "inside" explanation of their activities and nature is eagerly accepted. Activities of this sort are in turn regarded as heresies, later as psychological phenomena and at the present time as the result of social and economic forces. The pigeon-holing actually serves to aid concealment. Once labelled there is no further public interest, "the secret being now exposed".*

(Official science accepted Jung's psychological explanation of alchemy with relief. A troublesome thorn in rationalist flesh, it had been identified and labelled and was therefore respectable. There was no further need to regard it as something that needed attention.)

(19) *Apostasy from such organizations contains the suspicion of diversionary tactics.*

(Dervish orders who "went over" to Jenghis Khan. Mevlevis who agreed to put on a tourist pantomime for Kemal Ataturk.)

(20) *The available literature of such organizations seems to disappear after a time or is found in such a diversity of forms as to baffle inquiry. This peculiarity may suggest a deliberate policy of stirring up the pond to make the water muddy.*

(The quantity of surviving alchemical texts is enormous but the success in decoding is in inverse ratio to the amount of material included in any particular study.

After only seventy years it has apparently become impossible to unravel the origins of the neo-pagan Society of the Golden Dawn. There are now probably as many authoritative "final explanations" as there are researchers. Documentation of seemingly equal validity is available to prove that it derived from a "revelation" to Henri Bergson's sister and that it grew from a magical document lying on a book barrow in the Farringdon Road, London. Elucidation of Rudolph Steiner's source is no less enturbulated.)

From external analysis it seems impossible to arrive at any firm conclusion as to the theory of "intervention". As to the object of such historical operations as have been suggested, it would appear impossible to discover the aims and purposes which they could have.

If they are mounted to convert and organize masses of

people it seems clear that they have never succeeded. It is more likely (assuming that such activities take place) that the aim is to locate and act on selected people at various points in history and then to disband activity decisively.

It seems possible to detect vestigial traces of some activity of the kind suggested. The quality of such activity seems consistently arid and banal and may suggest the mechanical perpetuation of some format from which the essential quality has been fully abstracted.

Chapter Six

ALCHEMY: THE DISGUISED PATH

What is alchemy? Half a century ago there was little doubt in the West. It was a superstition among ignorant ancients that, by certain manipulations, base metals could be turned into gold.

Then, when Freudian and Jungian ideas began to circulate in Europe, a new, enlightened view of alchemy became fashionable. Alchemy, it was now said, was really human psychology. The alchemists were psychoanalysing themselves. They were sublimating and calcining their own subconscious. Their real aim was not to make gold but to make a non-aberrated man.

As pursuits of this kind in the Middle Ages overlapped territory which the Church held to be its own, the alchemists had been obliged to conceal what they were really doing behind an apparently lunatic attempt to turn lead into gold.

Even for the new psychological *avant-garde* this explanation was not entirely satisfactory, because it was well known that even in the 20th century highly intelligent men in Fez, Cracow, Damascus, Paris and London were currently engaged in attempts to make perfectly tangible yellow gold. They had given up charcoal furnaces and were using Calor gas, but they were manifestly doing something with pots and pans, and not with Egos and Ids.

Perhaps all external ideas about the nature of alchemy could be put into four views, separately or in combination:

First View: It is possible to transmute one element into another. One such transmutation is lead or iron into gold. From some unimaginable antiquity, a mighty secret has been handed down which shows how to do this. It is the most closely kept secret in human history.

Second View: Alchemy is the science of purifying man's inner nature and arriving at a non-aberrated individual. Such an individual would have, by comparison with ordinary men, certain advanced powers. For political reasons, this exercise had to be concealed in a pseudo-science of metal refining to which the Church would have no reason to object.

Third View: Metals *can* be transmuted. Lead *can* be turned into gold. An alchemist knows how to do this, and also knows a greater secret. If he is in a certain relation to the crucible in which the process happens, a comparable transmutation takes place in his own common presence. As lead turns into gold in the crucible, the operator's mind is transformed. He is subjected to something like nuclear radiation. Also, certain chemical by-products in the crucible are capable of being stored and used either to make more gold or to transform other men. Hence legends of "The Sly Man's Pill" and the Elixir which Saint-Germain is supposed to have offered Casanova when he was dying.

Fourth View: An alchemist is a man who knows an immensely powerful method of cleaning the Augean stable of his own subconscious mind. Pushed far enough, this process gives rise to a true soul-body inholding the properties of a different order of things. If this soul-body is directed on the base metals in a certain way (projection), it will accomplish a comparable transmutation in inorganic matter.

It should be said at once that no one outside the select circle of successful alchemists (if there are such) knows which of these, separately or in combination, approximates to the truth, but some hint may be contained in the first article of the Hermetic declaration, the Emerald Tablet of Hermes Trismegistus. "True it is, without falsehood, certain and most true. That which is above is as that which is below, and that which is below is as that which is above to accomplish the miracle of one thing."

Whether as a quick way to a fortune, as a process of psychological development, or as a holy science of soul-making, alchemy captured the imagination of Europe for centuries and at certain levels does so still, though in such circles there is now a widespread belief that there has been an interdict upon the complete operation since about the end of the 18th century. There are reasons to believe, however, that occasional breakthroughs still occur.

Alchemy may be derived from the Arabic *al-kimia*. The allegedly Egyptian origins of the art suggest that the "chem" root may come from the Egyptian name for Egypt, meaning black, referring to the black soil which distinguished it from the desert sand. It may also come from the Greek word for fusing.

Alchemy, at any rate, is of great antiquity, whether credit for the first historical record should go to China or Egypt. There are records of Chinese alchemy – or anti-alchemy – laws in 144 BC, and some reason to pre-date Chinese alchemy to the 4th century BC, at least.[1]

There were considerable exchanges between the Far and Near East, and Middle Eastern alchemy may well have come from China. On the other hand, Chinese alchemy was very largely esoteric and concerned with producing a medicine to give long life or immortality. Middle Eastern alchemy prior to Islam had a preponderantly exoteric reputation, and was seemingly concerned to manipulate metallic alloys. It has been pointed out that if China transmitted the idea of alchemy, it would have been an alchemy of medicine, and not of metallurgy.

If, however, we take the viewpoint that alchemy is the translation into "material" terms of information about non-causal events obtained through access to higher consciousness, there is no historical difficulty.

Both sources, Chinese and Middle Eastern, would penetrate to the same insights, but would translate them into whatever "material" terms appealed to their own psychology; in one case, medical, in another metallic, in a third, a combination of both.

Almost from the foundation of Islam, alchemy became a Moslem science, though Holmyard makes the point that this is true only linguistically. Arabic was the cultural language of the Islamic empires, and therefore the language of art and science. The texts dealt with might, however, be in any language: Persian and Greek, for example. Listing Stephanos, Apollonius, Archelaos and others, Holmyard says: "Islam appropriated Greek alchemical authorities *in toto.*" Certainly it would seem that Islam was the agent for reissuing a great

---

[1] E. J. Holmyard, *Alchemy*, Penguin, London, 1957.

amount of alchemical work from a much more remote past, but that, in addition, the Arab alchemists made their own highly original contributions.

The first translation of alchemical texts (from Greek and Coptic) are said to have been made on the order of Khalid, son of the Umayyad Caliph Yazid I, in the first half-century following the death of Mohammed.

Armed with these translations, the young Khalid studied the subject at Damascus under Morienus, said to be a Christian monk of Alexandria.

The Nestorian Christians at this time were celebrated for their work in assisting translation of past knowledge into Arabic, but this was a transition phase of Saracenic development. By the 8th century, the Arabs had produced a wide range of scholars able to read Greek. After this the transmission of past learning became rapid.

In alchemy this phase is associated with the name of Jabir ibn Hayyan, otherwise Geber. His style of writing (intended to enlighten those who already possessed the key to alchemy, while remaining exasperatingly obscure to those who did not), became known as the Geber style and gave the word "gibberish" to the English language.

Jabir was an orphan, whose father Hayyan was beheaded for instigating revolt against the Umayyad dynasty. In consequence the boy was befriended by the Shi'ite faction. Little is known about his early life except that his master was a scholar called Harbi al-Himyari. Jabir appears as a fully-fledged alchemist at the court of Haroun al Rashid. His protector was the Shi'ite Imam, Ja'far al Sadiq.

Accounts exist of Jahir curing one of the ladies of the court with "a certain elixir", so it is clear that the medical aspect of alchemy associated with the Chinese stream was known to the Arab alchemists by the second half of the 8th century.

Jabir was a scholar of great range. As well as books on alchemy, he wrote papers on astronomy, logic, medicine, automata and magic squares, (some of which were translated in Spain by Gerard of Cremona).

Coded material seems to be inseparable from these magic squares, and it is possible that matters concerned with the rival factions claiming the true mandate of the Prophet are involved in these cipher puzzles as well as material deriving from the objective science of alchemy.

Considering the nature of the material deriving from Mohammed it may be that the two aspects are inseparable.

Scholars dispute the attribution of much of the "Jabirian corpus" to Jabir, but it seems clear that he was the author of much of it, though his texts were probably expanded or even slanted by the Ishma'ilite sect in the 10th century for reasons connected with the double streams of occultism and politics which are apparently inseparable from this tradition.

Jabir's ground plan of nature involved four basic elements (earth, air, fire and water), in line with Aristotelian belief, but he developed these in terms of hotness, coldness, dryness and moisture. In the presence of these qualities and under planetary influences, metals were formed in the earth by the action of sulphur and mercury. Holmyard feels that this represents Jabir's major contribution to alchemy and that it influenced the development of experimental chemistry till the 17th century.

Holmyard, perhaps as a result of a visit to an alchemical laboratory at Fez, appears to have more than a purely academic attitude, and notes that when Jabir wrote sulphur, he meant "sulphur". Holmyard almost makes a leap into the mystical background of alchemy when he writes "(these were) hypothetical substances to which ordinary sulphur and mercury formed the closest available approximation".[2] Perhaps interesting comparisons with the "hydrogens" of G. I. Gurdjieff might also be made.

The combination of mercury and sulphur, absolutely pure and in a certain proportion, give rise, Jabir believed, to gold. In various degress of impurity and in various proportions they give rise to all the other metals.

One of Jabir's apparent endeavours was to arrive at a formula which would give the various balances. One such table, which he published, turns out to be a "magic square" which was known to the Neo-Platonists and, says Holmyard, "had associations for the Sufi mystical society of which he was a member".

[2] E. J. Holmyard, *Alchemy*, Penguin, London, 1957, p. 73.

And there we have it. Jabir was not an Arab with a bee in his bonnet about naive chemistry and magic squares. He was a Sufi.

The most open-minded scholars are continually baffled by a certain seeming incongruity. Throughout history men who are clearly intellectuals and who have, from internal evidence of their work, a high I.Q., are associated with what appear to be childish pursuits. They draw magic squares and fuse metals in bowls trying to manufacture gold. It is a disquieting picture, rather like coming upon Einstein seriously trying to get nuclear fission with a magnifying glass.

Yet the contradiction would seem to resolve when viewed against the background of all alchemical pursuits, which is clearly mysticism.

Jabir, reputed to be the greatest alchemist since Hermes, is a Sufi. He is associated with a technique of entering a different kind of consciousness. He has, in consequence, access to an inductive and not a deductive method. Instead of observing the results of experiment and deducing the laws which apply, he observes the laws in operation at noumenal level and induces their experimental application.

Since there is no everyday knowledge of such a process, there is no ordinary vocabulary to describe it. The alchemist is reduced to talking about sulphur and mercury and elixir and stone. If he lives at a time when there are no inverted commas, he cannot easily suggest the symbolic nature of these terms.

At the same time, there are many alchemical authorities who appear, from internal evidence, to be fully knowledgeable yet who deny completely that the transmutation of metals and hence gold-making in the ordinary sense is possible at all.

One such was Abu Ali Ibn Sina whose name was Westernised to Avicenna. He was regarded as the greatest intellect since Aristotle, and for centuries the medieval world regarded him as a genius whose word upon any subject was final. A famous work "On Minerals", long attributed to Aristotle himself, was discovered in 1927 to be a condensation of one of Avicenna's books.

Now Avicenna held the same basic ideas as did Jabir about the constitution of matter; but he went out of his way to assert that transmutation of minerals, and hence gold-making, was an old wives' tale.

There are several possible explanations. The first is that men of exceptional intellect, working pragmatically, arrived at certain conclusions by deduction from experiment. Such men would be in effect materialist scientists before their time.

The second is that certain exceptional individuals associated with genuine schools of human development added to the sum of the practical knowledge of their time because they had access to higher consciousness and could induce the application of natural laws to practical events.

The third is that men of this latter category chose to conceal the source of their knowledge by deliberate mis-direction.

The Sufic tradition appears to contain many examples of this, and it is said that reality can sometimes be best approximated, at temporal level, in terms of apparently irreconcilable opposites. "It is necessary to note that opposite things work together even though nominally opposed," said the great Sufic sage Rumi. Both Rumi (died 1273) and El Ghazzali in the 11–12th centuries, acknowledged Sufi giants, referred to mystical knowledge as alchemical transformation.[3]

Holmyard makes the point that alchemy, like printing, reached its highest pitch of perfection while still in its infancy, an observation in line with Rodney Collin's theory of cellular development. "Islamic alchemy," says Holmyard, "never surpassed the level it attained with one of its earliest exponents, Jabir ibn Hayyan."

Certainly an enormous amount of all subsequent alchemy in Europe derived from the Latin translations – in various degrees corrupted – made from the Jabir alchemical corpus.

So, from Egypt to Greece, to Islam, to Europe. The great transition to modern times took place after 1100 and was centred round the famous College of Translators at Toledo, founded by Archbishop Raymond. Robert of Chester, collaborating with another "student translator", Hermann of Dalmatia, undertook to translate the Koran at the request of Peter the Venerable, who was a Cluniac.

When they had finished this – it took two years – Robert of Chester then began the translation of an Arab treatise: *The Book of the Composition of Alchemy*. He recorded the completion of this

---

[3] One of Ghazzali's most important works is *Kimia-i-Saadat*, *The Alchemy of Bliss*.

task on February 11, 1144, so that the literary date of this alchemy passing into Europe is known precisely.[4]

Chester noted that no Latin words existed corresponding to some of the Arabic alchemical vocabulary, and he was forced to use simple transliterations.

In this way, many words like alkali, alcohol, athanor, elixir, matrass and naphtha passed from Arabic into Western European languages.

Adelard of Bath translated another alchemical text and Gerard did several from the Greek, one by Razi, and very probably *The Book of Seventy* by Jabir.[5]

The mystery of the alchemical process was now about to engage the whole of Europe, and this it proceeded to do in the 12th and 13th centuries.

Among the first of the European alchemists was Albertus Magnus. Albert, Count of Bollstadt (1206 or 7–1280) was the prototype of many strange figures of the Middle Ages who combined an eager, questing intellect together with a "certain something" which served to earn them election to the mysterious company of Secret People.

He refused to believe that knowledge ended with Aristotle, and insisted on the primacy of personal observation and experiment, whatever ancient texts had to say. "He is the first Christian who is prepared to accept a rational treatment of natural phenomena".[6]

A Dominican monk – in spite of his independent mind – he travelled all over France and Germany on foot, lecturing on philosophy before finally returning to Cologne to study and write in seclusion.

Albert was one of these apparently ambivalent intellects which are such a sore trial to the logical mind. He seems to have asserted on the one hand that the alchemical transmutation of metals was impossible, and that alchemists succeeded only in dyeing metals to look like gold. In another book attributed to him, he declares a subjective insight into the alchemical process "given him by the Grace of God", and goes on to describe recipes for performing transmutations!

[4] E. J. Holmyard, *Alchemy*, p. 103.
[5] ibid., p. 106.
[6] Gordon Leff, *Medieval Thought*, Penguin, London 1958, p. 208.

Albert's fame was such that young scholars came from all over Europe to get his teaching. One such, and the most famous of all, was Thomas Aquinas.

Whatever is to be made of his apparently contradictory views on alchemy, Albertus was no simple pragmatist. Legend associates him not only with constructing one of these famous "talking heads", but with making an entire artificial man, a task which occupied him for thirty years.

As Idries Shah[7] has disclosed, "making a head" is a Dervish code phrase for a certain exercise of inner development, and it is inconceivable that such a legend should have attached to a man who was not, alchemically speaking, on the inside.

That he possessed other powers associated with a level of development beyond the ordinary – instantaneous hypnotism, for example – is suggested in another legend. He is said to have invited a royal party to a banquet in mid-winter and then proposed holding it in the open air. Suddenly the royal guests saw the snow disappear. The sun came out, the trees were covered in foliage, the grass became midsummer green and fruit appeared on the bushes. As soon as the banquet was over, the sylvan scene vanished and the party found themselves shivering in the winter cold.

Clearly Albertus had the practice as well as the theory.

That there was a network of transmission behind the scenes so that knowledgable people, whether clerics or laymen, could contact one another, may be suggested by the family circumstances of Albert's greatest pupil, Thomas, later Saint Thomas, Aquinas.

To glimpse this it will be necessary to flash back briefly to a strange little empire in the Mediterranean, where a whole world, largely unsuspected by the rest of Europe, continued to inject apparently alien standards into European history.

In the 11th century, armies on the way home from the Crusades began to take part in the struggle for power in Southern Italy. Some of them, under Tancred de Hauteville, conquered part of South Italy, and took Sicily from the Saracens. Out of this operation grew a royal dynasty with Roger II established as the monarch of a combined kingdom of Apulia and Sicily.

[7] Idries Shah, *The Sufis*, p. 227.

This court was a strange mixture of the cultured and the barbaric, of East and West, of Christianity and Islam. Half European, half Oriental, it had a combined tradition of Greek, Latin, Moor and Jew. Roger kept a harem and had eunuchs.

A daughter of Roger II married the Holy Roman Emperor, Henry VI, and had a son, Frederick. The office of Emperor was elective, but with the support of Innocent III, the young Frederick was elected Emperor as Frederick II. As the Sicilian kingdom was hereditary, Frederick became both Emperor and King of Sicily.

The Pope's support for Frederick had been conditional on his mounting a Sixth Crusade. Frederick promised, but never quite got round to it. A later Pope, Gregory IX, excommunicated him and invaded his domains in South Italy. Frederick sailed for the Holy Land, but had an interview with the Sultan of Egypt, as a result of which it was agreed that Christian pilgrims should have access to the holy places for ten years. Frederick apparently achieved as much in ten minutes as all the Crusades put together. H. G. Wells regards this interlude as an outstanding example of simple commercial sanity in an era of supercharged religious emotion.

Frederick much preferred his Sicilian court to his German one. An amazingly well educated man, he spoke six languages, including fluent Arabic, and he gathered round him philosophers of all persuasions. Among his court scholars was Michael Scot, who translated both Ibn Rushd ("Averroes") and Aristotle.

From the court of Frederick, it is claimed, Arabic numerals entered the West. Called by his contemporaries "The Wonder of the World", Frederick was an astonishing mixture of scientist, philosopher, linguist, traveller and sybarite. He was a patron of the arts, valued beauty for itself, and was apparently interested in everything. In 1224 he founded the University of Naples, the first secular university in Europe, and he enlarged the medical school at Salerno. For light relief, he founded a zoological garden.

When the Provençal Troubadours were fleeing from the Albigensian terror, he set up a refuge for them. From this grew a Sicilian school of poetry, which later spread north. Out of it, it is claimed, grew the poetry of Dante. Frederick himself was a poet in the Italian vernacular.

It is fairly clear that Frederick was engaged in enterprises which went deeper than appearances. The Saracenic empires were undoubtedly the cover for the Sufic operation into Europe, by which certain evolutionary gains were being attempted, and the hidden inner activity spilled over into many forms. Whether Frederick was knowledgeable about the inner processes working through the history of the time it is impossible to say: but some indication may be glimpsed from the fact that when building castles in Southern Italy – for example, Castel del Monte in Apulia – these were designed as perfect octagons. This, says one historian, was a non-functional design and must therefore have been purely aesthetic.

Those who have noticed the recurrence of the octagon motif in various connections may suspect that it was not aesthetic at all.

The strange and haunting legend of Barbarossa – the monarch who sleeps in a deep cavern, his beard growing round a stone table, and who will awaken when the time is right for him to restore peace in a disordered world – this legend is normally ascribed to Frederick I.

H. G. Wells suggests that the legend should rightly be attached to Frederick II, and that it was subsequently antedated to enhance the religious prestige of the Crusader, Frederick I.[8]

If, as Wells suggests, the legend of Barbarossa should properly refer to Frederick II, some interesting speculations arise.

The legend of the great figure who sleeps till an appointed time has counterparts in Egyptian legend, in the story of Melchizedek, of Arthur, Merlin, Rip Van Winkle, and perhaps the Wandering Jew. That a legend of such an obviously archetypal nature should attach to a man who exhibited the qualities of Frederick II and who built octagonal castles for no apparent reason, is interesting indeed.

Was the influence of Frederick II purely local, a quixotic injection of alien Oriental ideas which startled Western Christendom as a nine days' wonder and then faded out of

[8] H. G. Wells, *The Outline of History*, Cassell, London, 1920, p. 678.

history? Or did his influence later emerge in underground and unsuspected ways?

One of the major influences on medieval Christianity was undoubtedly Thomas Aquinas, whose orthodox piety incorporated a resolute attempt to reinstate reason as a legitimate component of religious faith. His efforts made an impression on Church dogmatism from which, perhaps, modern attitudes of thought became possible.

Was it coincidence, therefore, that Thomas's family had distinguished themselves in the service of Frederick II? Or that, after an elementary education at Monte Cassino, he went to the University that Frederick had set up? Or that Thomas found his teacher in the person of Albertus Magnus who was clearly involved in activities which were not discernible on the surface?

It seems likely that certain influences from the court of Frederick II were well known in Thomas's family, and that he was destined for the rôle he had to play.

A not dissimilar family link may also be suspected in the career of Raymond Lully who, so far, has just failed to attain the award of canonization accorded to Aquinas.

Thomas went from Frederick's University at Naples (where his masters were Peter the Irishman and Martin of Denmark), to become a Dominican monk – a move of which apparently his family disapproved. This may, however, have facilitated his meeting with Albertus at Cologne. For the three years subsequent to 1245, Thomas studied under Albertus and emerged a "philosopher" and an alchemist. He then went to Paris, where in 1256 he was admitted as Master of Paris University.

This appointment brought to a head the clash between the alchemist scholars and the Church. One of Thomas's aims was to correlate all known learning of his day, an aim which has a familiar ring against the tradition which includes the Encyclopaedists of Basra and Roger Bacon. Reason and faith, he claimed, were both concerned with the same object. The former starts with sense-data and attains to a knowledge of the existence, goodness and will of God. The latter rests on revelation. Each requires to take into account the knowledge arrived at by the other. The Church now took its stand.

"Rationalism", it was felt, had gone far enough.

Thomas's writings were condemned by various European churchmen including the Bishop of Paris and two successive Archbishops of Canterbury. Their objection largely centred on Thomas's view of the human soul as "a single substantial form of the human body" – a view which apparently represented an attack on an article of faith.

The fight, however, was really between Aristotle and Rome. Aristotle had been regarded as an almost superhuman authority so long as he was known only in Greek. When his thinking became available in Arabic and, through the Translators and the alchemist scholars, in Latin, his system was suddenly seen to be a self-sufficient cosmology that did not require Christianity. The alarm bells rang.

Thomas apparently believed in the reality of alchemical transmutation; but his attitude contained an interesting factor not much hinted at before his day.

The Great Work, he believed, was dependent on a "celestial virtue", which was not always at the alchemists' command, and part of the alchemist's task was to arrange conditions under which this virtue would be most likely to function.[9]

An echo of this idea appears in our own day in the analysis of alchemy from external sources made by Pauwels and Bergier.[10]

Here it is conjectured that the alchemical process, whether related to the inner development of man or the transmutation of metals, is dependent upon some seemingly arbitrary factor which the authors suggest may be the intensity of cosmic rays at a particular place and time.

It may be that Pauwels and Bergier have an insight here, though their identification of the arbitrary factor with cosmic rays may be fanciful.

It is significant that initiate tradition in the Sufi stream insists that certain operations, though the procedures may be correct, will be effective (or, as they say, "developmental") only under a combination of circumstances which they summarize as "right effort by the right people at the right time and the right place". In the absence of these conditions, there is no "occasion".

[9] E. J. Holmyard, *Alchemy*, p. 114.
[10] *Dawn of Magic*, Gibbs and Phillips, London, 1963.

Whatever reality is concealed in this formula, it would explain recurring references throughout the whole of alchemical literature to an intangible which many alchemists were never able to find, and in the absence of which their efforts were endlessly vain.

Both Albertus and Thomas Aquinas were engaged, it seems, in a perilous exercise of hunting with hounds and running with hares.

They probably knew, because of their contact with a genuine esoteric source, that "known" truth and theological dogma need not, by any means, coincide. They were probably engaged in trying to reintroduce the original developmental force of Christianity, while gently diluting the organizational accretions which had all but smothered it. They tried, as a beginning, to show that rationalism and intuitive insights could be harmonized with theology.

Historically, it would seem that the effort failed. Yet behind the scenes much must have been achieved. "There is evidence that at the deepest levels of Sufi secrecy there is a mutual communication with the mystics of the Christian West," says Idries Shah.[11]

This behind-the-scenes communication is being increasingly recognized by modern Arabists and other scholars, but they tend to interpret the discovery so as to square with prior assumptions. They now incline to the view that there was something "behind the scenes" and that it was good, but they think this was so because of the effect of Christianity on the expositors of the ancient teachings.

"The discovery that Christian contemplatives used Sufi books, Sufi methods, and Sufi terminology has stimulated the inevitable results . . . Sufism, it is now declared, is able to produce true mystical experience because the Sufis revere Jesus. Further, Sufism was profoundly influenced in its early days by Christianity. The implication is that Sufi ideas are not to be rejected. If St. John of the Cross and Lully could use them, there must be some good in them. The scholastics have retraced a part of their path, and are rewriting their history to allow for uncomfortable facts."[12]

[11] *The Sufis*, p. 245.
[12] ibid., p. 246.

If men like Albertus and Thomas were in touch with some aspect of the Directorate, they would have the effect required on their contemporaries and their environment, and it is impossible, therefore, to judge their success or otherwise from externals.

Much was certainly achieved. The developmental secret hinted at by the alchemists was incorporated in many media from folk-practices to art and architecture.

The true nature of the Gothic cathedrals as textbooks of human alchemy was suggested in many ways. The idea that a whole stupendous spiritual reality existed behind the veil of everyday life was carefully injected by the few who knew. It continued to be reproduced in forms of increasing dilution through Illuminist, Rosicrucian and Masonic ideas all through the centuries.

Hints about the inner content of Gothic architecture continue to drip into the European consciousness to the present day; as, for example, in the cathedrals chapter of P. D. Ouspensky's *New Model of the Universe*[13] and in *Le Mystère des Cathédrales* by Fulcanelli (see fn. 1, p. 82).

Some significant material appears to have been introduced under the very eyes of official ecclesiastical authority and even to have been unwittingly given official approval, though the ideas, if presented openly, would probably have produced a reaction of official horror.

Thus the *Burial of Count Orgaz* by El Greco appears to be a devout religious work by a painter of genius, which it undoubtedly is.

Its composition can, however, be dissected to show reincarnation concepts, something like the equivalence of conscious and sexual energy and the plurality of "I's" in a human personality. These are not concepts which an ordinary clerical sponsor would have approved had he known of them.

Perhaps another example of devotional art being not quite what it seems is given by the 14th-century fresco *The Triumph of St. Thomas*, attributed to Andrea da Firenze in Santa Maria Novella in Florence. In this, St. Thomas is the focus of a pictorial allegory on learning. Above his head are the four

---

[13] Routledge, London, 1931.

cardinal virtues and the three theological virtues. Flanking him are the evangelists, among them St. John, and the Prophets, including Moses. At the foot, a row of female figures personify the theological sciences and the liberal arts, including arithmetic, geometry, astronomy and music.

St. Thomas is the centre of all. He sits enthroned and holding the Wisdom of Solomon open at a passage which says: "I prayed and understanding was given to me."

But below St. Thomas and apparently supporting him there are three small figures all but lost in the decoration. In *The Flowering of the Middle Ages*[14] in which a detail of the fresco is reproduced, these figures are identified. They turn out to be Ibn Rushd and the two arch heretics Sabellius and Arius. The nature of the structure on which St. Thomas rests can hardly be avoided.

Contemporary with Albertus and Aquinas was Roger Bacon, the almost fabulous "miraculous Doctor" (1214–1292), who wore Arab dress at Oxford and was said to "make women of devils and juggle cats into costermongers", a reputation which has gone some way towards concealing one of the greatest of the European intellects and one of the most outstanding figures of all time.

Influenced by Robert Grosseteste, Bishop of Lincoln (and first Chancellor of Oxford), Bacon became a Franciscan in 1247.

His heterodox views about almost everything early brought him into conflict with his clerical superiors. He had in mind a vast encyclopaedia of all knowledge then possessed in the world (once again an echo of the Basra Encyclopaedia) and he proposed, in a secret letter to the Pope, a major institute of learning, sponsored by the Church, which would centralize the enterprise.

The Pope apparently misunderstood and concluded that the encyclopaedia already existed. He expressed interest in it, and wanted to see it. Bacon, in a panic, sat down to write it.

He had to work without the knowledge of his own superiors, and it is some indication of the quality of his mind that in these circumstances and against the clock, as it were, he produced his

---

[14] Edited by Joan Evans, Thames and Hudson, London, 1966.

Alchemy: The Disguised Path

three monumental works, the *Opus Major, Opus Minor* and *Opus Tertium*. In these he outlined a scheme for research and experiment in languages, mathematics, optics, alchemy and astronomy. The Pope, Clement IV, died, however, in 1268, and with him went Bacon's dream of introducing the natural sciences to the universities of Europe.

Bacon professed to believe that the totality of human knowledge and possibilities was contained in the Bible; but unlike his contemporaries he did not believe that the Bible was an open book. To understand it, a certain kind of inner study was necessary and this involved a knowledge of alchemy, astrology and magic.

Clearly he was on dangerous ground and his volatile personality did little to reconcile his views with orthodoxy. He apparently paid for his views with a 14-year period of imprisonment by his own Order. He lived to return to Oxford, but died soon afterwards, in 1292.

That Bacon, like some others, was engaged in building, secretly, a bridge between the outward form of Christianity and its increasingly dilute inner content is suggested from many circumstances.

He cited the *Wisdom of Illumination* by the Sufi master (and martyr) Suhrawardi. The latter had declared that his philosophy was that of the inner teaching of all the ancients, Greek, Persian and Egyptian. It was the science of Light and through it man could attain to a state about which he could not normally even dream. Bacon repeated this claim and declared that the same secret had been held by Noah, Abraham, the Chaldean and Egyptian masters, Zoroaster, Pythagoras, Socrates *and the Sufis*.

Of speculative alchemy, Bacon said: "And because this science is not known to the generality of students it necessarily follows that they are ignorant of all that depends on it concerning natural things, namely, of the generation of animate things, of plants and animals and men, for being ignorant of what comes before, they are necessarily ignorant of what follows."[15]

Bacon, like Albertus, was clearly in touch with some genuine

---

[15] E. J. Holmyard, *Alchemy*, p. 117.

esoteric source. Unlike Albertus, he knew Arabic. It seems clear that the source, for both of them, was a Sufi one.[16]

Thus in suggesting that the work of alchemy may produce results other than those apparently being sought (e.g., making gold from lead) he uses an analogy which is in fact a straight lift from a Sufi teaching-story.

Bacon knew about "the right people in the right place at the right time", and implied the prime necessity of a living transmission in all developmental processes.

The West of his day (and ours) could not understand this concept – that a developmental situation has to be of an organic nature and subject to precise laws. He was in consequence regarded as sailing very close indeed to the wind of heresy.

Bacon had insights of a peculiar kind, much like those of Michel de Nostredame and the Scottish seer Coinneach Odhar (The Brahan Seer) centuries later. Bacon described in the plainest possible terms the steamship, the motor car, the aeroplane, the submarine and the cantilever bridge. He may also have been hinting at the helicopter. He also described two inventions which are not yet with us; one, a small power source capable of lifting enormous weights. This might perhaps be identified with the so-called Dean Device in which the familiar action and reaction laws of forces are inoperative. The theory of this has been the subject of much secret discussion in Europe and America for the last ten years.

Bacon also described a device "by which one man can draw a thousand to himself by violence against their wills and attract other things in like manner". That, so far, has not been discovered in the West, though hints of such a force can be found in certain esoteric traditions.

Albertus, Aquinas, Bacon . . . strange figures indeed. They were associated with a high order of intellect. They made a deep impression on their age and they contributed material which had a quality of persistence in various guises through many centuries.

The early alchemists were probably "knowers". They had learned techniques which gave them access to an enhanced level of awareness. From this level they knew the inner content

---

[16] Idries Shah, *The Sufis*, p. 200.

of religion. They discovered that all true religions are one. They experienced the laws of nature, which give rise to form and phenomena.

We have suggested that this source of inner development should be identified with Initiates serving the Directorate and called at this period of time, Sufis. This source was concerned with achieving certain evolutionary gains in the 12th and 13th centuries, and it was quite indifferent to whether the cover for its activities was orthodox Islam or orthodox Christianity.

Men who served this source – whether at first or second remove – found themselves living in two worlds. To declare the truth as they knew it – that there was an inner reality in Islam and Christianity which had been overlaid with dogma and organization – would have seemed apostasy. They had to work in secret, doing what they had to do but clothing their activity in some form nominally acceptable to the orthodox church.

They were men who knew they had to build a bridge, but it so happened that bridge-building was illegal. The bridge builders had to pretend they were engaged in some other activity – like digging holes in the road. Not unnaturally, the holes were incomprehensible to their contemporaries and have remained largely so ever since.

This bridging activity of the early Western alchemists is perhaps seen most clearly in the life of Ramon Lull whose name was anglicized to Raymond Lully. He succeeded in discharging his mission while remaining on such good terms with both Islam and Christian orthodoxies that he is regarded virtually as a saint by both.

Lully was born in Palma, the capital of Majorca, in 1235. The Mediterranean island – held by the Saracens for 700 years – had been reconquered by King James of Aragon six years earlier, with the aid of the Knights Templar.

Tradition has it that Raymond's father was "one of the knights who took part in the conquest of Majorca by El Rey Jaime". As the young Raymond later became tutor to the king's sons, it would seem that he was *persona grata* with the Aragon Establishment.

The association of the Templars with an Initiate tradition is well attested, so it seems likely that Raymond Lully was born into a family connected with an esoteric influence.

Lully became a master of the Catalan language and, after nine years' study with a Moorish slave, a master of Arabic as well. He was a poet, philosopher, scientist and prodigious traveller. He visited the Papal courts, was well known in scholarly circles in Paris, Padua, England and Germany.

He visited the cities of North Africa and very probably made less publicized visits to the East as well.

Lully was a devout Christian, but whether his devotion was to the orthodoxy which hailed him as its exemplar, or to an inner tradition of esoteric Christianity unsuspected by his peers, is in hindsight a matter of some conjecture. His praise of "Los Sufies" was one of the stumbling-blocks to his canonization though he is beatified as "The Blessed Ramon Lull".

With the material now available, it is very hard to avoid the suspicion that Lully, like Albertus and Aquinas, had work to do and was very content to accept the label of orthodoxy if and when such "cover" made his task easier.

That he was brilliantly successful in this ambivalence is shown by the fact that he was beatified by Rome. That some later doubts have arisen is suggested by the Church's evident reluctance to accord him full sanctity.

Lully taught Arabic in a college of oriental studies which he founded, close to where Robert Graves now lives. He invented a binary computer; wrote poetry; is credited with inventing the chemical process of rectification by distillation with limestone,[17] and built for himself such a reputation for gentle wisdom, benevolence and humanity that his life and work were still influencing men like Pico della Mirandola and Leibniz centuries later.

Lully's apparent orthodoxy was so complete that a scholar of the calibre of Friedrich Heer[18] can say of him:

"The writings of this remarkable man are still read and commented upon and not only in his native Spain. Large in mind and generous in spirit, ready to embrace the whole world in his sympathies, Lully held that conversion to Christianity as the sum of earthly truth would inevitably follow from the

[17] A. C. Crombie, *Augustine to Galileo*, Vol. I, *Science in the Middle Ages*, Heinemann, London, 1961.

[18] *The Medieval World*, London, 1961.

spread of enlightenment: in fact, that true enlightenment and conversion to Christianity were identical. Faith and reason, mystery and rationality were indissolubly wed."

What reasons, then, exist for supposing that Lully was more than a benevolent original thinker and missionary?

Perhaps through his family connection, Lully was in touch with a developmental source from his childhood, but he was forty before some decisive experience occurred. This would seem to have been an illumination and is said to have occurred when he climbed Mount Randa (near Palma).

This account may indeed be literal, but ascending a mountain is a well-known figure of speech for a less literal kind of ascent.

His illumination, wherever it took place, seems to have allowed him to see the laws of nature in operation, and he returned to ordinary consciousness with the idea of encapsulating his insights in a sort of universal machine which would be capable of solving all human problems.

That Lully was a genius capable of developing some sort of non-electronic cybernetic computer seems to be admitted. Modern scholars, while remaining a little reserved about computers in the form of talking heads, have accepted completely the idea that Raymond Lully did invent an early cybernetic machine. The machine is mentioned in *The History of Cybernetics*, and Martin Gardner in *Logic, Machines and Diagrams*[19] has a chapter on the "Ars Magna of Ramon Lull". In *Archaeologia* (74 Series II)[20] O. M. Dalton describes Lully's computer as a portable dial in the form of a book. A special issue of *Studio International* in 1968 cites Lully as a pioneer of the computer.

Friedrich Heer in *The Medieval World*[21] describes it thus: "It took the form of what can only be described as a computing engine which linked up the basic principles or 'ground words' of all knowledge by a mechanism consisting of concentric circles segmented by radii and of geometric symbols. It seems to have been what might be called a cybernetic machine prepared to unravel every problem, every science, even faith

[19] McGraw Hill, New York, 1958.
[20] Oxford, 1925.
[21] Weidenfeld and Nicolson, London, 1961.

itself. Here in rudimentary fashion were anticipated the great universal formulae of Einstein and Heisenberg which have provided man with the mathematical keys to the problems of matter, light, energy and fundamental laws of the cosmos. A miracle machine or, as later scoffers were to say, a wind machine, tossing empty words about. Leibniz was, however, not among the mockers. Lully's vision came too close to his own dream of finding a universal scientifically viable language which would enlighten all men impartially, the prerequisite of universal peace."

This, then, was Lully's attempt to translate an insight into the mechanism of the universe in terms of a philosophical machine.

If Lully was an illuminated man, what was the source of his illumination? From many pieces of internal evidence, it appears that Lully was quite simply a Sufi. In him the strains of alchemy, Saracen science, mathematics, the Cabbala and Sufi methodology converge in a most striking manner. His *Book of Contemplation* was written in Arabic, and his *Book of the Lover and the Beloved* is admitted to be modelled on esoteric Arab originals.

In the *Blanquerna* (translated into English in 1926[22]) his Sufic affiliation is stated openly. In it he speaks with admiration of a devotional methodology from "the Sufies" whom he describes as "religious men among the Saracens".

Lully's theory of the descent of man is practically the same as that of Rumi, where categories of stone, plant, animal, man, angel and God lie along an evolutionary scale.

This is remarkable, either as a coincidence or as a suggestion that Lully and Rumi were in correspondence. It is even more remarkable when viewed against repeated suggestions in Sufi material that advanced men of a certain tradition in the East transmitted learning by telepathy to men in the West who were able to sustain the communication. A reference to one example of this is contained in Aflaki,[23] where it is said that "the Dervish of the West" was in communication with Rumi. Was "the Dervish of the West" Raymond Lully?

The possibility of such communication and some hints of the

---

[22] Trs. E. Allison Peers, Jarrolds, London, 1926.
[23] Aflaki, *Munaqib al-Arifin*, London, 1881, reprinted as *Legends of the Sufis*, Coombe Springs Press, Kingston, 1965.

method and mechanism will be touched on later when we consider indications of Sufi influence on the modern world.

The real nature of Lully's mission and message is a matter of much contention among scholars and religionists.

Friedrich Heer notes that "Lull had a great appreciation and love of his Islamic adversaries and would have liked to revive the disputations formerly held between representatives of the three great religions. In his *Libro del Gentil* (which appeared in Arabic in 1272), a Jew, a Muslim and a Christian expound the chief points of their respective faiths. In his *Liber de Sancto Spiritu*, a Greek and a Latin converse in the presence of a Muslim ... Lully thought it an advantage for the children of Christian Europe to gain some insight into the Jewish and Islamic worlds. He was convinced that European Christendom needed to be educated afresh so that people's eyes might be opened to the beauty of alien worlds." Heer concludes that for Raymond Lully "true enlightenment and conversion to Christianity were identical".

Professor Guillaume[24] discusses the Christian and Moslem partisanship for the right to claim Lully's allegiance. He seems to decide on balance in favour of the Arabs. "Anyone who considers that Lully was the founder of the School of Oriental Studies, that he wrote and spoke Arabic and that the great aim of his life was to commend the Christian faith to the Saracens on intellectual grounds, and that he is said to have met a martyr's death preaching to the Arabs of Tunis, will probably feel that to exclude direct Arabian influence from his life is to narrow unduly the range of his overflowing sympathies. . . . Certainly in the theological or rather devotional section of his writings, he borrowed a great deal from the Arabs. . . . His treatise on the hundred names of God speaks for itself, and in *Blanquerna* he writes his manifest approval of the Marabout or Dervish system of exciting devotional and ecstatic states by the rhythmical recitation of certain words."

A modern Sufi in private correspondence has this to say: "Modern scholastics seem to be fighting like cat and dog to decide who is a rat. Professor Guillaume, unlike the French scholastics, concedes the Arabic influence, but does not realize

---

[24] *Legacy of Islam*, 1961, p. 272.

that the Saracenic civilization was the cover for a penetration of Sufic ideas into the West. The Catholic religiosity which is read in relation to Raymond Lully need not be taken too seriously. His life appears to parallel very closely that of many Sufis of the Middle East who had also to cloak heterodox interests in great religiosity. Lully's mission to convert the Saracens to Christianity . . . is in the familiar tradition of the 'cover story'."

On his third missionary visit to Africa, Raymond Lully is said to have been seriously injured when he was stoned at Bougie while preaching Christianity to the Arabs. He is said to have died when his ship was in sight of Majorca.

Says Heer: "Such a man, it will be objected, was an Utopian dreamer. He was indeed. But he was also an universal genius, a bold anticipator of the thoughts and problems of the future. . . . Few visitors to Majorca are aware that the vast cathedral of the island's capital is the last resting place of this great European."

In his life there seems little to associate with alchemy in the popular sense of the word. But in the next chapter when we look at the historical record, we shall see that Lully, gold-making and England are related in one of the strangest legends in the whole story of alchemy.

CHAPTER SEVEN

WHAT GOLD DID THEY MAKE?

For centuries after Albertus, Bacon and Lully, the light of alchemy flickers eerily all over Europe.

Strange figures appear in the courts of kings and princes, in monasteries and in market places.

They are hailed as superhuman, as charlatans, as religious geniuses, as philosophers, as spies. They write "gibberish", but their writings are superstitiously copied, hoarded, sold, ridiculed. The commonalty of Europe can interpret none of this, but it feels a strange haunting echo of something important beyond reason.

Among the alchemists themselves, there is a freemasonry of understanding. Texts are written to take students one degree further and to baffle more completely those below the level for whom the text is written.

All seems confusion and contradiction. Are the alchemists engaged in making metallic gold? Or are they talking about a whole range of metaphysics that has nothing to do with literal gold?

Even when they seem explicit, alchemists contradict each other. Petrus Bonus, an Italian, in the 1330s, writes *The Pearl of Great Price*, and claims that the whole art of transmutation can be learned in a single day. Yet Albertus Magnus took thirty years to make his "artificial man".

Bonus, though an erudite and earnest student, admits that he did not, in the end, succeed in The Great Work. It is interesting that he regarded the "astrological" factors in the process as irrelevant, and it is tempting to suggest that "astrology" represents the intangible factor which so many alchemists sensed but could not reach.

Paracelsus, on the other hand, had no such illusions and it seems clear that he, unlike Bonus, had made contact with a genuine source – perhaps in both Spain and Turkey – and consequently knew better.

In the figure of Theophrastus Bombastus von Hohenheim, who called himself Paracelsus, it is impossible to miss the feeling of certainty and assurance of one who truly knows. He seems to tower over the "theoretical" alchemists who puff their furnaces all through the centuries.

A restless, intolerant genius, Paracelsus stalks through Europe like a giant, endlessly fulminating against the conspiracy of ignorance that was the medicine of his time; endlessly misunderstood; endlessly trying to give away the spiritual gold he had accumulated. His career very closely approximates that of certain Initiates who take "the path of blame", and parallels between Paracelsus and many similar figures in the East could probably be found.

One scholar has said of him: "Those who imagine that the medicine of Paracelsus is a system of superstition that we have fortunately outgrown will, if they come to know its principles, be surprised to find that it is based upon a superior kind of knowledge that we have not yet attained, but into which we may hope to grow".

C. G. Jung had this to say: "We see in Paracelsus not only a process of chemical medicine, but also ... of an empirical psychological healing science."

Paracelsus' father was a doctor who taught his son "medicine and alchemy". Here again, as in the case of Lully and Aquinas, there is a hint of a family connection with esotericism. Paracelsus' father was the illegitimate son of Ritter Georg von Hohenheim (near Stuttgart), a Commander of the Order of the Knights of Jerusalem. His presence in the East in 1468 is recorded.

The Knights Hospitallers, like the Templars, are associated with a secret tradition under their outward humanitarian activities. It is known that Ritter Georg thought highly of his illegitimate son, and it seems probable that certain matters would be tacitly understood in the family.

After learning what he could from his father, the young Paracelsus went on an endless series of wanderings, accounts of which are confused and contradictory, but he is associated at one stage with the name of Johann Trithemius, a celebrated alchemist monk of Wurzburg. He says himself that he learned from abbots, bishops, doctors and many alchemists. He spent some time – perhaps significantly – in Granada in 1518, but his journeys took in Germany, France, Belgium, England, Scotland, Denmark, Russia, Tartary and Lapland! He seems to have served as an army surgeon on more than one occasion and certainly got an MD from the University of Ferrara.

Back in Strasbourg between journeys, he cured a prominent citizen of Basle, and so brought himself to the notice of Erasmus, who sponsored him for the post of Medical Officer of Basle.

Paracelsus suffered from a congenital inability to suffer fools gladly and his attacks on clerical superstition and medical ignorance ensured a sort of self-renewing anti-Paracelsus lobby from one end of Europe to the other.

"Magick is a teacher of medicine far preferable to written books," he said. "Magick alone – that can neither be conferred by the universities nor created by the award of diplomas, but comes direct from God – is the true teacher, preceptor and pedagogue in the art of curing the sick. And if our physicians did indeed possess these powers, all their books might be burnt and their medicines thrown into the sea – and the world would be the better of it."

Statements like these were as little likely to endear him to the leeches and apothecaries of Europe in the 16th century as they are to commend him to the General Medical Council of today.

But to Paracelsus, magic and medicine were opposite sides of the same coin. He is said to have invented the mercury therapy for syphilis, but it should be remembered that an alchemist's mercury is to be understood in quotation marks.

Yet he was beyond any doubt a pioneer in both science and medicine.

Holmyard[1] sums him up thus: "Paracelsus believed that sickness and health are all controlled by astral influences and that sickness can be driven out and health restored by 'arcana' or secret remedies. The function of the arcana is to restore a celestial harmony between an inner astrum or star in man and a heavenly astrum; they must therefore reach out to heaven, that is, be volatile and incorporeal. The actual medicine must be material, but the arcanum it contains is spiritual."

[1] E. J. Holmyard, *Alchemy*, p. 167.

From views like this it is sometimes claimed that Paracelsus invented modern chemotherapy, but it would be equally plausible to claim that he invented – or rediscovered – homœopathy 250 years before Hahnemann. This idea would be supported by the legend that Paracelsus cured the plague with a "similimum" made from infinitely diluted faeces. Whether or not he used the homœopathic "magic of the minimum dose" or the gross allopathic dose, Paracelsus knew principles of inoculation. He may have learned them in Turkey where they were known from ancient times. Lady Wortley Montague brought the technique to England from the Middle East in 1721, seventy-eight years before Dr Jenner was credited with vaccine inoculation. But a homœopathic attitude seems more likely. It is indeed all but explicit in the following: "For we teach that what heals a man also wounds him, and what has wounded him will also heal him."

Two centuries before Franz Anton Mesmer, Paracelsus was investigating the effects of magnetism on disease, and in his saying: "There is ice in the sun", he seems to have anticipated Hoerbiger by four hundred years.

He came close to postulating the equivalence of mass and energy: "Know therefore, that the said mass is nothing but a box full of force and power."[2]

Over and over again Paracelsus foreshadows modern attitudes alike in science and "fringe" medicine. "The newly-born and self-begotten spirit shadows forth its knowledge and intelligence in a figure and by a figure – that is, an image – so long as that figure or image is firmly held without wavering, fluctuation or dissolution within the seat of the imagination. . . . The first step is to beget the spirit from the star by means of the imagination."

Modern "positive thinking", the "New Thought" of Henry Thomas Hamblin, the "imaginals" of Douglas Fawcett's philosophical system, the "creative realism" of Rolf Alexander and the "imprisoned splendour" of Professor Raynor Johnson can all be ante-dated to Paracelsus; and to the source from which he obtained his development.

Is anything known about this source?

[2] *Buch Meteororum.*

Paracelsus called his longsword Azoth. This sword has become an Aladdin's lamp to Paracelsian legend. The sword was said to remain by his side at all times, even when he slept, and that it had encapsuled in its hilt a djinn which would serve him in all things – for example, bringing him a handful of gold crowns when he was low in funds.

If this seems preposterous in the 20th century, it might be noted that a book by a practising magician published in Austria within the last ten years gives the procedures in great detail whereby such elemental power may be harnessed. To the personal knowledge of the present writer an almost identical story attaches to a modern ring (now in a museum).

To its former owner, the elemental content of this ring was associated with the appearance of an entity which obtained information, found missing objects and even arranged the manipulation of material events.

The Azoth of Paracelsus gives a significant clue to the source of his capacities. "Azoth" is the transliteration of a Persian and Arabic Sufi term for "essence", the inner quality capable of transforming the nature of man. This inner quality is hidden, secret and forbidden. "Hidden, forbidden" comes from the same consonantal root as "stone". So Paracelsus' "Azoth" equals the hidden transformative substance in man, equals the Philosopher's Stone.[3]

Paracelsus, who is on record as preferring water as a drink, had the reputation of being permanently drunk. Almost certainly this derives from his use of wine in analogy. Wine is the symbol of the impalpable force which the Sufis call Baraka and is to be found throughout the whole range of Sufi poetry. In his *Philosophia Occulta*, Paracelsus gives almost literal versions of Sufic teaching material.

Paracelsus certainly visited Spain, but it may be that the sources he was seeking as a young man were no longer available in the familiar locations of Toledo and Granada, and he had to follow the trail to a source in Turkey. The Sufic origin of his development, at any rate, is clear.

Paracelsus did not deny the possibility of "literal" alchemy. He simply indicated that it was not for him. His particular

---

[3] Idries Shah, *The Sufis*, pp. 195, 204.

access to higher insights was interpreted in terms of his chief interest, which was to see the nature of disease and to apply the counter-measure indicated by his insight.

When appointed to some university lectureship his possession of knowledge of a totally different kind was so self-evident that he attracted vast crowds of students; but his polemics against self-appointed experts in every field always produced a new crop of dedicated enemies. Within months his students would be under pressure to desert him and presently Paracelsus, exasperated and generally a bit bedraggled, would be on the road to somewhere else, stopping only to make some urgent addition to the medical, astrological and philosophical writings on which he was always engaged.

His collected writings were printed in Basle 50 years after his death, and the whole corpus was translated into modern German early this century.

At the end of a life which was meteoric, troubled, frustrated and short (he died at forty-eight), Paracelsus returned to Salzburg old and frail before his time.

He made his will on September 21, 1541, and is said to have died three days later.[4] His enemies have prevailed to the extent that the word "Bombast" was his middle name.

The legends that surround his life are pale beside the legends that surround his death. One such says that after making his will he went to stand on a rocky ledge overlooking Salzburg when assassins, hired by his enemies, hurled him to his death.

This story was apparently supported by the discovery when his body was exhumed in the early years of the 19th century, that he had a fractured skull. Further examination in the 1880s however, showed that this was not a fracture but the result of rickets.[5]

According to another legend, Paracelsus, after making his will, is said to have taken aside his pupil, Dr André Wendl, and told him that in death he would perform his greatest alchemical experiment.

Wendl was to promise that he would dissect his master's corpse and place the pieces in a wooden chest for three days. Then at daybreak on the third day he was to open the chest.

[4] John Hargrave, *Life and Soul of Paracelsus*, Gollancz, London, 1951.
[5] E. J. Holmyard, *Alchemy*, p. 166.

The dismembered corpse would then be seen to have reassembled itself and from the chest Paracelsus would rise in the form of a young man renewed and immortal. Wendl is supposed to have opened the chest (in an outhouse of the White Horse Inn in the Kaigasse) too soon. The transformation was all but complete, but the reconstituted skull was still incomplete, and as Wendl watched, the process went into reverse and the corpse reverted to that of the dying, 48-year-old alchemist.

About such a legend there are echoes of a resurrection drama which is associated with a very high order of things, and it is significant that this legend seems to be, uniquely among European alchemists, attached to the person of Paracelsus.

For 700 years the threads of alchemy seem to connect a whole fabric of European literature, medicine, science and art. As we shall see presently, the tradition continues during the Second World War, and up to the present day.

Chaucer reported alchemical matters (a little disingenuously perhaps) in the Canon's Yeoman's Tale. George Ripley (of Harrowgate) studied with the Knights of St. John of Jerusalem. Thomas Norton, who was probably a Privy Counsellor to Edward IV, seems successfully to have made the "Elixir", but to have had it stolen from him by a woman – a suggestion which may be symbolic at several levels. Thomas Daulton went right to the steps of the scaffold refusing to divulge the secret of alchemy and was then magnanimously released, his courage having touched his captors, courtiers of the Edward IV court.

Churchmen, including a canon of Lichfield and a Prior of Bath, were engaged in alchemy and seem to have maintained a sort of intelligence network within the Church, for the most part unsuspected by officialdom.

The Elizabethan court was suffused in a – perhaps secondhand – glow of alchemical activity associated with that doubtful Fellow of Trinity, John Dee (who advised Elizabeth on the astrological aspects of her Coronation), and his more dubious partner Edward Kelly, who is said to have found the Philosopher's Stone in a cavity in the ruins of Glastonbury Abbey.

The Bacon–Shakespeare–Marlowe enigma which is still reducing scholars to incoherence seems clearly to derive from the presence in Elizabethan times of a group engaged in using literature for the injection of developmental ideas into the 16th century. As always, the identity and location of such activity is deliberately concealed in such a way as to ensure that the details remain impenetrable collectively. Individually they lead to a maze of false trails which are mutually exclusive.

In Scotland, the alchemical tradition was represented as early as the 1200s by Michael Scot of Kirkcaldy. Scot had a place in the Sicilian court of Frederick II, and his reputation as a magician (he foretold the details of the Emperor's death and of his own) brought him a mention in the *Decameron* of Boccaccio and in Dante's *Inferno*.

Sir Walter Scott repeats the tradition that Michael returned to Scotland and is buried with his alchemical books in Melrose Abbey.

In all European countries these strange figures are seen engaged in some extraordinary activity, disappearing in strange circumstances and leaving even stranger legends behind them. But did any of them do what they were ordinarily supposed to be doing: make tangible gold?

Holmyard in *Alchemy* gives a fascinating review of the historical "facts" of the "hard-line" alchemists.

The most startling and seemingly documented of these is Alexander Seton, an East Coast Scotsman who in 1602 in Basle apparently turned a crucible of lead into gold, and had as witnesses a Professor from the University of Freiburg and Jacob Zwinger, a noted Swiss scholar of the time.

Throughout the operation, Seton touched none of the material, merely sitting back and directing the other two, Professor Dienheim and Zwinger, in the proceedings. Seton repeated the same feat with a merchant named Koch who threw into a crucible containing mercury, a pinch of powder and wax handed to him by the alchemist. The result was reported as six ounces and three grains of 23-carat gold.

This became regular practice with Seton. He provided the "Stone" and allowed others to make the transformation. Sometimes he had as many as six witnesses. In one case he transmuted a pair of iron pliers into a pair of gold pliers.

He made gold before witnesses in Rotterdam, Amsterdam, Munich, Frankfurt, Strasburg, Hamburg and Basle.

If this was conjuring, it was superb. It was also motiveless, for Seton seems to have sought no rewards.

Christian, Elector of Saxony, heard of this incredible series of performances and invited Seton to call and demonstrate. The alchemist was on his honeymoon, but with masterly oneupmanship, he sent his Scots servant, William Hamilton, to the court with a pinch of powder. Hamilton, surrounded by the Elector's court, promptly made a crucible of undoubted gold.

The potentiality of such a human gold-mine roused the worst instincts in the Elector. Honeymoon or no honeymoon, Seton must be brought to court. The alchemist, apparently without suspicion of what impended, yielded. Immediately Christian had him in his power, he was seized and put to torture. Only when at the point of death was the torture stopped, and Seton thrown into a dungeon.

Some hint of the intelligence service which existed within the alchemical freemasonry may be suspected from the fact that a student of alchemy, Michael Sendivogius of Moravia, at once made his way to court and using the influence of friends, succeeded in visiting the alchemist in his dungeon. Using bribery and wine, Sendivogius succeeded in immobilizing the guard and getting the seriously injured Seton clear of the jail. Picking up Seton's wife on the way, the trio fled to Cracow, where shortly afterwards Seton died of his injuries. Not, however, before bequeathing to his rescuer a quantity of "Stone".

Sendivogius married Seton's widow and, using what was left of the precious "powder of projection", went on to make gold at public demonstrations all over Europe. At one, before the Emperor Rudolph II, he handed the Emperor the requisite amount of powder and allowed him to make the transmutation himself.

What is to be made of such a story? The facts are historical, but Holmyard is driven to say: "Rejecting, as we must, the hypothesis that Seton effected genuine transmutations, there would seem to be no alternative but that he was an extremely adroit and plausible imposter."

Such a conclusion seems a little shaky on the question of motive. Seton, if he was a "con man", gained nothing from his imposture but mutilation and death. Nor does he seem ever to have tried to gain anything. Was William Hamilton, the red-haired Scotsman, also an impostor – equally adroit and plausible? And did the gift of Seton's powder automatically turn Sendivogius into a master illusionist? In this triple conjunction the theory of collusion and imposture seems strained to breaking point.

Those who accept the "hard-line" theory of alchemy have suggested that Seton did have the great secret and regarded himself as a missionary charged with demonstrating to a sceptical Europe the physical aspect of a mighty truth. This sort of motivation in an alchemist of a certain degree may not be wholly absurd. It might be echoed in the incident associated with the name of Johann Schweitzer who, in the then fashion of scholarly Latinizations, was known as Helvetius.

Schweitzer was a sceptic about literal alchemy and had written scathingly about gold-making claims. He was a man enjoying a reputation for the highest integrity, and in addition to being an eminent citizen of The Hague, in 1666 was physician to the Prince of Orange. Helvetius had no possible motive for concocting the story of transmutation which he described. In fact it discredited his previous, published, views and lost him face. His own account of the incident survives and the circumstances appear to be of a degree of attestation which would probably be admitted as evidence in a modern court of law.

Two days after Christmas, 1666, Helvetius opened the door of his house to find a stranger on the doorstep. The latter began to talk about alchemy and took Helvetius to task for his scepticism. The doctor invited the man indoors, and was soon captivated by the visitor's seriousness and culture. In the parlour the stranger produced a carved ivory jewel-box inside which, lying on a bed of velvet, were three pieces of what looked like resin or crude glass. Each piece was as big as a walnut and of pale amber colour. These, said the stranger, were made of the Philosopher's Stone and were capable, used all together, of making twenty tons of gold.

Helvetius was allowed to handle one of the pieces, but, not unnaturally, continued sceptical.

Much as he would like to give Helvetius conclusive proof of his claims, the stranger said, he could not do so without permission. This he would try to obtain, but in any case he would call again on Helvetius in three weeks' time.

Against all expectations, the man did come back three weeks later. This time he broke off a little scrap of the material and gave it to the doctor. The latter thought this minute scrap, even if it were genuine, was probably too insignificant to have much effect, and said as much. On hearing this, the stranger took back his gift and broke it in half with his thumb nail. He gave the doctor the half fragment and said that even this was more than sufficient.

There is a suggestion in the conversation at this point that the stranger was testing Helvetius in various ways. Helvetius wrote down the whole conversation from memory in his diary, and it is of more than superficial interest.

Regrettably, the stranger said, he could not do a transmutation tonight; but he would return at nine in the morning and would then give the doctor conclusive proof that alchemy was no hoax.

The stranger did not return at nine the next morning, or any other morning. Helvetius never saw him again. When the doctor and his wife had given up all hope of his return, they took the only action that suggested itself. They would try for a transmutation themselves, using the tiny scrap of material the alchemist had left.

They got a crucible and melted half an ounce of lead over the kitchen fire. When it was fully molten they enclosed the scrap of "Stone" in a pellet of beeswax and threw this into the lead-pot.

Before their eyes the entire mass turned into what looked like brightest gold.

The crucible was still too hot to handle with comfort, but somehow the pair ran through the streets with it to a goldsmith who assayed it and pronounced it genuine. Within hours the story was all over the Hague and within weeks it was all over Europe.

The official goldsmith to the Prince of Orange asked permission to test the gold and subjected it to various standard procedures. One of these consisted of mixing in a quantity of silver filings with the gold and treating the whole mass with *aqua fortis*. To everyone's astonishment, some of the silver was then converted to gold, the virtue of the "Stone" being not wholly expended in the original transmutation. Helvetius ended up with more alchemical gold than he had made in the first place.

The story was of course a sensation. Many plausible and implausible explanations were offered, but at no time does the integrity of Helvetius appear to have been questioned.

Not the least interesting part of the story is the conversation between Helvetius and the alchemist. This includes a number of very significant sentences. One such is: "Nay, without the communication of a true adept philosopher, not one student can find the way to prepare this great magistery." In explaining that alchemy could perform other transformations than that of gold (he listed the production of precious stones as one example) the alchemist appears to be merely describing a process of material chemistry. Between the lines, however, he is clearly describing another process altogether. The two aspects are cunningly interwoven: but it would appear that the doctor failed to pick up the symbolism.

Other parts of the conversation could have been in the nature of a test, and in saying that "the student must know the whole matter from head to heel", and in using flowery metaphors about the seal of Hermes, the alchemist was probably going as far as he dared.

Helvetius, it would seem, did not make the right responses, and perhaps the stranger had to write him off as a possible candidate for this reason.

Perhaps at that particular time a man interested in alchemy and possessing Helvetius' integrity was needed. Perhaps also some popular demonstration as to the veridical nature of material alchemy was also called for. In failing to find in Helvetius the degree of preparedness he had hoped for, the alchemist settled for his second aim and achieved it through the scrap of material he donated to the doctor.

The conversation must rank as one of the most significant in the whole published annals of European alchemy. It establishes the stranger as a man who knew the spiritual nature of the process, and it leaves in the historical record an endorsement of "Holy Alkemie's" literal counterpart.

In the record of gold-making one of the most enduring legends is that Raymond Lully came to England sometime in the second half of the 13th century, made alchemical gold for Edward II and "founded the Bank of England".

Lully's visit to England, his association with Abbot John Cremer of Westminster, the production in the Tower of London of enormous quantities of gold from which the coins *Nobles de la Rose* were struck – all this is regarded by many scholars, including Holmyard, as apocryphal. Holmyard doubts that there ever was an abbot John Cremer. Mary Atwood, who was a very able scholar indeed, accepts the story and cites the kernel of the legend in an MS (*Ultimum Testamentum*) attributed to Lully himself. There would certainly appear to be contemporary or near-contemporary references to the incident in works by other writers, including Olaus Borrichius R. Constantius, Dufresnoy and Dickenson (de Quintessentia).[6]

According to the story, Lully, while in Vienna, was invited to England by Edward II. The Blessed Raymond refused. Abbot Cremer, who had laboured unsuccessfully at alchemy for thirty years, set off to meet Lully, who had moved on to Italy. There they met, and there Lully is supposed to have transmitted to Cremer the key to the mystery. Cremer then persuaded Lully to change his mind and come to London.

Lully was immediately introduced to the King, who promised to mount yet another Crusade if Lully would agree to finance it with alchemical gold. In a private chamber in the Tower of London, Lully is said to have produced 50,000 lbs. of purest gold. The "Testament" attributed to him says *converti una vice in aurum 50 millia pondo argenti vivi plumbi et stanni.*

On receiving this enormous treasure "converted from mercury, lead and tin", the King then broke his promise to conduct a Crusade, arrested Lully and demanded more gold.

Lully, aided by Cremer, managed to escape from the Tower and fled the country. Contemporary writers relate a further incident – that when the cell in the Tower from which the alchemist had managed to escape was searched, a quantity of "Stone" was found concealed in a wall and with this the workmen succeeded in transmuting lead into gold.

Whatever the literal value of this story, it may not be without symbolic significance. "The Bank of England was founded by

[6] M. Atwood, *Suggestive Inquiry*, Trelawney Saunders, London, 1850.

Raymond Lully". If "Bank of England" is taken to symbolize the later emergence in Elizabethan times of England as a temporal power which has played a decisive part in world history, the message would appear to be that this impulse derived from some action by Raymond Lully. Perhaps the separation of spiritual gold from literal gold, like the alchemical separation itself, is one that eludes historians.

Is there no authentification of "literal alchemy" more recent than seven hundred years ago?

Indeed there is, and within the past few years. Morag Murray – an expert on the esoteric perception system known as *Kaif* – is a Scotswoman married to an Afghan. She has seen alchemical gold made by an alchemist in N.W. India and has given a notarized account of it to Idries Shah, the author. It is given verbatim in Shah's book, *Oriental Magic*.[7]

Morag Murray was taken to meet a Pathan called Aquil Khan, somewhere in the Khyber area.... The alchemist, a most taciturn and slightly disreputable individual, took her and her companion on an expedition to collect about a quarter of a pint of the juice of the plant which looked like a large dandelion. This may have been the so-called Soma plant, which figures *ad nauseum* in Vedic recipes for both alchemy and longevity, and has been tentatively identified as *asclepias acida* or *gyanchum viminale*.

Next day the alchemist collected a large ball of clay by scooping up selected handfuls from the bed of a running stream. From this clay he made two deep bowls six inches across.

On the third day, the party collected some dark-red, hard kindling wood, and on the fourth day some large grey, nearly square stones.

On the fifth day, they built a fire (started with paper on which certain symbols had been written), and progressively fed it with the hardwood sticks, charcoal and the dried blood of a white goat.

The fire, lit on the first night of a new moon, was kept burning for seven days, the party taking turns to stoke it. The two clay bowls were placed on a large square of linen on the

---

[7] Octagon Press, London, 1969. (Reproduced by permission. Further reproduction without permission is forbidden.)

ground. Then strips of new cotton were cut an inch wide from a large sheet and laid on the linen. Morag Murray then describes the actual gold-making.

> What remained of the clay was mixed with spring water (carried five miles in a new jar), to the consistency of thick cream. A piece of stone the size of a large apricot was placed in one bowl, with a piece of silver the size of a sugar-lump. Over these was spread two tablespoonfuls of the "milk" sap we had gathered. All the time the gold-maker kept looking at the stars – restlessly, like a man consulting his watch. He now placed the other bowl on the one containing the stone, silver and juice, and formed a kind of circle of the two.
> The whole thing was then carefully wound round with the long strips of cotton, dipped in clay which stuck like glue.
> This was continued until all the cotton was used up, and the mass was greatly enlarged. Lastly, more of the clay (ordinary clay) was moulded round the package, and the whole was put into the heart of the glowing fire. Hot charcoal was spread over this, and the vigil began.
> The "bowl" had to remain at white heat for seven days and seven nights. Fortunately it was not necessary to sit over the fire all the time; but we had to keep a constant shared watch of it. This was because "Satan cannot make gold, and if this gold in the making were left unwatched, he would come and steal it in its present form, and learn the secret". Even Ahmed and I – the uninitiated – had by this time formed the habit of looking anxiously at the stars. Excitement ran high in my mind. Aquil crushed that: every experiment of this nature must be treated as a matter of course: no talk, no laughing, no optimism, no doubt. No eating or drinking on duty!
> The weary days and nights passed. Aquil removed the red ball from the fire, and laid it aside in a pile of sand to cool. It took twelve hours to cool sufficiently. Not all the cotton, we noticed, had burned, due to the presence of the clay, as Aquil unwrapped it.
> At last the bowls were prised apart, and within lay a piece of yellow metal. Aquil handed it to me: "Take it to a jeweller and see if it is gold."
> When I hesitated, thinking that there must be some trickery, he went into the back of the cave, and brought out a large cotton bag. Out of this he turned about fifty other nuggets, just like the one which lay in my hand. "These are some, there are many more."
> "I would have doubted, once, as you doubt. It took me thirty years to learn this. Thirty years . . . of water and nuts, berries and

starvation, contemplation and experiment. I had to learn to read the heavens, tame animals, know signs. All I had when I started was a formula which was garbled, and I had to put it right. As to the finding of the places where the right ingredients are . . . that took years."

I asked him what he wanted to do now. "Now? It is five years since I perfected the system. I have been making gold ever since. I cannot do anything else. And I do not want to. But what is the use of it all? I set at naught all my old Master warned me against. It becomes an obsession. The very fact that I can do what none other can (except a few) is my joy, and I do not want anything else.

What is the good of gold? Can it restore life? I am its slave. I cannot get away from it. There, my friend, is my story. The fascination has me in its grip. I cannot, will not, give the gold away, sell it or let anyone else have it. I do not know why this is, either."

I took the gold to the jeweller. He offered to buy it. It was not mine. I took it back to Aquil. He threw it like a piece of coal into the back of the cave. "Go back to London," he said. I have no way of knowing to this day what the answer to all this is.

It is tempting to speculate about the relevance of this futile gold-making to a conversation between G. I. Gurdjieff and his pupils, reported by P. D. Ouspensky in *In Search of the Miraculous*.[8]

Talking about different paths of human development, Gurdjieff said: "It must be noted that in addition to these proper, legitimate ways, there are also artificial ways which give temporary results only, and wrong ways which may even give permanent results – only wrong results. In these ways a man also seeks the key to the fourth room and sometimes finds it. But what he finds in the fourth room is not yet known. It also happens that the door to the fourth room is opened artificially with a skeleton key, and in both these cases the room may prove to be empty."

Whether the search leads to an empty room or not, the search is not confined to ancient and medieval times. An alchemical legend, as powerful as any from the past, attaches to the mysterious Fulcanelli, who has never been finally identified; but who is believed to be alive still, and in Spain.

Pauwels and Bergier in their book *The Dawn of Magic* (Matin des Magiciens)[9] piece together an extraordinary story which in

---
[8] Routledge, London, 1950.
[9] Gibbs and Phillips, London, 1963.

various forms has been circulating in Masonic and Rosicrucian circles for the past two decades. Sometime between 1920 and 1925, a mysterious individual in France approached Eugène Canseliet, a student of alchemy and occultism, and asked him if he could arrange publication of a manuscript which he had written.

Canseliet agreed and carried out his task, but, the book published, the mysterious stranger failed to reappear. This manuscript was the now famous *Mystère des Cathédrales*. It purports, among other things, to be a key to the architecture of the Gothic cathedrals, showing them to be enciphered textbooks of the alchemical technique.

In 1937, Jacques Bergier, co-author of *Dawn of Magic*, was a student studying nuclear physics under the famous André Helbronner (later killed in Buchenwald by the Nazis). Bergier was visited one day by a mysterious stranger whose manner conveyed an impressive authority. For various reasons Bergier has since concluded that he was in the presence of Fulcanelli. The visitor hinted that Western science was on the verge of discovering the ultimate structure of matter. The forces which would then become available would imperil the whole planet.[10]

The stranger said:

> M. André Helbronner, whose assistant I believe you are, is carrying out research on nuclear energy. M. Helbronner has been good enough to keep me informed as to the results of some of his experiments, notably the appearance of radio-activity corresponding to plutonium when a bismuth rod is volatilized by an electric discharge in deuterium at high pressure. You are on the brink of success, as indeed are several other of our scientists today. May I be allowed to warn you to be careful? The research in which you and your colleagues are engaged is fraught with terrible dangers, not only for yourselves, but for the whole human race.
>
> The liberation of atomic energy is easier than you think, and the radio-activity artificially produced can poison the atmosphere of our planet in the space of a few years. Moreover, atomic explosives can be produced from a few grammes of metal powerful enough to destroy whole cities. I am telling you this as a fact: the alchemists have known it for a very long time.
>
> I know what you are going to say, but it's of no interest. The

---

[10] *Dawn of Magic*, p. 77, English edition.

alchemists were ignorant of the structure of the nucleus, knew nothing about electricity and had no means of detection. Therefore they have never been able to perform any transmutation, still less liberate nuclear energy. I shall not attempt to prove to you what I am now going to say, but I ask you to repeat it to M. Helbronner: certain geometrical arrangements of highly purified materials are enough to release atomic forces without having recourse to either electricity or vacuum techniques. I will merely read to you now a short extract...."

He then picked up Frederick Soddy's *The Interpretation of Radium* and read as follows: "I believe that there have been civilizations in the past that were familiar with atomic energy, and that by misusing it they were totally destroyed."

He then continued: "I would ask you to believe that certain techniques have partially survived. I would also ask you to remember that the alchemists' researches were coloured by moral and religious preoccupations, whereas modern physics was created in the 18th century for their amusement by a few aristocrats and wealthy libertines. Science without a conscience.... I have thought it my duty to warn a few research workers here and there, but have no hope of seeing this warning prove effective. For that matter, there is no reason why I should have any hope."

Bergier has never been able to forget the sound of that precise incisive voice, speaking with such authority.

He ventured to put another question: "If you are an alchemist yourself, sir, I cannot believe you spend your time fabricating gold like Dunikovski or Dr Miethe. For the last year I have been trying to get information about alchemy, and find myself surrounded by impostors or hearing what seem to be fantastic interpretations. Now can you, sir, tell me what is the nature of your researches?"

"You ask me to summarize for you in four minutes four thousand years of philosophy and the efforts of a lifetime. Furthermore, you ask me to translate into ordinary language concepts for which such a language is not intended. All the same, I can tell you this much: you are aware that in the official science of today the role of the observer becomes more and more important. Relativity, the principle of indeterminacy, show the extent to which the observer today intervenes in all these phenomena. The secret of alchemy is this: there is a way of manipulating matter and energy so as to produce what modern scientists call 'a field of force'. This field acts on the observer and puts him in a privileged position *vis-à-vis* the Universe. From this position he has access to the realities which are ordinarily hidden from us by time and space, matter and energy. This is what we call 'The Great Work'."

"But what about the philosopher's stone? The fabrication of gold?"

"These are only applications, particular cases. The essential thing is not the transmutation of metals, but that of the experimenter himself. It's an ancient secret that a few men rediscover once in a century."

The story as told by Pauwels and Bergier is only part of the "Fulcanelli corpus" which circulates in Rosicrucian and Masonic circles. According to this, Fulcanelli was a member of the former French Royal family, the Valois, who were kings of France from 1328 to 1589. He and his brother, both students of alchemy, lived anonymously in Belgium under the name of Dujols. The brother who later assumed the pseudonym of Fulcanelli succeeded in "making the Stone" when he was seventy-two – in 1928. He is still alive, aged 118 (1974), but has the appearance of a man of forty-five.

According to Canseliet's prefaces to the several editions of *Le Mystère des Cathédrales*, "the Master" disappeared while Canseliet was preparing the first edition for publication, and has never been seen since. A different account is current in various occult circles. This alleges that at least one former pupil of Fulcanelli has had subsequent contact with him in Spain. One man is said to have been summoned to Seville. Met there by an intermediary, he was hypnotized and conducted on a long journey to a mysterious valley in a mountainous region. There he was reunited with Fulcanelli, who emerged as the leader of a strange colony of people living in simple but elegant conditions and all dressed in 16th-century style.

After receiving instruction appropriate to his level, this man was conducted back to Seville. Apart from the specific instruction given him and the general impression he retained of the colony and its remarkable people, all other details were removed from his mind by hypnosis and no further clues to the whereabouts of Fulcanelli have ever been recovered.

Even in circles where the Fulcanelli legend is much discussed, the mysterious Spanish colony is regarded as exceeding probability. It is, however, worth noting that members of Sufi groups are sometimes deprived of memory as part of their own development or mission.

Only when deprived of the support which memory would

give, can the individual be driven to the extremes of effort necessary for a particular phase of his work. A Sufi may be sent "to a far country" and obliged to begin a critical phase of his work there, without memory of his own past. An actual example of this is known to the present writer. The parallel between this procedure and the loss of memory at birth is obvious.

In some quarters the whole Fulcanelli legend is regarded as an allegory in modern terms. Others claim that it is factual. Subtending the whole Fulcanelli corpus is the idea that he has achieved election to the same category as the mysterious Count of Saint-Germain. Fulcanelli is supposed to be waiting now in Spain for the beginning of a new phase in European history when benevolent (but technocratic) monarchies will be the general form of government. He is destined for the throne of a new France which he will ascend as Europe's first Initiate Monarch since Frederick II.

This part of the story is not popular in French Masonic circles, however, monarch being a concept not in good standing.

However fantastic the elaborations of the Fulcanelli legend, the "secret valley in Spain" is at least of symbolic interest. It echoes strangely with George Borrow's report of a similar legend where a group of people retaining ancient customs and ancient knowledge is said to survive in some secret Shangri-la in Spain.

Borrow is popularly supposed to be talking about either Jews or Gypsies, but there may be reasons for supposing that he is talking about neither.

Between the lines in *The Bible in Spain*,[11] it seems clear that Borrow was engaged in some activity altogether separate from the distribution of copies of the Gospels to the Spaniards.

He repeatedly mentions people who talk about "the affairs of Egypt". This phrase is supposed to refer to the tenuous communication system of the Gypsies throughout Europe and contemporary writers have picked it up – presumably from Borrow – and fed it back to the Gypsies. Gypsies now talk to newspaper interviewers about "the affairs of Egypt".

[11] Dent, Everyman's Library, London, 1961.

From other sources it can be discovered that the phrase was in fact a recognition signal among Sufis in transit.

Borrow incidentally was an accomplished orientalist and in 1884 translated from Turkish into English some of the Mullah Nasrudin corpus of "jokes".

It is now well known that the Nasrudin stories are teaching material used in Sufic schools as part of a process to awaken a dormant activity of the human mind.[12]

That Borrow knew of the secondary nature of the Nasrudin corpus is indicated in some guarded sentences with which he ends his translation: "Some people say that whilst uttering what seemed madness, he (Nasrudin) was in reality divinely inspired, and that it was not madness, but wisdom that he uttered."

Fulcanelli – Borrow – Spain, gold-making – alchemy: and behind all a single connecting thread: the Sufic impulse.

England, last century, saw a very strange chapter in the story of alchemy and one that passed almost unnoticed. It is the story of an English country gentleman and his daughter, who, working entirely from the theory given – or concealed – in alchemical texts, ancient and modern, apparently uncovered the basic secret of alchemy. They concluded that the aim of true alchemy was "experimentally to transmute the gross nature and baser elements of man into incorruptible life". They also discovered, in all except the minutest of details, the nature of the practice by which this aim could be achieved.

Mary Anne South (later Mrs. Atwood) of Bury House, Gosport, Hampshire, was born in 1817. She grew up her father's favourite and became in turn his secretary, pupil and collaborator.

Thomas South had been interested in alchemy all his life, and had early become quite convinced that behind all the "gibberish" of the texts, there lay concealed not only a complete philosophical system, but a technique of realizing it in practice. He had scholarship, seclusion, patience and a private income and he devoted all to his quest for the inner secret of alchemy.

Together he and his daughter began to compare alchemical texts from a certain viewpoint. In one text a certain aspect is massively concealed. In another the same point may be in

[12] Simac, R., *In a Naqshbandi Circle*, Hibbert Journal, 65–258, Spring, 1967.

relatively plain language. By overlapping a large enough number of texts, certain basics may be extracted. This is said to have been the method whereby the complete masonic rituals were uncovered some twenty years ago.

The Souths lived at a time when magnetism, electricity, mesmerism and spiritualism were confusedly associated in the public mind; a sort of psychological interim period that was trying to bridge ancient superstition and emergent modern science. South and his daughter came to the conclusion, according to W. L. Wilmshurst, that "both the physicist and the psychical empiricist were rediscovering and exploiting obscure natural forces, the existence of which had been perfectly familiar to philosophers, metaphysicians and enlightened occultists of the past, but the manipulation of which had been kept carefully concealed . . .".

By 1846 father and daughter had pieced together their tentative conclusions and were confirming them daily with mounting excitement. Almost of itself, a book took shape. Perhaps without deliberately intending it, Mary found that she clothed her writing in a kind of code. She discovered that she was writing – just as the alchemists had done – in a way that protected the secret from most, while partially clearing the way for those who were ready to understand. Early in 1850 the book was ready for publication. She called it *A Suggestive Inquiry into the Hermetic Mystery* (see p. 65). The proofs came back from the printer. The sheets were bound, the first copies came from the presses. One hundred volumes went out to learned societies and libraries. Then something happened.

Some believe that during the week when distribution of the book was starting, one or other had some mystical experience in which they saw deeply into the alchemical mystery.

What is known is that one night father and daughter could think and talk about nothing except the culmination of so many years of devoted toil. The next, both were in a state of shock – a continuing panic to *prevent the book appearing*.

They bought out the printer's interest, called in all issued copies. They cancelled distribution and by offering as much as ten guineas for a single copy of their own book, they succeeded in assembling at Gosport *almost* every copy in existence.

And there, in the back garden of Bury House, they made an

enormous bonfire in which, in the period of a few hours, was consumed the devoted labour of a lifetime.

Not all the copies were recovered, and from a surviving copy the book was reprinted in Belfast in 1918. Even this edition is something of a collector's item.

It is clear that Mary South and her father concluded – from what source is not known – that the practical technique was inadequately concealed in the book. Like the Chinese alchemist who feared even the fly on the wall, and like Fulcanelli (if it was he) who dreaded the discovery of nuclear fission, Mary South and her father were suddenly terrified of the responsibility they incurred should the technique fall into unworthy hands.

Perhaps the secret does protect itself, as the alchemists say. It is safe to say that a 20th-century reader going through the work would dismiss most of it as simple nonsense. The suggestion that in the Bible the phrase: "Thus saith the Lord" is a code, indicating the presence of a mention of Hermetic practice: the interpretation of the word "adultery"; even a pointed reference to Ezekiel, Chapter Eight, would hardly stir a modern reader, conditioned to believe that the ages before modern science were ages of unrelieved ignorance.

The present writer suspects that a mention of "the stone that the Builders rejected" comes closest to a possible plain language betrayal of an operative technique, but even so, the missing element which so many alchemists endlessly sought in vain remains missing.

It is difficult to avoid the feeling that Mary credited her posterity with greater intuition than they have proved to possess.

Some glimpse of the heights of Mary South's penetration of ultimate mysteries may be gleaned from the following scraps of conversation which Mary's companion, Elizabeth de Steiger, noted and preserved:

> The [alchemical] process takes place in and through the human body in the blood, changing the relation of its component parts or principles, and reversing the circulatory order so that the sensible medium becoming occult, the inner source of its vitality is awakened and the consciousness at the same time being drawn centrally, comes to know and to feel itself in its own true source, which is the Universal Centre and source of all things.

Alchemy is Divine Chemistry, and the transmutation of life; and therefore that which is the medium between soul and body is changed and the soul freed from the chains of corporeity. The body is left as a mere husk. These people put on their bodies as mere coats.

The moment men begin to reduce the ontological ground taken by adepts to physical science, they begin to twaddle.

The spirit teaches its own Art, and according as it is obeyed the artist goes on developing the way for him to advance itself to perfection.

When one life being fermented throws its life to another equally fermented, a greater perfection is produced in the patient than was before in the agent who imparts it. That is the law of progression of the vital force: *sic itur ad astra*.

There is no such thing as truth absolute in nature, because she has no true conceptive vehicle: all her conceptive life is deformed and falsified, so that, as Raymond Lully says, "the pure matter of the philosophers is not to be found on earth".

The speech of Mind uttered into the pure ether qualitates and specificates. The ether is two-fold; the mundane which is full of the false forms; the pure which is not of this world but is connected with the suprasensual life.

In the Philosophical Dissolution, body, soul and spirit are separate; the body lies without breath; the other two are united to it as by a thread and this continues until the refixation takes place.

The outward form of Masonry is too absurd to be perpetuated, were it not for a certain secret response of common sense to the original mystery.

It may seem strange to say so, but too much haste to be good or perfect involves a self-willed action which defeats the end. . . . "Be not righteous overmuch," says Solomon, showing we should not exceed the capacity that is given.

The whole work is an action of agent upon patient, and the reaction of patient, advancing, on agent. The work is gradual, but always progressive; each fermented spirit advances upon its origin.

Kirchberger says for de Saint Martin that there is no true government but a Theocracy.

Intellectual seekers get quickly deeper, but have more to overcome.

The wonderful part of the process is that the spirit, becoming freed from the body, carries on the perfection and purification of her own vehicle, the soul.

Before leaving alchemy and alchemists, it would be interesting to look at a legend which appears to consolidate the entire alchemical corpus into one.

The French diplomat, Louis Jacolliot, spent a large part of his posting to India investigating ancient legends. He wrote a number of remarkable books, and it may be that he was able finally to draw on more than theoretic deduction. His books include *Voyage aux Ruines de Golconde*, *Voyage au Pays des Bayadères*, *Voyage au Pays des Perles*, *Voyage au Pays des Eléphants*, *Voyage au Pays des Fakirs Charmeurs* and *Voyage aux Ruines de Betjapour*.

Jacolliot uncovered the Legend of the Nine Unknowns. According to this legend, the Society of the Nine Unknowns was created by the Indian Emperor Asoka in 273 BC. Asoka wished to encapsule all human knowledge of the time and to ensure that all further research into the real psychology of man and the ultimate nature of matter would be confined to men incapable, because of their advanced state, of misusing the knowledge.

Pauwels and Bergier in *Dawn of Magic* trace the transmission of this legend through Talbot Mundy, the English novelist who spent much of his life in India.

The Nine Unknowns, according to Jacolliot, are still alive, and he implies contact with them. In suggesting the range of their activities he cites powers which were certainly unknown in the West in 1860, such as psychological warfare, sterilization by irradiation, and something like the release of nuclear energy.

Each of the Nine Unknowns is supposed to be responsible for the security of one entire branch of human knowledge. These branches include physiology, microbiology, transmutation of elements, extra-terrestrial communication, gravitation, cosmology, light, and the evolution of human society.

The science of judo is supposed to have resulted from a "leak" from the Book of Physiology and alchemy from the Book of Transmutation. It is also suggested that liaison between the guardian of transmutation and the Unknown in charge of human evolution allows for the release of alchemical gold to alleviate distress locally, following natural calamities or social upheaval.

Says Pauwels: "Having power to mould the destiny of the human race, but refraining from its exercise, this secret society is the finest tribute imaginable to freedom of the most exalted kind. Looking down from the watch-tower of their hidden glory, the Nine Unknowns watched civilization being born, destroyed and born again, tolerant rather than indifferent – and ready to come to the rescue – but always observing that rule of silence which is the mark of human greatness. Myth or reality? A magnificent myth in any case."

Allowing for the colouration of detail perhaps inseparable from a Hindu (and French!) transmission, this legend is accommodated with surprising ease in the theory on which this present book is based: the theory of the Hidden Directorate.

It is echoed in a remarkable passage from the *Kashf al-Mahjub* of Al Hujwiri, the Afghan Sufi who died in 1063. Hujwiri, strangely enough, spent most of his life in India.

> ... Traditions have come down to this effect and the sayings of the Saints proclaim the truth thereof and I myself, God be praised, have had ocular experience of this matter. But of those who have power to loose and bind and are the officers of the Divine Court, there are three hundred called Akhyar and forty called Abdal and seven called Akbar and four called Awtad and three called Nuqaba and one called Qutb or Ghawth. All these know one another, and cannot act save by mutual consent.[13]

A remark by Idries Shah in *Oriental Magic*[14] seems to refer. There is, he says, a chief of the entire Sufi corpus. His identity is known to a few and he maintains contact only with the Heads of Orders – and that telepathically.

A schematic diagram in the same book showing the world Sufi hierarchy taken together with even slight acquaintanceship with the evolutionary aims which lie behind all Sufi activity, is probably sufficient to place the Legend of the Nine Unknowns in true perspective.

[13] Translated by R. A. Nicholson, published E. J. W. Gibb Memorial, 1911.
[14] *Oriental Magic*, Octagon Press, London, 1969, Chapter 7.

CHAPTER EIGHT

GURDJIEFF AND THE INNER CIRCLE OF HUMANITY

The idea of a directing influence behind the historical process has not gone entirely unsuspected. In Napoleonic times, the French group who called themselves the *Sophiens* obviously suspected something of the kind, and it led them to search for a directing source in the East.

However, after six years, they concluded that the initative lay with those who directed such matters and not with aspirants, however well intentioned. They decided that all their efforts had been a waste of time, and with remarkable candour they said so and wound up their society.

In recent times, Lewis Spence has noticed significant elements in history and has tried to link them together in *The Occult Causes of the Present War*.[1]

A most ambitious (though not perhaps very perceptive) effort on the same lines was made by a group, said to be apostate Freemasons, in London in the 1930s, published anonymously as *The Trail of the Serpent*. The author has recently been tentatively identified as Mrs H. T. Stoddart, a member of the Golden Dawn.

Such inquiries necessarily begin with the only material available, i.e., those parts of genuine operations which become visible after the original "occasion" has been abandoned and the medium is in decay. Such studies as Lewis Spence's and the anonymous author of the *Trail of the Serpent* illustrate, if nothing else, the essential invisibility of the material they are trying to detect.

As we have tried to suggest, genuine operations, once terminated, leave "traces" invested with powerful energies. These act as a magnet for well-intentioned ordinary people who seek to perpetuate what is in effect an empty form. It has been claimed that virtually all occultism known to the West is of this variety.

[1] Spence, *The Occult Causes of the Present War*, Rider, London, 1941.

Such pseudo-movements are "involuntary". The personality, negative emotions, vanity and wish-fulfilment urges of those involved, proceed, as in ordinary life, to mechanical and perhaps finally destructive ends.

Due, however, to the illuminating and magnifying nature of the original idea to which they are attached, such organizations have an apparent vitality much in excess of ordinary social and political groupings.

Since it is only "remainder" forms which are available for investigation, it is not surprising that such inquiries as have been attempted converge on some theory of an historical influence which is for the most part sinister.

According to the author of *The Trail of the Serpent*, the higher grades of all hermetic societies "require that the adept be enslaved by some astute outside mind or group of minds which, it would seem, seek to rule the nations through hypnotically controlled adepts ... for one and all of these modern Mysteries are ruled by some unknown hierarchy...."

Lewis Spence moves tentatively to the conclusion that some evil forces permeate European Freemasonry (but not English Freemasonry!), concluding, for example, that Cagliostro engineered the French Revolution for the advantage of a sinister illuminist group opposed to monarchy.

The Trail of the Serpent starts by collecting facts, but finishes by attributing most of humanity's woes to the Jews and the Elders of Zion.

Pauwels and Bergier see the Russian Red Dragon Society contriving the Russian Revolution and the assassination of the Czar; and Haushofer, with Gruppe Thule, animating the empty shell of Hitler in a bid to provoke a Satanic apocalypse. ("He will dance, but we will play the tune.")

It is probably safe to assert that all attempts to discern and connect the elements which might provide a unified theory of history must fail so long as inquiries are confined to the visible shadows and not the invisible substance. The substance, however, has a built-in invisibility; or so it seemed till very recently.

Since the early 1950s, a great deal of hitherto unknown material has become available, and in the nature of things this cannot have happened by accident. If it has leaked, it is because those in charge of it have decided to "leak" it.

Separately, the various hints amount to little. Taken together, they suggest, for the first time, the nature of the organization, long suspected but never identified, which is concerned with injecting developmental possibilities into the historical process at certain critical points.

On the basis of internal evidence, it may be legitimate to suggest that this organization is the expression of one of the Centres inferred by J. G. Bennett as directing the evolution of the whole human race. Twelve thousand years ago, these Centres withdrew for some 80 generations to prepare for the début of modern man. The suggestion is that one of these, immediately responsible for the West, has decided to come, partially at least, into the open in the second half of the 20th century. It may be that the intellectual development of the West is now at such a stage that the parent can only guide the offspring further by taking it into its confidence.

To glimpse the steps by which the first hints of this have passed into the public domain and to guess at the possible purpose of such action, it will be necessary to go back to last century and to the little Caucasian town of Alexandropol.

There in 1872 was born George Ivanovitch Gurdjieff, certainly one of the most remarkable figures ever to appear in the West.

The Caucasus region has been a mixing bowl of cultures for thousands of years. European, Slavonic, Turkish, Roman, Mongol, Persian and even more ancient cultures have flooded into this area and then receded, each leaving some contribution. It was into this fusion of influences that Gurdjieff was born.

His family were Greeks who had emigrated from Caesarea in the 16th century. His father was a bard whose recitations preserved legends of remote antiquity, including Assyrian and Sumerian traditions.

It was these that probably first suggested to Gurdjieff the idea of some hidden influence that linked all the generations of men in a way ordinarily unsuspected.

Late in life he discovered that the archaeological recovery and translation of ancient cuneiform inscriptions endorsed in minutest detail the account of ancient history preserved in his father's poems. In other words, there exists an unsuspected oral transmission of history as accurate and at least as enduring as any orthodox historical record.

As a youth, Gurdjieff became obsessed with the idea that there was a purpose and aim behind human life which was hardly ever glimpsed in the ceaseless generations of man. He became convinced that in former epochs man had possessed genuine knowledge of such matters, and that this knowledge was still preserved, somehow, somewhere.

Together with a number of others, like-minded with himself, Gurdjieff began a search (lasting decades) for traces of this knowledge. His "society" of seekers, singly and in groups, went on pilgrimages to remote places where traces of this ancient knowledge might survive. The members – some actual, some possibly allegorical – met at intervals of years to compare results. Their survey took in Africa, Persia, Turkestan, Tibet, India and the Far East as far as Malaya.

Some of his friends were killed. Some remained with brotherhoods they had discovered in unimaginably remote corners of the world. Gurdjieff and some others made a contact which they regarded as significant in the highest degree and they underwent a long and arduous training.

This period seems to have finished by about 1908, and during his lifetime nothing appears to have been known about his activities between 1908 and his appearance in Moscow in 1914.[2]

There he occupied the rôle of teacher and gathered round him a group which included the Russian writer and philosopher, P. D. Ouspensky. The subsequent activities of Gurdjieff and his pupils is given in Ouspensky's *In Search of the Miraculous*[3] and in a flood of books by pupils, former pupils and interested bystanders published in recent years.

During his period in France, Gurdjieff came under scrutiny by many intellectuals of the West, who tried to assess what was going on in the only terms available – their own.

The result is a motley collection of impressions and "assessments" which variously show Gurdjieff as a superman, a

---

[2] Much new material has recently come to light from the researches of J. G. Bennett (*Gurdjieff, Making a New World*, Turnstone, London, 1973).

[3] Routledge, London, 1950.

magician and something like a madman. He had an incredible capacity for puncturing people's egoism and was seemingly wholly unconcerned about the vituperation this produced.

If there is one impression common to all, it is that Gurdjieff was not an ordinary man. He possessed powers which ordinary people did not possess, and he had an aim before which all other considerations were wholly unimportant.

Those who were close to Gurdjieff for longer than a single afternoon are unanimous in testifying to the extraordinary effect he had upon them. Outraging all ordinary standards of good manners and behaviour, and sometimes using language which by social standards was unpardonable, he could nevertheless leave an impression of some unbearable nostalgia; a hint of some unknown level of humanity; an impression of holiness. The experience of meeting Gurdjieff could never be forgotten.

For years, while earning a living as a business man in Paris, he conducted his classes at Fontainebleau, supervised the coming and going of thousands of pupils from all over the world, taught his dance movements and his music and wrote two books and part of a third.

The first book, *All and Everything*,[4] which was in proof before his death (October 29, 1949), probably confirmed the literary world in its belief that Gurdjieff could be written off as a madman.

But behind the extravagance of language, the deliberate confusion of chronology and the absurd allegories of ravens as space scientists, there is a significance which is certainly not to be appraised superficially.

The drama of the universal process, the nature of time and an exposition of the transflux energies associated with life, are linked to a cosmology that is mind-daunting. There is every reason to believe that Orage and C. S. Nott are right, and that *All and Everything* is a work of objective art comparable to the Mahabharata.

The book produces effects upon the reader at several levels. On people whose lives have been based entirely on the satisfactions of personality, the effect is sometimes overwhelming.

---

[4] G. I. Gurdjieff, *All and Everything*, Routledge, London, 1950.

Gurdjieff was often asked about the source of his system and the origins of the teaching it contained. This he would never divulge, but sometimes pointed to the indications contained in his second series of writings, *Rencontres avec des Hommes Remarquables*.[5]

This carried the suggestion that the members of Gurdjieff's society of seekers had travelled in virtually unexplored areas of Central Asia.

"Gurdjieff's people" all over the world included writers, scientists, artists, doctors and professionals of many kinds. Many of them sensed that in *All and Everything* there were revelations about the mechanism of nature which could be translated into practice in the technological world of the 20th century.

A quarter of a century after his death this appears to be happening. Ideas, all unacknowledged, have crept into psychology which clearly derive from *All and Everything*.

In England and America, a new science of "structural communication" is being applied to such diverse activities as teaching machines and naval strategy. This, though the origin is not suspected by educationalists or industrialists, derives from Gurdjieff's "occult" teaching.

In the early years before Gurdjieff's death, all was confusion among the many "Gurdjieff groups" in England, America, France, Germany and elsewhere.

Several "successors" to Gurdjieff appeared, all implicitly or explicitly claiming that they had been given the charter by "G" himself.

People who for years had worked on themselves to transcend ordinary personality limitations, behaved in thoroughly "unobjective" ways. There was name calling and vituperation. There was, on one hand, a tendency to look outward, and, on the other hand, a tendency slavishly to continue the "work" taught by Gurdjieff himself.

Behind most of this there was probably fear. Most sincere pupils realized that their studies and practice had taken them beyond the most childish patterns of ordinary personality behaviour, but they had not for the most part

---

[5] Julliard, Paris, 1960.

reached a level from which they could make further progress on their own.

Some of the most independent people sought to meet the next phase half-way – if there was a next phase.

Many elaborate deductions were made. In *All and Everything*, it was related, for example, that seven centuries before the "Babylonian events", a genuine Messenger had incarnated on earth. His name was Ashiata Shiemash. This "Most Very Saintly, now already Common Cosmic Individual", had concluded after very long deliberation that all the methods used by Genuine Messengers in the past, namely, one or other of the sacred impulses of Faith, Hope and Love were no longer applicable. Certain accretions in the soul-body of humanity had become so dense that the inspiration of a Messenger employing one of the familiar sacred impulses was no longer adequate to achieve the catharsis from which evolution could proceed.

Ashiata Shiemash decided that Conscience alone remained uncontaminated in the human presence, and he proceeded therefore to work on methods of activating Conscience.

This chapter in *All and Everything* had always made a profound impression on people, and some of the Gurdjieff groups deduced that it was the key to the future. "Seven centuries before the Babylonian events" was, they decided, a typical Gurdjieff "blind". Various Messengers and Prophets known historically might be identified with efforts based on faith, hope or love, but none was known who had made his appeal to human conscience. . . . From this it was decided that Ashiata Shiemash *was still to come*.

Near the end of his life Gurdjieff had been asked what would become of the Gurdjieff people after his death. He was said to have replied: "Another will come. He is even now preparing." Other hints placed this expectation in India, or some country with Indian associations.

This combination of clues led a large number of Gurdjieff people in America, England and France to identify the Indonesian teacher Mohammad Subuh with "Ashiata Shiemash", and this was almost certainly a factor in the rapid spread of Subud in the West.

Other groups associated with the Gurdjieff material, but centred more on his pupil, P. D. Ouspensky, declined to make this identification, but found reason to identify with the Indian mystic, Maharishi Mahesh.

Various lecture courses at present advertised throughout the country for subjects far removed from anything metaphysical apparently derive from yet another attempt to identify Ashiata Shiemash. It is difficult to avoid the conclusion that this represents the ultimate example of looking for a caravan in an empty oasis.

In addition to such attempts to identify Ashiata Shiemash, several attempts were made to make contact with Gurdjieff's source in the East. These were without success, but the experience of those who tried probably underlines the principle that such sources cannot be found unless they want to be found. When they do, there is little difficulty. As it transpired, they *did* want to be found – but not apparently before 1961.

In that year a journalist and traveller seeking material for an article on Sufi practices met a Sufi in Pakistan and was unaccountably introduced to every facility for getting material for his article. This journalist, Omar Burke, found himself allowed to visit a secret Dervish community whose location has been identified as Kunji Zagh ("Raven's Corner") in Baluchistan.

He spent some days there, and gathered various impressions of the community's activities. Soon afterwards he wrote his article, which appeared in *Blackwood's Magazine* in December 1961.

Burke, in his description of the day-to-day life of this community, described various practices and one particular exercise which were clearly identifiable with Gurdjieff's system.

The article was read, by chance, by a member of one of the London Gurdjieff groups who realized that one trail to Gurdjieff's "source", long thought to be concealed beyond hope of discovery, was in fact being given openly in a literary magazine!

It is perhaps possible to imagine the excitement and the behind-the-scenes activity which this discovery produced. Contact was finally made with Akhund Mirza, the wandering Dervish who had so fortuitously met Burke in Pakistan, and additional information asked for. The reply was, if anything, more startling than the original discovery of a possible clue to Gurdjieff's source. The London group were told that it would be pointless to come to Baluchistan as the current focus of activity was not in the East at all, but in England.

A little later, but independently of the Burke incident, a seeker writing under the name of Rafael Lefort, was to solve the same mystery in a much more direct way.

This man had come to the conclusion that the section of the Gurdjieff movement with which he was associated was pursuing activities which were sterile and futile. He also felt that from being developmental under Gurdjieff, the activity had now become totalitarian.

Braving the heretic label which his action would undoubtedly give him, he went to Turkey and sought the trail to Gurdjieff's source by the simple and direct method of going about asking people: "Did you ever hear of a man called Gurdjieff?"

In a short space of time he realized that his inquiries were being passed back in some way, and were leading to opportunities for him to meet people who *had* known Gurdjieff and who also knew a great deal about associated matters.

Lefort's book *The Teachers of Gurdjieff*[6] is an outstanding example of achieving big results by employing methods so simple that nobody else apparently thought of them.

Lefort was passed along a line of a dozen contacts, at each of which his motives were tested and his vanity deflated. In the end he came to the same source as the London group had arrived at by different methods.

By 1962 the great mystery had thus been solved twice – although the solution had apparently been available all along.

The whole story of the search for Gurdjieff's source is much like the Eastern story of the blind men and the elephant. People had touched a trunk, an ear, a tail and had built up a theory of the nature of the beast. But the search was for bits and pieces. Nobody was looking for a complete elephant.

---

[6] Gollancz, London, 1966. It has recently been pointed out with some authority that this is in the nature of a series of fables put together to illustrate a point of view and should not be taken as a factual account. If this is the case it may however do no more than illustrate a Sufic aphorism which, roughly rendered, says "It doesn't have to be fact to be true".

The search also shows European scholarship in an unflattering light. Gurdjieff talked about teachings in Kafiristan. The Sufi tradition of Haji Bektash says the same thing. Anyone who had suspected the Sufic origins of G.'s system could have found this reference in a book published during the period of G.'s stay at Fontainebleau.[7]

G. also published a pamphlet, copies of which still exist, naming several Sufi Orders and groups as the source of his dramatic presentations.

While excellent minds in England, France and Germany were trying without success to arrange pieces of an intractable jigsaw puzzle, the existence of the completed picture was almost common knowledge in the East.

An inner circle of humanity which kindles or restrains human activity is associated with the Sufi concept of the Abdals ("Changed Ones"), and this is openly referred to in both oral and literary sources.

The idea that Dervish or Sufic brotherhoods represent a more or less visible link in this organization is part of common acceptance among quite ordinary people in the East.

In fairness, it should be mentioned that the Sufic link seems to have been considered, but to some extent passed over. Rodney Collin had noticed certain significant points in Dervish literature, and even published in Mexico a booklet[8] containing Dervish material. This was a selection from the *Lives of the Gnostics* by Aflaki, who was a disciple of the grandson of Jalaluddin Rumi (1207-1273), founder of the Mevlevi Order[9] of Dervishes. Rumi was the author of the great poem, the *Mathnawi*, which expresses the mystical path which the Mevlevis tread.

Gurdjieff had taught "movements", a stylized dance technique which requires extended energies of attention. The association of the G "movements" and the Mevlevi whirling was perhaps unavoidable, but we shall find reason to suspect, presently, that the "movements" have a different source, although G. dressed his disciples in Mevlevi outfits, perhaps for "misdirection" purposes.

[7] J. P. Brown, *The Darvishes*, O.U.P., London, 1927, p. 166.
[8] *The Whirling Ecstasy*, Ediciones Sol, San Antonio Abad, Mexico, 1954.
[9] Mevlevi means "of the Master".

Before Gurdjieff took over the Prieuré at Fontainebleau, P. D. Ouspensky, the Russian philosopher and G.'s pupil, had decided that Gurdjieff's exposition was unsatisfactory on intellectual grounds. He believed that G. lacked the ultimate key to the system he taught. He believed, further, that G. had taken, or was about to take, a wrong turning which, instead of obliterating egoism, would create it into an entity with grave consequences for all associated with him. He parted from G., and formed his own groups of pupils. Ouspensky's decision to work independently seems today, even from the sidelines, to have been rash. He proceeded to exclude entire elements from the practice taught by Gurdjieff – a practice which, according to Ouspensky, was already defective.

Ouspensky's hope was that by sheer intensity of personal effort, he would attract the attention of the Source. Instead of looking for it, the Source would look for him.

By 1938, it had become apparent that this expectation had not been realized.

Like other intellectuals who had studied Gurdjieff material, he was fascinated by the word *Sarmoun*, a secret brotherhood that Gurdjieff had mentioned and from which he had clearly obtained important gains.

Ouspensky, like many others, suspected that the Sarmoun monastery was, if not the actual Source, on the threshold to it.

For some reason, he believed that the Mevlevi Order of Dervishes held the entrée to Sarmoun.

In the 1930s it is believed that Ouspensky made contact with the Mevlevis and asked them to send someone to England. This they declined to do, but indicated that they were prepared to receive a representative from him. One of Ouspensky's senior pupils was ready to leave for the East in 1939 when War broke out and the project was abandoned.

Although one section of Ouspensky's pupils are convinced that he broke through to a certain level of development as a result of almost superhuman efforts made in the last few months of his life, others are equally convinced that he died wholly disillusioned.

Sufic sources have since indicated that the whole search for Gurdjieff's Source – and later for his successor – was watched from various points in Central Asia with compassionate, if wry, amusement. One of their reported comments is: "The Western European and American phase of the Gurdjieff – Ouspensky operation was heroic in intensity. The Source is not attracted by heroism, but by capacity and ability to respond to its messages."

The seekers were quite right; a key was missing. But it was not the kind of key they imagined. What was missing was the realization that "interventions", designed to inject a developmental impulse into the historical process, are discontinuous.

"Occasions" relate to the fortuitous presence of energies on a much vaster scale and perhaps from outside the planet. It is as though a solar wind blows on the earth at intervals. When it does, agents of the Directorate – represented for the past 1,000 years and more by some Sufic organizations – can act to straighten out involutionary trends and produce an evolutionary gain. In the absence of this "solar wind", there is no possibility of "work", and hence no activity on the historical scale.

The matter is not at the discretion of those who organize the field-work, much less of aspirants to participate, however industrious and well-intentioned.

Both lines of search which finally traced back the source of Gurdjieff's teaching, came to the same conclusion: it was a Sufic source. They also discovered that examination of the Gurdjieff material would have shown this all along.

The central figure of *All and Everything* is an archetypal figure called Beelzebub, who in his youth committed an indiscretion. By dint of conscious labour and intentional suffering of a heroic nature, he purifies himself to the point where he can be received back into the hierarchy of cosmic beings.

Beelzebub describes his experiences on earth to his grandson, "Hassein". Two major historical figures in the East are Hassan and Hussein, grandsons of – Mohammed. Further, Beelzebub is the anglicized version of *B'il Sabab*, which is Arabic for "the man with a motive, aim".

Another example of this play on meaning is the famous Ashiata Shiemash. When the leadership of a Sufi school is transferred from one teacher to another, the transfer is signalled by the phrase, *Ya Shahim Sahiest*.[10] As an anagram,

---

[10] "It is prepared, O my Shah!"

Ashiata Shiemash is virtually intact even in English transliteration.

In his writings, Gurdjieff repeatedly mentions meetings with dervishes. One of the most seemingly absurd accounts relates to a hermit living in primitive conditions in a cave. This man, however, lights his cave with electricity and gas. He also produces an abscess on the leg of a visitor by playing certain notes on a musical instrument, and then causes the swelling to reduce and finally disappear by playing another sequence of notes.

While not perhaps discouraging speculation about possible symbolic meanings of the story, Gurdjieff told several of his pupils that it was a factual account of an incident he had himself experienced.

One possible conclusion to be drawn from the story is that certain people who live in primitive conditions may possess sophisticated modern technology. They may also possess powers unknown to science and medicine because they have fallen heir to a wholly different kind of knowledge.

The hermit in the cave is a dervish, that is, a member of a Sufi order. His name is Asvatz-Troov. B'il Sabab (the man with the aim) is introduced to Asvatz-Troov by another dervish, the Hadji Bogga-Eddin of Bokhara.

"Bogga-Eddin" is a Russianized version of Bahauddin, the Russians substituting "g" for "h" (Gitler for Hitler). If we note that a very famous Sufic teacher was called Bahauddin, and that he came from Bokhara, the concealed reference to the origin of the dervish's powers becomes clear.[11]

Bahauddin Naqshband was a Sufi teacher in the Khwajagan ("Masters") line whose school greatly influenced the development of the Mogul and Turkish empires. The transmission from Bahauddin is known as the chain or the Masters of the Design. He died in 1389, but his spiritual power or baraka is said to sustain, among other organizations, the Brotherhood of Sarmoun!

Sarmoun, it will be recalled, was believed by many of Gurdjieff's followers to be the key to his teaching. Recent hints

[11] The second great Central Asian Sufi Master named Bahauddin Shah is buried near Kabul in Afghanistan. He belonged to the same Sufi family as the Hindu-Kush Sayeds located by *The Times* correspondent in Kafiristan.

suggest that the word may also identify the "powerhouse" through which developmental activity, in respect of at least part of the world, is maintained.

Hints of this are now appearing in ordinary sources. The American travel author, Peter King, in *Afghanistan: Cockpit in High Asia*[12] notes:

> Nor is the Snowman the only mystery in Nuristan (*area of Afghanistan, till second Afghan War called Kafiristan*). Somewhere in these mountains are to be found the hidden monasteries or training centres of what Afghans refer to as The People of the Tradition. These people, about whom one can learn little, are supposed to be the custodians of the secret traditions which are the bases of religion and man's development. In the most inaccessible spot of all is said to be the Markaz or "powerhouse" of the People. The Sufis in Afghanistan are closely connected with these People, but no one will tell an outsider anything more than that these monasteries exist. They say that the only outsider to have penetrated into the outer ring of monasteries was a Russian-Greek, George Gurdjieff, whose contacts enabled him to be accepted as a pupil. This is the same Gurdjieff who had some success with a form of philosophical teaching in the United States and Europe in the 30s. Said to have been trained by Bahauddin Nakshband, one of the "outer masters", Gurdjieff mastered some of the teachings and tried to teach them in the West. This teaching did not really catch on, and after his death his converts carried on in a desultory fashion and introduced some things to freshen up the image. It was not, apparently, till the 1960s that a group of his former students re-established contact with the original Source of the teaching. This was both a shock and an ecstatic experience for them, for they found that the dervishes did not accept all the important successors of Gurdjieff as being worthy of being taught, let alone to teach. ...

Clearly, in the last ten years, information which has been held in impenetrable secrecy for centuries – perhaps millennia – is emerging into common knowledge. It is equally clear that this has not just happened, but has been engineered.

It seems inconceivable, for example, that a Western newspaper reporter should just happen to discover extensive details of something that has never been more than a whispered hint all through history. Yet this happened in 1964.

[12] Geoffrey Bles, London, 1960.

The London *Times* on March 9 of that year published an account by its own correspondent of a visit to a highly significant monastery in Kafiristan. The article includes the name of the Abbot and – virtually – directions for getting there.

Earlier, in January 1961, in a weekly English-language cultural periodical published in Delhi, S. Brook White described the operation of Sufi methodology all over the world, and revealed that it is active in England.

In December, 1965, the English magazine *The Lady* published an article by Major Desmond Martin in which the author describes what amounts to a facility trip to a monastery of the Sarmoun Brotherhood.

In 1961, a doctor[13] was given facilities to watch an hitherto unknown form of medicine being practised in a remote community in Afghanistan. The method involved hypnosis, but was far removed from the mere removal of symptoms by post-hypnotic suggestion. It recalled classical accounts of the Greek "Temple of Sleep" technique which is ordinarily supposed to be symbolic.

The practitioners, who trained for 16 years before being allowed to practise, were Sufis.

In a book review in the London *Evening News* (February 10, 1969), the writer noted a number of significant hints that had been appearing in recently published books, and seemed to suggest that these references were part of a deliberate policy of releasing information.

From all of these published accounts and from other sources, it may be possible to suggest some tentative conclusions.

In summary, these would be:

The legend of the "Secret People" has recently received considerable confirmation. Such matters do not, by their nature, "leak" by accident, and it is to be concluded that information has been deliberately released.

A number of centres associated with this activity can be deduced.

(1) In Baluchistan, in a place referred to as Kunj-i-Zagh ("Raven's Corner").

[13] J. Hallaji, in *The Nature of Hypnosis*, Eds. R. E. Shor and M. T. Orne, Holt, Rhinehart and Winston, New York, 1965, pp. 453ff.

(2) By a waterfall locally known as Nimtout in the Paghman range, which begins about 20 miles north-west of Kabul.
(3) At an unidentified location in Northern Afghanistan "looking up to the Hindu Kush". This is the legendary monastery of Sarmoun, the acting head of which is a Sufi, identified as Baba Amyn.
(4) Adjoining the above, a similar community for women.
(5) Northern Afghanistan, a location given as Abshaur.[14]
(6) A centre in Persia.
(7) A centre in Iraq.

The references from which the above list has been deduced may overlap, and it is possible that two at least are separate descriptions of the same location.

One possible reason for deliberately exposing the general location of communities which have for so long been kept secret would be that the real activity associated with them has been moved elsewhere. Such an idea seems almost explicit in an incident reported by Major Martin in his magazine article already referred to. He was allowed to see certain possessions of the Sarmoun community which had never before been shown to the uninitiated. He reports: "They had been 'deconsecrated', as it were, because a new phase of teaching *somewhere to the West* had superseded the ritual to which they belonged. Henceforth they would be merely museum pieces" (our italics). Several speculations might arise from this. At the turn of the 12th century the Mongol invasions took place, a turning point in history, the significance of which is not perhaps fully allowed by historians. In the Sufic hierarchy – at any rate above a certain level – this event and its long-term consequences were foreseen and steps were taken in advance (a) to limit the worst excesses of the new régime at the level of everyday life, and (b) to turn adverse conditions to ultimate advantage. When Jenghis Khan swept through Central Asia and destroyed Balkh, "the mother of cities", Sufic organizations had already acted in a certain way. One-third emigrated. One-third, seemingly, came to terms with the invaders. One-third went underground.

There would seem to be at least the possibility that a

---

[14] Means "waterfall".

similar situation is foreseen in the 20th century. If this is so, the "Cockpit of Asia", lying as it does between China and Russia, would probably be untenable for the organization of "The People of the Tradition".[15]

The theory of such a contingency, with its element of emigration, would be supported by the circumstance that something subtended by the Sarmoun and associated traditions began to establish in the West, including England, from about 1952. The Sarmounis ("the Bees") believe that the teaching they follow pre-dates the Flood. They assert that objective knowledge is a material substance and can be collected and stored like honey. This is done during periods of history when the world does not value honey. At critical junctures, the Sarmouni distribute the honey throughout the world by the agency of specially trained emissaries.

Associated with the organization of the Sarmouni is a symbol called the No-Koonja (literally, "nine-pointed diagram"), also known as the Naqsh (seal or design) which "reaches for the innermost secrets of man".

Social structures set up in various parts of the world by the agents of the Tradition are later taken over by people without understanding. Such, the *Times* correspondent was told at Abshaur, become in time only "philosophical grinding mills", and from that stage become cursed.

The Sarmoun tradition regards as degenerate dervishes who teach through Moslem scriptures, and dervishes who give public displays of dancing, etc.

Such activities of the Sarmoun teaching as are sometimes detected "outside" are of a nature which leads Christians to regard them as disguised Mohammedanism, and Moslems to regard them as disguised Christianity.

Certain activity throughout the world apparently causes concern. Due to recent trends of immigration, Asiatic populations in Western countries have tended to set up social and racial groups using Sufic terminology and Sufic forms of organization. To the Western mind which has experience of such

---

[15] A communist revolution took place in Afghanistan in the spring of 1978.

communities, the word Sufi tends to be associated with this imitative activity. Agents of the Tradition are concerned about the effects of this. Since they used other labels of identification before the 7th century, it may be that the members of the Tradition will be constrained to relinquish the word Sufi – a word which among themselves they seldom use.

*   *   *

We have suggested that there is behind visible history a hidden influence which is concerned with evolutionary aims for the whole human race. We have suggested that recently clues to the identity of this influence have become deliberately available, and we have tried to show that the clues converge upon Afghanistan and associated geographical areas.

Chapter Nine

FREEMASONS, SUFIS, INITIATORY SOCIETIES

We have seen that several independent lines of research, attempting to trace the source of Gurdjieff's teaching, led to the conclusion that the source was a Sufic one centred in Asia, probably in Afghanistan.

The material we now have to consider suggests that Afghanistan is the source of a great deal more than Gurdjieff's system; that it is in fact the prime source of a whole range of esoteric systems which the West – and the East – have wrongly attributed elsewhere.

The material now to be considered was the first general summary of the investigation made by the group of five people mentioned in an earlier chapter. Each member of this group had a personal interest in one branch of esoteric tradition and had pursued his or her speciality to the point where further back-tracking seemed impossible. At this point the five people came together.

One of the group was interested in witchcraft and its possible connections with secret societies of other kinds. Another was working on the distribution of Hindu and Buddhist esoteric beliefs. A third had been looking for clues which might establish a source for Western Freemasonry. The fourth had done research on the teachings of Gurdjieff, the Indonesian cult of Subud and the philosophy of Ouspensky and his followers, including Dr. Maurice Nicoll, Dr. Kenneth Walker and Rodney Collin. The fifth had made an extensive study of Theosophy and Anthroposophy, alchemy of the psychology variety, and Vedanta.

On pooling resources, it was soon apparent that behind all the separate researches there was a common factor. Historical, topographical and psychological evidence pointed strongly to the conclusion that all of these cults originated in the East.

Later a more startling possibility began to emerge – that all of these systems had a common parentage.

The Vedantist theory of the Gurus as teaching masters could be traced beyond the borders of India in two waves – and probably a third. While Western students of Vedic teachings were content to ascribe the centre and origin of Vedanta to the traditional wisdom of India, the Hindus themselves regarded their teachings as emanating "from beyond the mountains".

The Hindu scriptures were written during the period when the Hindu tribes were an agrarian community in the Asian heartland – which embraces Afghanistan, Khorasan and what are today parts of Russia. The magico-religious references of the Vedas date from this place and epoch.

When the Hindus settled in India they still looked to their original homeland for spiritual inspiration. The Sanskrit and Tibetan *Shambala*, mythologized into a place beyond the earth, has been identified by no less an authority than Madame Alexandra David-Neel with Balkh – in Afghanistan – the ancient settlement known as "the mother of cities".[1] Other places long considered to be legendary have been identified by historians and geographers with localities within the boundaries of present-day Afghanistan.

According to Alice Bailey,[2] the Theosophist, "Sanyat Kumara" (generally identified with the Biblical "Ancient of Days") lives in Shambala. Below him is a triad of world government: Manu, Maitreya and Manachohen, jointly responsible for creating and dissolving racial types and the rise and fall of civilizations – surely a symbolic representation of the idea of a physical Centre which we have deduced.

Present-day folklore in Afghanistan asserts that after the Moslem conquest, Balkh was known as The Elevated Candle ("Sham-i-Bala") which is evidently a classical Persianization of the Sanskrit Shambala.

Nor did the esoteric associations of Balkh disappear with its Islamization. It became a centre of scientific activity and mysticism. Jalaluddin Rumi, the great 13th century mystic and originator of the "Dancing Dervishes", was a native of Balkh. His teacher, Sanai, was from nearby Ghazna. Omar Khayyam

---

[1] Alexandra David-Neel, in *Les Nouvelles Littéraires*, No. 1390, 1954, p. 1.
[2] *Initiation, Human and Solar*, Lucis Press, New York, 1933.

studied at Balkh; it was the birthplace of Avicenna (Ibn Sina). Adelard of Bath translated a great astronomical work by Abu Ma'Shar, the scientist, of Balkh.

During the Middle Ages and in several later waves, Sufi missionaries spread through India. They came from Afghanistan. The techniques, beliefs and practices which they brought were adopted alike by the Hindus and by the Moghul rulers and their Moslem subjects. One Moghul prince, Dara Shikoh, averred that Sufic teaching was the same as that which underlay the Vedas and he wrote several books to prove the point. He eventually paid with his life for infidelity to the official definitions of Islam.

The origin of Rudolph Steiner's anthroposophy has been the subject of endless speculation in the West. Implicit in the researches of John Symonds, the biographer of the infamous Aleister Crowley, is the idea that Steiner did not just happen to have the inner development which led him to form a world-wide esoteric movement. He apparently had earlier training in a secret society called the *Ordo Templi Orientis* of which he was at one stage the Austrian Grand Master.

Such diverse results as the esoteric philosophy of Max Heindel and the modern society of AMORC – which advertises for recruits in the newspapers – have been traced by some to the source with which Steiner was associated prior to about 1911.

The sequence appears to be as follows.

In the 1890s a high-grade Viennese Freemason called Karl Kellner was initiated into an Eastern secret society about which almost nothing is known. Kellner had made contact with three members of this society, one of whom, at least, was an Arab.[3]

Kellner returned to Germany and with three fellow Masons, Hartmann, Klein and Reuss, created in 1902 the *Ordo Templi Orientis*, which it was claimed "possessed the same secret as the Templars and the Illuminati". It apparently dealt in the same technique of magic as had been independently developed in England by Aleister Crowley after he had secured the expulsion of MacGregor Mathers from the *The Golden Dawn* society.

The Golden Dawn (Crowley's version) and the German O.T.O. of Kellner, Hartmann and Reuss for a time amalgamated and it

---

[3] J. Symonds, *The Great Beast*, Rider, London 1951, p. 104.

may well have been the presence of Crowley in the combined organization which led Steiner to resign from the O.T.O.

The O.T.O. was one of a considerable number of European secret societies of the period which fell under the general classification of "Rosicrucian". They included the Rosicrucian Society of England (later The Golden Dawn), the Red Rose and Golden Cross (mesoteric section of the G.D.), the Argenteum Astrum (esoteric G.D.), Licht, Liebe, Leben, and others.[4]

The modern Rosicrucians seem in general to be without any real knowledge of their origins. Manly P. Hall in *The Riddle of the Rosicrucians*[5] says that with the exception of a few vague generalities, no real information can be gathered from these sources. "Each group had its opinions, but was woefully lacking in the documentation necessary to justify its pretensions."

Traditional opinions in Rosicrucian lodges converge on the belief that the movement was founded by a German, Christian Rosencreutz, who was initiated in Palestine *by an Arab group*.

When it is realized that the Sufi teacher Suhrawardi of Aleppo had a teaching method called The Path of the Rose and that the Sufic word for a dervish exercise has the same consonantal root as the word for a rose, the Sufic origin of the Rosicrucians may be inferred with some confidence.

According to Steiner's Anthroposophical lore the Baghdad Caliph Haroun el Rashid tried to create an esoteric centre in the ninth century. His chief lieutenant was Jafar the Barmecide whose family, the Parmaks or Barmaki, were the traditional custodians of the Buddhist religious shrines of Afghanistan. All roads, it would seem, lead to Balkh.

Haroun is known to have had contact with Sufis, notably one teacher in Mecca and another in Basra, both of whom warned him against his activities. One of these was no less a personage than Fudail, son of Iyad, a major Sufi sage.

Ibn al Atahiyya (died 828), another of the Sufi teachers who had contact with Haroun el Rashid, has been traced as an important influence in the "witchcraft" cult in Western Europe. Although "witches" probably have an unbroken

---

[4] According to Rosicrucian legend, the founder of the order obtained his knowledge in Arabia, Fez (Morocco) and Egypt.

[5] Philosophical Research Society, Los Angeles, 1951.

tradition since Neolithic times, witchcraft as it was known in the Medieval West owed its form to something which it acquired from the East. In the next chapter, when the consequences of leakages in developmental techniques are discussed, we shall try to identify this factor.

There is no discernible connection between the followers of the Vedic teachings and European witches, but they appear to have evolved – or involved – from a common influence which was Sufic in origin. The organization may well have been used as a vehicle.

Similarly, the connection between the Tibetan form of Lamaism and the Dancing Dervishes remains unsuspected until a common connection is noted with Balkh in Afghanistan: and the fact that the Dalai Lama traditionally is escorted to his palace by five dervishes.

Recent research has suggested a connection between Freemasonry and Sufism,[6] and there have been repeated suggestions of a connection between the Rosicrucians and the Masons.

Links between Freemasons and the "Illuminati" have also been established.[7]

In the Balkans, the Bektashi Sufis claim that they are Masons,[8] and the known techniques of the European Illuminists are almost identical with those of the Roshania ("the Illuminated") sect of the Afghan hinterland.

The Bektashis were founded by Haji Bektash of Khorasan and the Order has connections with Kafiristan. Moslem historians, referring to Bektash, suggest that the legendary link with Kafiristan must be a myth, as there is no record of Bektash having been there. However, some of the exercises taught by Gurdjieff in the West are identical with those of the Bektashi and Gurdjieff *is* known to have spent some time in Kafiristan. Thus Balkh, Khorasan, Kafiristan and the area where the illuminated Roshania are located, are all in the

---

[6] Idries Shah, *The Sufis*, p. 178 et seq., and see J.K. Birge, *The Bektashi Order of Dervishes*, Luzac, London, 1937.

[7] Anonymous: *The Trail of the Serpent*, London, 1936.

[8] "It is rather strange that the Dervishes of the Bektashi Order consider themselves quite the same as the Freemasons, and are disposed to fraternize with them" (Brown, *Darvishes*, Chap. II).

same general area of Afghanistan and indeed are not far from each other.

The Theosophical doctrine of the Himalayan "Masters" popularized by Madame Blavatsky is in most respects very close to the Sufi tradition of the Khwajagan (which means "masters"). The Theosophical Masters whom she indicates as being centred in the Himalayas, are at best a little intangible: but the Khwajagan teachers are entirely corporeal and literal, having been physically located in the Hindu Kush area since the 10th century. The Hindu Kush range is in Afghanistan: geographically, it forms the Western extreme of the Himalayas.

Professor Denis Saurat,[9] who did a computer-like analysis of the components of Theosophy, showed that all the distinct elements into which the system can be broken down already existed in European occult literature before Madame Blavatsky was born. She could, he infers, have created the entire Theosophical corpus without going outside a Russian library.

René Guénon, working on the data provide by A. P. Sinnett, the Theosophical leader, shows that to have had the experiences she claims at the dates indicated (she was 42 when she went to America in 1873), she would have had to start her travels shortly before she was born. He concludes that her seven years' sojourn in the Himalayas was pure invention.[10]

Yet *Isis Unveiled* and *The Secret Doctrine* are more than the sum of their parts – even if the parts already existed in European literature. The explanation may be that Madame Blavatsky was a member of the Italian secret society, the Carbonari, which beyond any question was *originally* a Sufic impulse.[11]

She was also, according to the Masonic historian John Yarker in his *Arcane Schools*, an initiate Druse. The Druses, according to Madame Blavatsky herself, were "the last survival of the archaic wisdom religion", and "had a close affinity with the Turanian Lamaists".

Whether they had or not, they are said to have been active within the famous "Abode of Wisdom" in Cairo in 1017, a subject which will be touched on more fully in the next chapter.

[9] *Literature and the Occult Tradition*, Bell, London, 1939.
[10] Guénon, *Le Théosophisme*: quoted in *The Trail of the Serpent*, Anonymous, London, 1936.
[11] Idries Shah, *The Sufis*, p. 178–181 et seq.

Afghanistan is therefore linked in the tradition of the "witches", the Anthroposophists, the Theosophists, the Buddhist Lamaists of Tibet, the Vedantists, the Masons and the "Illuminati". The single common factor is a Sufic impulse emanating from Afghanistan.

Roger Bacon, who lectured at Oxford on the Illuminist philosophy (but was careful to call it merely "Eastern"), was a Franciscan and there have been repeated hints of a Sufic-Franciscan connection. The known career of St. Francis and the nature of the Franciscan teaching suggests contact with a source in the East – a matter which neither side seems anxious to confirm.[12] In recent times a book by an Italian doctor (Count Alberto Denti di Pirajno) who is not specifically concerned with metaphysics, has a curious passage referring to the friendship of a Catholic (Franciscan) Bishop and a certain Sufi master.[13]

Nor would the Franciscans appear to be the only Roman Catholic Order with unsuspected fraternal associations. Ameer Ali has suggested that the Jesuit training as well as the Jesuit organization derive from Fatimite societies in Cairo.[14] More, various Christian saints act (and write) in a fashion that has curious echoes with notable Sufi figures.

In recent years a Catholic scholar has published a book in which he suggests (with ecclesiastical permission) that Christians and Sufis might go back together to their common origin.[15]

In addition to the claim of such great Sufi teachers as Hallaj to be "the real Christians", Afghanistan is the seat of a community which claims descent from the *Nasara* who also call themselves "the real Christians". Sufi literature abounds in tales of Jesus as an Initiate.

Settlements of this community extend into the mountains of Kafiristan. There is even a shrine and tomb in Kashmir, Yuz Asaf, between Kafiristan and Tibet, where it is claimed "the teacher, Jesus, died". Robert Graves has interested himself in this tradition.

A persistent claim is made by the Afghans to be descended

---

[12] *The Sufis*, pp. 228 et seq.
[13] A. Denti di Pirajno, *A Cure for Serpents*, trs. Kathleen Naylor, Reprint Society, London, 1955.
[14] Ameer Ali, *Spirit of Islam*, Methuen, London, 1965.
[15] Cyprian Rice, *The Persian Sufis*, Allen and Unwin, London, 1964.

from the Lost Tribes of Israel. Those claiming this call themselves the Beni Israel and have been noted to observe Jewish customs. In view of the Moslem conquest, which was not exactly pro-Jewish, this is a remarkable attitude indeed. Writers noting this curiosity have stressed that the Afghans, who are fanatical Moslems, would hardly admit such a thing, much less claim it, unless it was a deeply-held tradition. The Beni Israel tradition is said to date from an emigration to Afghanistan from Babylon. The Victorian Jewish-Christian traveller, talmudist and visionary, Dr. Wolf, in his *Bokhara*, accepts the claim.[16]

Sufi influences have been traced in the formation of the Sikh religion,[17] and it is well attested that the Baha'i religion grew from a once-Sufic group. Baha'i history offers a remarkable example of myth-accretion, suggesting how formalized components enter a source which was originally developmental.

Abdul-Baha, son of Baha'u'llah, said to have been the founder of the Baha'i faith, was in 1918 a prisoner of the Turks in the Palestine fortress of Akka. A young British officer in Intelligence learned that the Turkish C.-in-C., whose headquarters were then between Haifa and Beirut, had threatened to execute Abdul-Baha should the Turkish forces be obliged to evacuate Haifa.

None of the British military personalities of the time had any interest in Abdul-Baha and the efforts of the young major to get them interested were unavailing.

The officer, risking court-martial, managed to get an uncensored telegram through to a personal friend in the British Cabinet with the result that Balfour, Curzon, Milner and Lloyd George discussed the political pros and cons of the situation should the Turks execute a man with a considerable religious following in the East. The result was that General Allenby was told to secure the safety of the Baha'i leader. The Intelligence officer, Major Tudor Pole, using underground contacts within

---

[16] The tradition is recorded in the Afghan document *Afghan Treasury*, by Niamatulla, and accepted by Elphinstone, Burnes and Raverty. It is doubted as a fact by Sir Olaf Caroe, who admits its wide currency as a belief "which, however unreasonable, it is hard to shake" (*The Pathans*, Papermac, London, 1965, p. 10).

[17] M. A. Macauliffe, *The Sikh Religion*, Oxford, 1909. Sikh scriptures actually contain quotations from Sufi sources.

the enemy lines, then circulated the story that considerable reprisals would follow any hostile action against Abdul-Baha and his family.

When the British forces overran Haifa, an advance party encircled the prison and Abdul-Baha and his family were released.

This action was greatly appreciated by the Baha'i movement and no doubt greatly enhanced British prestige in Persia and elsewhere.

Twenty years later, tourists were being shown the spot where the Turks, so it was said, had erected a cross on which to crucify the Baha'i leader who was saved by the intervention of God through the instrument of Wellesley Tudor Pole. It is clear that among the uneducated rank and file of Baha'is in the East, this item is in process of being incorporated into the Baha'i corpus and may well illustrate in our own days a process by which religious myths arise.

In later life, Tudor Pole and Abdul-Baha remained in contact and Tudor Pole was shown on more than one occasion some of the powers associated with a man of exceptional development. Once while sitting with Baha in his house on Mount Carmel, the interpreter was called away. Baha continued to speak Persian, Tudor Pole English. It was only some time later, when others of the party re-entered the room, that Tudor Pole realized that a two-way conversation had been going on in different languages and that he had understood perfectly. As we shall see, this is not an unfamiliar situation in the presence of Sufis above a certain grade.

Arkon Daraul[18] describes a sect in, of all places, the Putney suburb of London, where he was allowed to see the adherents, some sixty men and women, performing exercises before an eight-foot statue of a peacock. The cult, he learned, was brought to London in 1913, and may now have sixteen lodges throughout the country. Their rituals are based on Arabic numerology and their chief aims are social, humanitarian (like the Masons), the sharing of an emotional experience as a consequence of the dance movements, the expectation of success in ordinary life, and the development of mental concentration which may lead to a mystical experience.

[18] A. Daraul, *Secret Societies*, Muller, London, 1961.

The cult is associated with the Yezidis or Devil-Worshippers of N.E. Iraq and Kurdistan who, because they were not of the orthodox persuasion of Islam, were labelled heretics (and therefore worshippers of the Devil) by the Turks.

William Seabrook,[19] the travel writer, investigating the Yezidi sect, was told that the adherents knew a certain name which must never be mentioned. Daraul, investigating the Peacock sect in London, also learned of a name that must never be mentioned. Seabrook deduced that the name was *Melek Taos* which means "Angel Peacock". It was, he was told, the name for "the Spirit of Power and the Leader of the World".

According to the anonymous author of *The Trail of the Serpent*, the name of the power which must not be mentioned is Lucifer.

Seabrook learned that the cult believes in the existence of "the Seven Towers of Shaitan" or powerhouses which form a chain across Central Asia. This powerhouse idea, it will be recalled, was picked up by Peter King in Afghanistan when researching for his book.

The "Power House" idea was one which formed the background to many of the ideas of the novelist John Buchan: the same idea which we have identified with a series of hitherto secret monasteries in Afghanistan.

Some historians have suggested that Zoroastrianism arose in Afghanistan. Zoroaster spent much of his life in Balkh. The same origin (Afghanistan) has been claimed for Zen Buddhism. It is clear that the Buddhism of Japan was at least strongly influenced, if not actually introduced, by Afghan Buddhist visitors. Archaeologists have shown that certain Japanese statues are in a style derived from the Afghan shrines of Bamian. Further, the similarity of the Japanese Zen system to that of the Sufi training method may be due to oral transmission by the same route. In the next chapter when we try to deduce the nature of advanced Sufi powers, we shall see that the literature of Japan has many references to the powers of Zen masters which are almost identical.[20] Incidents involving

---

[19] W. Seabrook, *Adventures in Arabia*, Harrap, London, 1941.

[20] Since the Afghan Buddhist shrines and monastery complexes of Bamian were for centuries the world centre of Buddhism (Tibet came later and was always the centre for only a minority of Buddhists), few students find the idea of a diffusion to the Far East from Afghanistan difficult to conceive.

such powers, even to the type of occasion on which they are exercised, could sometimes be lifted straight from Sufi sources.

One important tradition has not so far been referred to. It has no readily recognized "label" in the West and is little known. It is the tradition which attaches to the Sayeds, the descendants of the Prophet Mohammed. This tradition may have two components: (a) the hereditary transmission of spiritual force (baraka) from Mohammed and (b) a secret training technique whereby members of the Hashimite family have been able to develop capacities normally dormant in mankind. These capacities are both worldly and spiritual. There are also hints that this dynastic tradition, properly implemented, reflects the structure of a hierarchic order of a non-material kind.

Some hold that both the baraka and the knowledge of how to apply it are common to all the family of Hashim. Others believe that is has become dilute or has been extinguished entirely in all but one branch of the dynasty – that known as the Hindu Kush Sayeds. Certainly for a thousand years the secret training system of the Hashimites seems to have ensured that rulers and highly placed advisers in cultures all over the East have been drawn, to a very large extent, from this one remarkable "Family of Hashim".

It is widely believed that the most inviolate security of this training system is necessary because of the power potentials involved. It is widely suspected that a single "leak", through the Ismaelis, was responsible for the aberration of Hassan Sabah and the creation of the tyranny of the Assassins which operated for two hundred years and was still echoed in India as recently as the end of the last century.

The Hindu Kush Sayeds, who are in some quarters believed to retain to this day both the spiritual transmission and the technique of deploying it, are descended from the Prophet's grandson Hussein. They settled near Paghman in Afghanistan in the 13th century. Once again traces of a mysterious influence track back to Afghanistan.

Very little is known about the nature of the secret training system of the Hashimites but some Moslem writers have openly expressed the view that it consists simply of the inner teachings of the Sufis. A number of indications in recent years combine to suggest that the man recognized at present as the titular head of world Sufis is a Hashimite and a member of the Hindu Kush Sayeds. *The Times* correspondent who reported on a visit to an Afghan monastery deduced that this man was its absent head.

In the (oral) *Traditions of the Prophet* there are two stanzas which could be highly suggestive set against the foregoing. They are: "The time will come when you are divided into seventy-two sects. A group among you will be my people, the people of Salvation." And: "I leave nothing to you except my family."

One further, rather strange, pointer remains to be noticed. In Islamic lore it is said that during the Prophet's lifetime he received delegations from Afghanistan. These delegations were given the title "The Rudder" by Mohammed himself. His visitors are said to have satisfied the Prophet that they represented a very ancient teaching. Thus, though the Afghans were not converted to Islam till centuries later, something came from Afghanistan and played some part in the early Moslem tradition. Behind such legends, the hint would seem unavoidable: that since very remote times, a mysterious influence has been centred in Afghanistan and that it emerges at infrequent intervals to exert an unsuspected but eventually significant effect at certain critical points in history. For the past 1200 years or so, this influence appears to be identifiable with the Sufi tradition but it seems abundantly clear that it pre-dated the Moslem religion to which it attached itself – as it had, under other names, in other days, attached itself to other religious impulses.

*   *   *

Some plausibility at ordinary level may be claimed for the idea that the history of the East has been decisively influenced by *something* centred in "the Cockpit of Asia". It would seem however to strain credulity to breaking point to suggest that this same something has been pervasive even in Europe and has influenced such an intangible as Western poetry. Yet this must now be suggested.

One of the group of five researchers mentioned in Chapter 8 had always been struck by a strange trend in English literature

– especially in poetry. He had noticed that in all examples of the poetry which by common consent is labelled "great", there was a thread which was in some way alien. He suspected that it was this "alien" component which gave this class of poetry its status. This he had never been able to identify, but in view of the many indications of unsuspected influences in the culture of the West emerging from the team's researches, he began to look at the matter again from this point of view. The team concluded that, almost alone among commentators, Professor Denis Saurat had noticed the same thing. Saurat's book *Literature and the Occult Tradition*[21] is in fact an attempt to analyse just this.

His conclusion is that virtually all great poetry in English owes its quality to the injection of an influence which he identifies – *faute de mieux* – as "neo-Platonic".

"One of the most curious phenomena of modern literature," he says, "from the Renaissance to the 19th century, is the existence among a certain number of great poets between whom there is often but a slight connection, of a common, non-Christian stock of myths and ideas. Spenser, Blake, Milton, Shelley, Emerson and Whitman in Anglo-Saxon literature: Goethe, Heine, Wagner, Nietzsche in Germany: Hugo, Vigny, Lamartine and Leconte de Lisle in France, would seem, after a close study of their religious ideas, to be like branches of the same tree. . . .

"Still more curious than the existence of ideas in common is the recurrence of certain myths and symbols which seem to have a particular fascination for these poets."[22]

In searching for some way of identifying the common factor, Saurat says: "The first natural hypothesis consists in seeing here one of the forms of the evolution of neo-Platonism. This hypothesis is not false but inadequate . . . a large number of the conceptions we have gathered together have their origin elsewhere. Especially is the doctrine of immanence, almost universal among our poets, contrary to neo-Platonism as it is generally understood."

Among all these poets there is, he says, a common ground not only of doctrine and myth, but also a common morality. This includes a certain remarkable idea: ". . . *the election of a certain*

[21] Bell, London, 1939.
[22] Saurat, op. cit.

number of beings in a further stage of evolution than the others" (our italics).

Saurat finally pins down the common factor to a single word. All of these poets without exception have been influenced by the Cabbala!

The importance of such poets is great. "It is certainly in the philosophical poetry of a race that its very soul can be seen.... From time to time there arises some superior genius, who from the summit of the assembled results of specialized branches of knowledge obtains a vision of the far-off goals, expresses anew for his time the desires of his fellow men, marks out the distance already covered or tries to divine the future ways.... The philosophical poets remain more than any other order of minds best qualified to represent the entire aspirations of their race, the very soul of their humanity."

In short, Saurat sees that all the great philosophical poets of the West are concerned with the idea of man's possible evolution and with the existence among men of more highly developed individuals, *and that they derived these ideas from the Cabbala.*

As we have seen, the Jews themselves credit the production of the Cabbala, in the form known in the West, to the Sufic school called the Brethren of Sincerity. In other words, the most profound poetic ideas in European literature owe their genesis to the Sufis.

Persuasive arguments have been advanced for the idea that "Shakespeare" was the pen-name of a group devoted to injecting certain ideas in the cultural stream of Elizabethan England,[23] and C. S. Nott[24] has suggested that the different qualities of the members of this group can be detected from the contributions they make to different plays. The head of this group was responsible for various passages – perhaps in Lear and Hamlet – passages that stand out as the insights of an altogether exceptional intellect.

Professor Nicholson has pointed out that certain portions of the Shakespearean corpus have an uncanny resemblance to passages in earlier Sufic material.[25]

[23] John Evans, *Shakespeare's Magic Circle*, Barker, London, 1956.
[24] C. S. Nott, *Journey through this World*, Routledge, London, 1969.
[25] R. A. Nicholson, *Selected Poems from the Divani Shamsi Tabriz*, Cambridge, 1952.

Sufic originals for Robinson Crusoe (Hayy, son of Yakzan: the Living One, Son of the Aware) and for much of Don Quixote and Dante have also been uncovered.

The realization that so many separate cults, religious forms and literary impulses lead back to Sufic sources – and when the tracks are clear enough – to Afghanistan, required a distinct effort of readjustment by the five people of the team. They recognized that the ordinary followers of each of these cults regards his own as in some way special, a stage higher than the others, a more privileged approach to truth. One member of the team wrote: "It was a strange experience and a humbling one to discover that the originating principle of all these beliefs converged on a single source and it was exciting to think that we had apparently uncovered it. We were left also with a sense of wonder that this source had been able to give to the outward appearance of each of these beliefs such a characteristic face as to be unrecognizable to all the others."

One more surprising fact fell to be considered. Almost all the discoveries the team had made derived from material already in print and freely available in Europe. In other words, the inter-relation of so many schools of belief and their common origin in Afghanistan was already on record. All the team had done was to link up existing references and draw the obvious conclusion. Almost anyone could have done this; but nobody apparently had,

Sufism, it seemed, has many faces. The faces belong to the members of a very large family who, not recognizing their kinship, are not on speaking terms with each other.

The realization that this was so suggested the next step and a further speculation. If an original single source could find expression in so many different forms, what was the nature of the original impulse? Would it be possible to make any discoveries about its nature by searching through Sufic literature?

Dictionary definitions and studies of Sufic practices by Westerners were unanimous in one thing: the Sufis were a cult within Mohammedanism. In view of the team's discoveries, it now seemed unwise to regard this as axiomatic. If Sufism had so many faces in the West, might it not have just as many in the East?

Was the Islamic form the ultimate nature of Sufism, or was this again merely a convenient wrapper for a wider spectrum operation?

With this possibility in mind, the team decided to approach Sufic literature with as few prior conceptions as possible – however widespread and authoritative such prior assumptions might be.

Many orientalists in the West have defined Sufism as a heretical movement within Islam with Christian overtones. Others regard it as an amalgam of pre-Christian and pre-Moslem ideas, but using the general form of Islam for its expression. Others, and they are not few, pontificated about Sufism almost entirely on the basis of what other scholars of their own general persuasion had written.

All such views failed to account for certain material found in the Sufic corpus itself. Such awkward facts, when they were noticed, were either ignored or treated as vagaries irrelevant to the central theme of Sufism. This reaction exactly parallels recent results in behaviourist psychology. Experts set to solve problems whose resolution depends on dropping prejudices canot solve the problems: they have the prejudices!

The team agreed to treat all Sufic material as having the same weight till such time as they could decide otherwise. If such diverse activities as alchemy and Freemasonry were facets of Sufic activity in Europe, would it not be reasonable to suspect that the basic impulse had just as many outward facets in the East? And that orthodox Islam was only one of them?

On-the-spot accounts of Sufism at the present day certainly seem to support the idea that the Sufis are pious Moslems. Dr. Martin Ling's *A Moslem Saint of the Twentieth Century* (London, 1961), presents a picture of orthodox piety and prayer of Medieval, if not Old Testament, intensity. The same atmosphere suffuses Carl Vett's *Dervish Diary* (Los Angeles, 1953).

This is not a picture suported by the recorded attitudes of the classical Sufi masters. If anything, they tended to warn their followers that pious adherence to the outward observances of religion was flummery. They also endorsed ideas and individuals who were of the utmost embarrassment to orthodoxy. They hailed Mansur Hallaj (who was widely regarded as both a magician and a demi-Christian and who was executed for blasphemy to Islam) as "One Who Was the Truth" and a perfected Saint.

Shattar was held by the Sufi classical masters to be in excellent standing. Yet Shattar wrote *The Five Essences* which, to outward understanding at least, is a book of magic spells – *something expressly forbidden by Islam*.

Sufism for a time prior to the 12th century was regarded with the utmost suspicion by the jurists of Islam. It was then rehabilitated by Ghazzali, who showed, some may feel with a little sophistry, that its activities were not inconsistent with the Party line. Sufism was thereafter in good standing. Yet Sufic activity continues to include material regarded as offensive to many in orthodox Islam. It seems clear that a corpus of "non-Islamic" material is both indigenous and necessary to Sufism and continues in use, though it canot be squared with Moslem respectability.

There are many instances of individuals who, by any ordinary test of Islamic dogma, were infidels, being openly approved by the Sufis. Their literature abounds with interpretations of the Koran which are, from an orthodox point of view, horrifying. Even the great Jalaluddin Rumi, lauded in every Islamic country as a pious man, says in his *Masnavi*: "We have taken the essence of the Koran and thrown the carcass to the donkeys." By Islamic standards, such a remark is an abominable heresy!

At this stage the team was only in process of establishing contact with a Sufic organization and its views up to this point were derived almost exclusively from literary sources. Nevertheless, these pointed unmistakably to a number of conclusions.

A large number of cultural traditions, which may be religious, humanitarian, literary, craft-orientated, artistic or psychological, are seemingly unconnected. They are in fact manifestations of a common activity which is certainly Sufic and probably, at least for a lengthy period, Afghan.

This impulse, infusing widely separate national and racial streams, has a mode of action which grafts into existing elements and works with existing materials.

There is probably no parallel for an inter-cultural influence working in this way.

The action does not result from any identifiable teaching. It is indirect, a "provoking of action" technique depending for its effect on what would now be called subliminal response. Its real action is therefore unnoticed and the connection between its many forms in many countries is unsuspected. This applies alike to adherents and to outside observers.

Outside observers, particularly in the West, start from the assumption that all phenomena must be describable in terms of known categories. Sufic activity is not amenable to this approach and seems to be organized to resist investigations which begin with such an assumption.

For example, Lucy Garnett, who was for a long time resident in Turkey, tried to investigate local Sufic activity impartially.[26]

She noted devotional elements, religious forms, a respect for women, some magic and some miracles. The totality refuses to fit any category with which she is familiar and she retires, baffled. The idea of an indirect action technique was unknown in Western thinking, at least in 1912.

A Methodist Minister, John A. Subhan,[27] is in a similar position. The plurality of approach which he sees exemplified in Sufism, defies categorization. It has no common denominator with anything familiar. He is reduced to noticing that Sufis are people who use supernatural procedures. The idea that in certain hands magic may not be magical but functional was outside any terms of reference he knew.

Even the adherents of many cults – particularly in the West –may be in no better position. They may have their own, sociological, motivation for membership, unsuspected by themselves, and may have no idea of the anterior nature of their own organization. The mystique of their particular speciality may be attributed to "higher levels", "extraterrestrial sources" and so on.

Such people are particularly insulated from any possibility of back-tracking to the source. The particular presentation which they advocate has become for them a cherished prop-

---

[26] L. M. J. Garnett, *Mysticism and Magic in Turkey*, Pitman, London 1912.
[27] *Sufism, its Saints and Shrines in India*, Lucknow, 1938.

erty and is related to the human psychological impulse of "havingness".

Any hint that their speciality might share a common origin with others amounts to a deprivation and hence a sense of loss. Such hints, if they arise, are rejected at subconscious level.

Where this situation obtains, the teaching has probably passed below the minimum level at which its original function can be discharged. It is no longer under the direction of its original source and has become "remaindered". It becomes a social phenomenon,

The outward structure will, however, continue, perpetuated by adherents who have a vested interest in asserting its uniqueness.

It seems abundantly clear that the originating source is aware that this deterioration is inevitable and takes it into account.

There are successive renewals, each new phase lasting a comparatively short time before being replaced by a different presentation, of the same basic nature but having a form which appears to be entirely new.

From all of this it seems reasonable to conclude that those responsible for such a subtle and many-sided process possess knowledge of social and cultural forces and the psychology and motivation of people far in advance of any knowledge observable in ordinary humanity at this time.

CHAPTER TEN

ASSASSINS, KALI-WORSHIPPERS, DERVISHES

The theory that we have approached in this book is that humanity has been continuously under the guardianship of an initiate tradition. The real nature of this tradition, its activities and its methods has always been the most closely guarded secret.

This does not mean that its agents have always been invisible. On the contrary, they have been part of life. They have been prophets and priest-kings in whom a superior role was explicit. They have also been artists and scientists, monks, handymen and tinkers, accepted as part of the common life, but unsuspected of their hidden role.

But in whatever form they have appeared, their real aim and the inner nature of their activity has always been massively obscured. From time to time, however, the powers possessed by such men have been suspected and these suspicions have been incorporated in folklore and the legends of magic. But the nature of the energies disposed at these levels and the training which leads to their incorporation in a human being have never been divulged.

The reasons are obvious. Atlantis (whatever reality, physical or otherwise is indicated by the word) is said to have ended in an apocalypse because knowledge of higher energies and the techniques associated with them leaked out to those in whom personal egoism was still the central motivation.

At some stage in the history of Egypt, the same is said to have happened. There, a pyramidic social structure ensured that every horizontal cross section of the pyramid contributed to the well-being of the level below and received sustenance from the level above. The base was in touch with the earth and the apex was a king-initiate in touch with another order of things outside life. Initiation, probably always a calculated risk, was at some stage unwisely conferred. Techniques then began to pass out of the control of purified sources and became available for egoistic ends. This was the magic of the self-will, the sorcery of the self against which Moses inveighed. "Egypt before the sands" began to go down.

Men of development, acting as the agents of powers outside life, have been known by many names; in turn initiates, priest-kings, prophets, masters, patriarchs, hanifs and many others now lost. If our assumption is correct, this range of activity has, since the 7th century AD, been the province of Sufic orders – or those of the Sufic orders which have not themselves succumbed to involuntary erosion.

This period of some twelve hundred years has not escaped its share of the disasters which follow the leakage of classified psychic material. The career of Hasan Sabah, the historical "Old Man of the Mountains", seems to provide an example.

Perhaps because the outward form of Islam was used to an exceptional degree as the instrument of a major developmental operation, there seems to have been a tendency for fringe information about psychic and spiritual techniques to become relatively public.

Knowledge of such techniques, fragmented but still potent, passed into the hands of factions struggling for political supremacy in the various caliphates. One such faction, the ancestors of the present day Ismaelis, tried to use psychological techniques deriving from genuine "School" for political and indeed criminal ends. One centre of such activity was the "Abode of Wisdom" in Cairo under the Fatimite Caliphs. There techniques either deduced or stolen from Sufic sources were employed to develop a secret society dedicated to political intrigue and assassination.

Bernard Springett (*Secret Sects in Syria*) quoting from *A Short History of the Assassins* by Ameer Ali[1] says. ". . . .the different degrees adopted in the Lodge (the Abode of Wisdom) forms an invaluable record of Freemasonry. In fact, the Lodge at Cairo became the model of all lodges created afterwards in Christendom." Elsewhere Springett claims that the constitution of the Knights Templar was a servile copy of that of the Assassins. As

---

[1] Quoted in the anonymous *Trail of the Serpent*, London, 1936.

is well known, there was considerable contact between the Crusaders and the Assassins.

It is widely believed that Hasan Sabah, the infamous founder of the Assassins was a renegade of the abode of wisdom. Whether he was or not he had certainly studied under a very famous teacher, the Imam Muwafiq. Other pupils at the same time have been said to include Nizam, a future Prime Minister to the Turkish Sultan of Persia and the now world-famous Omar Khayyam.

Of Hasan, Nizam was later to write: "He proved to be a fraud, hypocrite and self-seeking villain. He was so clever at dissimulation that he . . . completely captured the mind of the Shah."[2]

Hasan became in fact a sort of Hitler of the 11th century, equalling the latter in perfidy and certainly surpassing him in psychological knowledge.

Utilizing techniques apparently deriving from the Abode of Wisdom, Hasan maintained himself for thirty-four years as the undisputed autocrat of one of the most remarkable armies in all history – the Assassins. His troops were 70,000 fanatics reduced by a technique of brainwashing to military zombies.

From his castle at Alamut (described 150 years later by Marco Polo), Hasan engineered palace revolutions, assassinations and wars for his own advantage.

He made pacts with Saracens against the Crusaders and with the Crusaders against his own fellow religionists. He murdered, tortured and intrigued to the point where he was able through sheer terror to transfer Ishmaeli loyalty from the Caliphs to himself.

An Assassin recruit might be sent to work and live a thousand miles away, there to wait for years for the order to plunge his dagger into somebody whose death was essential to his master's plans. Hasan's agents extended through every country in the East, intriguing and killing at Hasan's orders till no life was safe and the shadow of an Assassin dagger seemed to hang over everyone in power from the Caspian to Egypt.

At one stage a representative of the Sultan reached Alamut bearing – a little optimistically – an ultimatum to Hasan. For

[2] Arkon Daraul, *Secret Societies*, Muller, London, 1961. Reprinted, Octagon Press, London, 1983.

answer, the Old Man of the Mountains raised his hand and a white robed guard standing on a rampart answered that he understood and obeyed – then hurled himself two thousand feet to the river in the valley below. Hasan had achieved such discipline among his subjects that he could command instant suicide.

Such extraordinary power seems even to have been transmitted. Henry of Champagne visited one of the Assassin castles a century later, and was given a similar demonstration by way of suggesting that Christian princes venturing in these parts were up against something qualitatively different from anything in Western military experience.

Hasan, at the centre of his empire of invisible terror, sent missionaries to Afghanistan and India and even farther afield. That so much is known about the cult is due to the circumstances of its destruction – or partial destruction – at the hands of the Mongol invader, Halaku Khan in 1335. Halaku's chief minister was ordered to complete a history of the Assassins, which he did, greatly helped by the fact that the written constitution of the Assassins was found in Alamut.

Not so well known is that the cult of Thuggee which bedevilled India during the whole period of British rule is an Ishmaelic derivation of the Assassin Cult, transferred in part to the Hindu goddess, Kali.

How was the fanatical Assassin discipline achieved? Western accounts turn on the idea that the Assassin recruits were drugged with Hashish – hence the word Assassin from "Hashashin (the addicts). According to this story, novices were first stupefied with the drug, then taken to a stage-set garden of startling beauty with marvellous flowers and water-courses. There they reclined while seductive damsels caressed them and fed them sweetmeats.

They were then doped again to unconsciousness and on recovering were told that by the favour of their leader they had been given access to a mystical experience which was a foretaste of paradise.

Assured that, provided they died in the service of their master, this bliss awaited them for all eternity, the recruits were prepared to obey any order and suffer any fate.

Modern psychologists would probably contest that such a procedure would produce the inexorable conditioned reflex of obedience which the Assassins undoubtedly exhibited.

It is therefore interesting that there is another explanation from Sufic sources. This alleges that at the acceptance ceremony of a new recruit, Hasan took a square of silk weighted at the corners with a coin. Blessing the newcomer Hasan swung it round the man's neck, at the same time exerting pressure on a nerve centre in such a way as to produce instantaneous hypnosis. In this state, the novice had communicated to him the contents of Hasan's mind – a technique of non-verbal suggestion which Rudyard Kipling seems to have known about.

The transfer of thought without verbalization is not known in the West generally, but the method of inducing a sub-catatonic state by nerve pressure definitely is. It was practised by a stage hypnotist within the last twenty years. He did it at several English variety theatres until privately warned to leave the country by a knowledgeable member of the British Medical Association.

Hasan's initiation technique had another subtlety. The representation of bliss induced in the recruit's mind included the suggestion that the experience could be enjoyed again – in the act of committing murder at the order of the Assassin chief.

Hasan's pupils were therefore under both a conscious inducement and a post-hypnotic imperative.

Known facts about Thuggee, the version of Assassin practice which grew up in India, appears to support this account in a remarkable way. Major General Sir William Sleeman, the Britisher who was (almost) responsible for stamping out Thuggee in India, discovered some very strange facts about Thug psychology. He found that they experienced an extraordinary sensation of pleasure in the process of ingratiating themselves with a band of travellers whom they intended to murder. They simulated friendliness and honesty to such an extent that they were quickly accepted by any travellers, however initially suspicious.

It is known that part of the curriculum at the Abode of Wisdom in the early 11th century included "intelligent dissimulation", a technique which enabled the Assassins who mastered it to ingratiate themselves in any social conditions.

For their murder by strangulation, the Thugs used a silk weighted generally with a coin. Sleeman discovered that the act of strangling a victim produced a moment of ecstasy in the Thug, which, he declared, made all other considerations in life seem unimportant.

When the full account of Assassin crime in the East 900 years ago is considered, and when it is recalled that Sleeman estimated Thuggee murders at 40,000 per year in the India of last century, the terrible consequences of occult knowledge falling into wrong hands are apparent.

The European witch cult may be a further example of an activity arising from the leakage of developmental knowledge. Like the Albigenses, the witches are known chiefly from the accounts of their enemies, and it is possible that no objective assessment of witchcraft, in its inner nature, exists. Certainly modern witches do not know the origins of their practices and researchers are constantly struck by the avidity with which present day witch groups seize on "origins" found for them by academic witchologists like Margaret Murray.

Modern apologists of the cult like Gerald Gardner[3] and Justine Glass[4] appear to be engaged in plausible whitewashing while the traditional Roman Catholic attitude, deriving from Inquisition material, is one of superstitious horror and vilification.

Material of the Malleus Maleficarum variety, i.e., intentional vilification, tends nowadays to defeat its own ends. Instead of confirming Satanic practices at physical level, it suggests rather a turgid excitation of the lower levels of the human subconscious: psychological rather than physical goings-on.

However, it seems undeniable that witchcraft has repeatedly shaded off into Black Magic of the most palpable kind and modern material from Huysman's *Là-bas* to current newspaper accounts of rural tombstone-turners confirms this.

The original nature of witchcraft remains in all probability unassessed.

Though something like the cult has probably existed since Neolithic times, the version of it familiar to medieval Europe

[3] G. B. Gardner, *Witchcraft Today*, Rider, London, 1954.
[4] Justine Glass, *Witchcraft: The Sixth Sense and Us*, Spearman, London, 1966.

suggests that the original impulse obtained a high octane fuel injection from a Sufic source.

Sufic/Witch parallels are overwhelming.

The ritual knife of the witches is called Athame. The same instrument of the Saracen Two-Horned cult is *Adh-dhamme*. The winding sheet in which members of the Two Horned dance their rituals is the *Kafan* which looks very like the origin of the word coven. Members of the Two-Horned call their meeting *Az Zabat* ("powerful occasion") which is almost certainly the witch *Sabbat*.

Thomas à Becket is rumoured to have been connected with a ritual sacrifice. The legend has resemblances to disguised teaching material. Becket is said to have had a Saracen mother.

There is some connection between the Order of the Garter and witchcraft,[5] and there are plain correspondences between Garter and Sufic ritual.

The areas in which witchcraft was strongest were the areas most strongly under Saracen influence. Spain was conquered in A.D. 711 and was not re-Christianized till 1492. Arabs were in Languedoc in 759 and in Provence from 889. They were strongly established also in Savoy, Piedmont and Switzerland – all areas associated with witchcraft.[6]

A Father Gualchelm of St. Albin's, Angers, reported in 1091 a great crowd passing him on the road. These, he decided, were the Harlechim "of whom I have heard but in which I did not believe". "Harlechim" may have been a corruption of *Aghlaqin*, a Sufic group known as The Silent Ones who wore patchwork clothes.

A tract of 1450, *Errores Gaziorum*, gives an account of a witch rite. *Gaziorum* would seem to be a Latinized version of *Gazair-ites* – the Arabic for "Andalusians". *Errores Gaziorum* re-translated into Arabic would give *Ghulat al Algazairyin*, "the Errors of the Andalusians" where "error" is an Arabic technical term for a sectarian belief.

The Sufic master Jalaluddin Rumi mentions "riding on a stick" which is a familiar witch idea.

[5] Gardner, op. cit.; Shah, *The Sufis*.
[6] J. T. Reinaud, *Invasions des Sarrazins en France*, Paris, 1836; Eng. trs., H. K. Sherwani, *Muslim Colonies in France, Northern Italy and Switzerland*, Orientalia, Lahore, 1955.

A witch cult leader apprehended in Sweden during a witch pogrom of 1668 wore a turban, and like witch leaders in England before and since, was invoked with the word Antecessor. "Antecessor" in Arabic is *Qadim* which means both "antecessor" and "ancient".

Robin is a recurring witch name. The word in Persian is *Rah-bin*, "he who sees the road", and in the Berber Two-Horned sect the leader is referred to as *Rabbans* ("our master").

A considerable number of other links are given by Idries Shah in *The Sufis*. The connection between witchcraft – at any rate from the 10th century on – and some sort of Saracen cult activity seems beyond dispute.

But what was the nature of the Saracen "injection" which gave rise to or so deeply affected the Medieval witch cult of Europe? It may be that in researching for his book *Witches and Sorcerers*[7] Arkon Daraul uncovered the exact occasion. Among Arab migrants to Spain around 1460 were a sect of Berber ecstatics called the Two-Horned. From the information given in *The Sufis* by Idries Shah, this seems to have been a Moroccan branch of a sect peculiar to the Aniza tribe of the Bedouins. They followed a teaching which had been given by a Dervish member of the tribe, Abu el Atahiyya, and because the Arabic for goat has the same consonantal root as Aniza, they adopted the goat as their clan-badge. This poor goat has been appearing ever since, and is used to this day when the cover of a lurid paperback has to convey the idea of black magic. Incidentally, the tribal camel-brand of the Aniza was a broad arrow which has appeared all through the centuries as "the witches' mark". The Aniza certainly started something.

According to Arkon Daraul, a branch of this sect moved from Morocco into Spain. They were a non-proselytizing cult and well disciplined; members could be cast out for an infringement of the rules.

About the time the Berber branch of this sect moved into Spain, some dissident members met a leader of the Spanish Jews, Rabbi Ishaq Toledano. Ishaq was the head of a Jewish group who had come together with the idea of seeing whether they could use traditional Jewish magic to stem the tide of

---

[7] Muller, London, 1961.

persecution by the Christians which was making Jewish life in Toledo all but impossible.

It would appear that the dissident members of the Two-Horned were welcomed eagerly by Rabbi Ishaq as being likely to make a knowledgeable contribution to the operation the Rabbi was trying to develop. In other words, the Two-Horned possessed genuine knowledge of a developmental technique and this could be used – or misused – for magical ends.

The combined organization which resulted, Jewish and Arab, appears to have amalgamated many of the components which the West was later to identify with witchcraft.

Ishaq knew the dangers involved for himself and his followers if details of his magic operations against the Christian enemy leaked out, and he realized also – from the example of his Two-Horned recruits – the force that could be carried over to another organization by apostates. He devised a method of binding his group together.

The idea was to commit his members to actions so atrocious that none would ever dare confess to them. In this way, the security of his "New Community" would be absolute. He required his members to perform evil actions and to destroy the persons and property of non-members – particularly Christians – as a trade test for advancement within the Community. He also introduced rituals involving sexual perversions and the eating of abominable material. Such activities were so far outside the accepted tolerance of ordinary people of any religion as to put participants outside the pale of humanity. He also used poisons and drugs which "cemented the bond".

The sect worshipped an idol (unspecified), and when members of the cult were possessed by the spirit of the idol, they engaged in flagellation and the exchange of obscene kisses.

A devout Moslem writer, Abdus Salam ibn Zumairi, who was deported from Spain 130 years later, left an extensive description of the cult which he implied was still flourishing in his day. Rumour had it that members of the sect could fly.

About the time apostate members of the Two-Horned were collaborating with Rabbi Ishaq, the Dominican Inquisitor of Carcassonne, Jean Vineti, produced a tract declaring that a new heresy had arisen which was unconnected with the old corpus of rural beliefs which the church had more or less tolerated.

Trevor Roper[8] regards this as a Dominican manoeuvre to get round *Capitulum Episcopi*. This was a sort of "common law" of Ecclesiastical Europe dating from the views of St. Boniface and Charlemagne in the 8th century. It said in effect that to believe in witches, much more to hunt and burn them, was an act of superstition unworthy of a Christian and should rank as heresy.

Trevor Roper feels that some zealous orders of the Roman Church felt that this seriously inhibited their efforts to extirpate heresy and the Dominicans at least intrigued with several Popes to rescind it and so provide Papal authority for large-scale witch-hunting.

The Dominicans apparently succeeded in 1484 when two of their number, Heinrich Kramer and Jakob Sprenger, obtained a Bull from Innocent VIII which authorized "his beloved sons" to extirpate witchcraft in the Rhineland.

Trevor Roper sees the tract of Jean Vineti, thirty years earlier, as the vital link in the chain of events which made this celebrated Papal Bull possible. By claiming that the witchcraft of the middle of the 15th century was an entirely new heresy, Vineti removed it from the protection of the *Capitulum Episcopi* of seven centuries earlier.

There seems little doubt that some Church orders were intensely interested in finding a way round the *Capitulum*, but it may be that Vineti was not so far wrong in claiming that something qualitatively different had appeared on the scene.

In the early part of the 15th century there was a purely local and unorganized form of witchcraft, which, with some exceptions, the Church put up with.

In the second half of the 15th century there was a witchcraft in the form which Europe was to have till 1650 and beyond.

In between there was Rabbi Ishaq and his New Community. The inference is not conclusive, but it is highly suggestive.

It is also interesting that the abominations alleged against the witches of the 15th and later centuries were in the same category as those developed for his own reasons by the Jewish black magician. The sequence of events strongly suggests that genuine developmental techniques possessed by a knowledge-

---

[8] H. R. Trevor Roper, *The European Witch Craze in the 16th and 17th Centuries*, Pelican, London, 1969.

able religious group were leaked by apostates to an outside source and gave rise to several centuries of evil and human suffering.

In the light of these illustrations it is not surprising that the nature of the powers latent in man is little mentioned and the techniques by which they may be developed are mentioned not at all. Such powers may belong to the evolutionary future of the race, and may probably be developed at this stage only legitimately when the agent has been purified of self-will.

As mentioned in the last chapter, the team of five investigators made contact with a Sufi Order and explained the nature of their research. Would it be possible for outsiders to see either examples of the rumoured Sufi powers, or of the training which was said to produce them? It was finally agreed to let the team have limited facilities of this kind – including introduction to other Sufic sources – on certain conditions. The chief condition was that they would be allowed to watch some Sufic procedures, to ask for explanations and to publish a report provided the team could find a prior reference to the same phenomenon or the same technique in already published material. As this condition extended to the literature of all nations, it was not as restrictive as it seemed at first.

It also allowed the team to use the well-known investigation technique of overlap. With reference to, say, telepathy, it might be possible to find fragmentary references in a dozen different sources. If these could be amalgamated to cover exactly the total incident witnessed, the team would be entitled to provide a composite picture in this way.

Perhaps the single most startling discovery made by the team was the Sufi attitude to telepathy. Sufic telepathic powers are used on a world-wide scale in such a way *as to discredit the idea that telepathy is possible*.

The team became convinced that controlled telepathy is possible and is used, in fact, as a practical communication system between individual Sufis and their group leader and also between different Sufi groups. It is also used to obtain information from people and places which it is impracticable to contact in any other way.

Telepathy is within the range of existing human mental powers, but for reasons connected with the overall evolutionary situation of mankind, it is vital that this should not be realized at the present time – or indeed within the foreseeable future.

Among Sufis, telepathy is invaluable as a means of communicating certain kinds of knowledge more efficiently than is possible by any other means: for example, to influence individuals and cultures as an integral part of the Sufi mandate to act upon the character and knowledge of man.

However, the chief function of telepathy among Sufis is – and here a direct quote was permitted – "to interfere with the success of telepathic experiment on the part of dangerous individuals". The team learned – greatly to its astonishment – that a protective telepathic countermeasure is manned by Sufis throughout the world. This is only occasionally breached by experimenters in the unauthorized category.

Sufis claim that their telepathy is actually used to induce scepticism about the possibility of telepathy in the minds of people who might misuse it – if they could develop it. It is also used to motivate people towards useless and futile telepathic and other "psychic" or parapsychological efforts in order to divert them from premature discoveries in the field of esotericism. Such a sophisticated concept was wholly unexpected by the team.

In this connection the reported activities of American and Russian military authorities would seem to be relevant. Considerable efforts are at present being made to discover whether it would be possible to use telepathy for military and espionage purposes.

Probably given impetus by the report by Pauwels and Bergier[9] to the effect that the Pentagon had conducted an experiment in telepathy between a control station and a clairvoyant in a U.S. nuclear submarine, the Russians intensified their work at two parapsychological research centres at Moscow (under Professor Asratjan) and at Leningrad (under Professor Vasiliev).

The Russians have declared that they consider telepathy a proven fact.[10] The suggested mechanism is that brain radiation having the same speed as light emanates from the agent and

---

[9] L. Pauwels and J. Bergier, *The Dawn of Magic*, Gibbs and Phillips, London, 1963.

[10] Interview with Asratjan, *Daily Express*, January 21, 1963.

triggers off nervous discharges in the brain of the subject which can be "rectified" to give the image originally transmitted.

Professor Vasiliev is reported to have succeeded in establishing telepathic communication between Leningrad and the Black Sea, but success to anything like operational standard appears to depend on special (rare) subjects and repeated hypnosis.

Well-informed amateurs claim that Vasiliev's work is far in advance of the much publicized researches of J. B. Rhine *but have aroused little or no scientific interest*.

Due to the private enterprise of an English man and wife team, Gregory and Khosen, Vasiliev's work was translated into English.[11] The Gregorys actually typeset, printed and bound the book themselves. Interest appears to have been almost nil and the conclusions of Vasiliev have been ignored.

From experiments the team were allowed to watch, it seems that the Sufis hold that a form of telepathy can influence plants, minerals and inanimate objects in such a way as to help or hinder projects which would be advantageous or otherwise to mankind from the standpoint of the Sufi mandate.

The team was told categorically that telepathic powers are currently used, and have been used through the whole of historical times, to influence human cultures in such a way that a tension and rivalry is maintained. This offsets natural inertia and ensures that cultures attain their norm of productivity over an historical period.

The team noticed that in admitting their use of telepathy and similar powers, the Sufis seemed to concentrate on broad concepts like the dynamics of human interaction and almost wholly to ignore sentimental concepts like "good people", "my country" and such-like local or limited classifications.

The Sufic attitude seemed to be that moral values were not of permanent validity, but should rightly be regarded as instruments for achieving evolutionary gains. Moral values which fail to make, or cease to make, such a contribution should be regarded as expendable and replaced with others.

It was asserted that both individuals and communities exist – generally unknown to the public – who possess telepathic and

---

[11] *Experiments in Mental Suggestion* by L. L. Vasiliev, Leningrad State University 1962. English version, Society for Study of Mental Images, Church Crookham, Hants.

paranormal functions and use these for selfish ends. Although they have limited success temporarily, these people in the end destroy themselves and the destructive influence extends to their associates in proportion as they have been attracted by similar motivation. The Sufis refused to claim that they were the only organization with the knowledge to invoke such paranormal powers. They said there was no point in making such a claim as it would only attract or repel the sort of people whom they did not want to contact – either in co-operation or in opposition.

It was categorically stated that all official and academic experiment in telepathy would come to nothing even though it might be possible to claim from time to time that proof of such a faculty had been established.

One Sufi allowed himself to be quoted: "Since we have prescience as well, it can be stated that the necessary effort and ingenuity to accomplish the art of telepathy will not be marshalled during the entire foreseeable period of generations in which this power could be a significant aid to humanity."

Methods of developing telepathic ability observed by the team were surprisingly simple, but the terms of their agreement prevent a description of the details. It was emphasized that this must be carried out under the immediate direction of a genuine Naqshbandi teacher. (Many imitators exist.)

No reference in literature could be found which was sufficiently germane to allow its use as an illustration of the Sufi practice.

Clairvoyance

One of the traditional procedures used by Sufis of all branches, involves obtaining information of things past, present and future by a form of divination. This capacity continually influences the behaviour of a Sufi teacher and explains some of the apparent "rationality" with which Sufic leaders are taxed.

When he acts in a way which appears to be unrelated to the problem in hand, it may be because he has, by instant perception, seen the matter in added dimensions. He sees the past of the incident and by looking into the future sees the effect which would be produced by various alternative actions on his part.

Although the processes which will now be suggested from accounts already published appear to be lengthy they really describe an elementary stage in the use of paranormal psychology. The Sufi master is able to achieve the end result instantaneously and even while carrrying on an ordinary conversation.

The best description of Sufic clairvoyance covering the team's experience appears in the *Modern Egyptians* of E. W. Lane.[12]

Lane presents the practitioner as "a magician", but there are reasons to believe he was a Dervish. The Sufis incidentally do not regard cognition across time and space as either miraculous or having any special sanctity. It is regarded simply as a procedure using ordinary known forces. In this connection the Sufis appear to be closer to Western materialist thinking than occultists. Lane describes his experience:

> I had prepared, by the magician's direction, some frankincense and coriander seed (he generally requires some benzoin to be added to these), and a chafing dish with some live charcoal in it.
>
> These were now brought into the room, together with the boy who was to be employed. He had been called in, by my desire, from among some boys in the street, returning from a manufactory; and was about eight or nine years of age.
>
> In reply to my enquiry respecting the description of persons who could see in the magic mirror of ink, the magician said that they were a boy not arrived at puberty, a virgin, a black female slave, and a pregnant woman.
>
> The chafing dish was placed before him and the boy; and the latter was placed on a seat. The magician now desired my servant to put some frankincense and coriander seed into the chafing dish. Then taking hold of the boy's right hand he drew, in the palm of it, a magic square, of which a copy is here given.
>
> $$\begin{matrix} 4 & 9 & 2 \\ 3 & 5 & 7 \\ 8 & 1 & 6 \end{matrix}$$
>
> The figures which it contains are Arabic numerals. In the centre, he poured a little ink, and desired the boy to look into it, and tell him if he could see his face reflected in it. The boy replied that he saw his face clearly. The magician, holding the boy's hand all the while, told him to continue looking intently into the ink and not to raise his head.
>
> He then took one of the little strips of paper inscribed with the

---

[12] Many editions. Quotation is from the edition of 1890, London, pp. 248–254.

forms of invocation, and dropped it into the chafing-dish, upon the burning coals and perfumes, which had already filled the room with their smoke. And as he did this, he commenced an indistinct muttering of words, which he continued during the whole process, excepting when he had to ask the boy a question, or to tell him what he was to say. The piece of paper containing the words from the Kuran he placed inside the fore part of the boy's takeeyeh, or skull-cap.

He then asked him if he saw anything in the ink, and was answered "No"; but about a minute after, the boy, trembling and seeming much frightened, said: "I see a man, sweeping the ground."

"When he has done sweeping," said the magician, "tell me".

Presently the boy said: "He has done."

The magician then again interrupted his muttering to ask the boy if he knew what a "beyrak" (or flag) was; and being answered "Yes", desired him to say "Bring a flag".

The boy did so, and soon said: "He has brought a flag."

"What colour is it?" asked the magician.

The boy replied, "Red."

He was told to call for another flag, which he did. And soon after that he said he saw another brought, and that it was black.

In like manner he was told to call for a third, fourth, fifth, sixth and seventh; which he described as being successively brought before him: specifying their colours as white, green, black, red and blue. The magician then asked him (as he did also each time a new flag was described as being brought) "How many flags have you now before you?"

"Seven," answered the boy. While this was going on the magician put the second and third of the small strips of paper upon which the forms of invocation were written, into the chafing dish; and fresh frankincense and coriander-seed having been repeatedly added, the fumes became painful to the eyes.

When the boy had described the seven flags as appearing to him, he was desired to say: "Bring the Sultan's tent; and pitch it."

This he did, and in about a minute after, he said: "Some men have brought the tent; a large green tent; they are pitching it." And presently he added, "They have set it up."

"Now," said the magician, "order the soldiers to come and pitch their camp around the tent of the Sultan."

The boy did as he was desired; and immediately said: "I see a great many soldiers with their tents. They have pitched their tents." He was then told to order that the soldiers should be drawn up in ranks, and having done so he presently said that he saw them thus arranged.

The magician had put the fourth of the little slips of paper into the chafing dish; and soon after he did the same with the fifth. He now said: "Tell some of the people to bring a bull."

The boy gave the order required and said: "I see a bull. It is red. Four men are dragging it along, and three are beating it." He was told to desire them to kill it, and cut it up, and to put the meat into saucepans and cook it. He did as he was directed; and described these operations as apparently performed before his eyes.

"Tell the soldiers," said the magician, "to eat it."

The boy did so, and said "They are eating it. They have done; and are washing their hands."

The magician then told him to call for the sultan, and the boy having done this said: "I see the sultan riding to his tent, on a bay horse, and he has, on his head, a high red cap. He has alighted to his tent, and sat down within it."

"Desire them to bring coffee to the Sultan," said the magician "and to form the court." These orders were given by the boy, and he said that he saw them performed.

The magician had put the last of the six little strips of paper into the chafing-dish. In his mutterings I distinguished nothing but the words of the written invocation, frequently repeated, excepting that on two or three occasions, when I heard him say: "If they demand information, inform them, and be ye veracious." But much that he repeated was inaudible, and as I did not ask him to teach me his art, I do not pretend to assert that I am fully acquainted with his invocations.

He now addressed himself to me, and asked me if I wished the boy to see any person who was absent or dead. I named Lord Nelson, of whom the boy had evidently never heard; for it was with much difficulty that he pronounced the name, after several trials.

The magician desired the boy to say to the sultan: "My master salutes thee, and desires thee to bring Lord Nelson; bring him before my eyes, that I may see him, speedily."

The boy then said so; and almost immediately added, "A messenger has gone, and has returned, and brought a man dressed in a black suit of European clothes. The man has lost his left arm." (Dark blue is called by the modern Egyptians "eswed", which properly signifies *black*, and is therefore so translated here.)

He then paused for a moment or two; and, looking more

closely and more intently into the ink, said: "No, he has not lost his left arm; but it is placed to his breast."

This correction makes his description more striking than it had been without it: since Lord Nelson generally had his empty sleeve attached to the breast of his coat. But it was his *right* arm that he had lost. Without saying that I suspected that the boy had made a mistake, I asked the magician whether the objects appeared in the ink as if actually before the eyes, or as if in a glass, which makes the right appear left. He answered that they appeared as if in a mirror. This rendered the boy's description faultless.

Whenever I desired the boy to call for any person to appear, I paid particular attention both to the magician and to Osman. The latter gave no direction either by word or sign: and indeed he was generally unacquainted with the personal appearance of the individual called for. I took care that he had no previous communication with the boys; and have seen the experiment fail when he *could* have given directions to them, or to the magician. In short, it would be difficult to conceive any precaution which I did not take. It is important to add that the dialect of the magician was more intelligible to me than to the boy. When *I* understood him perfectly at once, he was sometimes obliged to vary his words to make the *boy* comprehend what he said.

The next person I called for was a native of Egypt, who has been for many years resident in England, where he has adopted our dress; and who had been long confined to his bed by illness before I embarked for this country.

I thought that his name, one not very uncommon in Egypt, might make the boy describe him incorrectly; though another boy on the former visit of the magician, had decribed this same person as wearing a European dress, like that in which I last saw him.

In the present case the boy said: "Here is a man brought on a kind of bier, and wrapped up in a sheet". This description would suit, supposing the person in question to be still confined to his bed, or if he be dead.

A few months after this was written, I have the pleasure of hearing that the person here alluded to was in better health. Whether he was confined to his bed at the time when this experiment was performed, I have not been able to ascertain.

The boy described his face as covered; and was told to order that it should be uncovered. This he did, and then said: "His face is pale, and he has moustaches, but no beard." Which is correct.

Several other persons were successively called for; but the boy's descriptions of them were imperfect, though not altogether incorrect. He represented each object as appearing less distinct than the preceding one, as if his sight were gradually becoming dim. He was a minute, or more, before he could give any account of the persons he professed to see towards the close of the performance; and the magician said that it was useless to proceed with him. Another boy was then brought in; and the magic square, etc., made in his hand, but he could see nothing. The magician said that he was too old.

* * *

On another occasion, Shakespeare was described with the most minute correctness, both as to person and dress; and I might add several other cases in which the same magician has excited astonishment in the sober minds of Englishmen of my acquaintance.

A short time since, after performing in the usual manner, by means of a boy, he prepared the magic mirror in the hand of a young English lady who, on looking into it for a little while, said that she saw a broom sweeping the ground without anybody holding it, and was so much frightened that she would look no longer.

* * *

An historical incident involving Cagliostro offers a second illustration.

In the late 1770s, Cagliostro visited Mitau in the Courland province of Latvia and was entertained by a local Master Mason, Marshal von Medem. Cagliostro demonstrated what is sometimes called *Colombe clairvoyance*. The incident had many witnesses and was recorded in several contemporary reports. It is given in semi-fictional form by Frank King.[13]

> Having anointed the head and left hand of the child with a special "oil of wisdom", he inscribed some mystic letters on the anointed hand and commanded the pupil to look steadily at them. Hymns and prayers followed until the little fellow became

[13] *Cagliostro: The Last of the Sorcerers*, Jarrolds, London, 1929.

strangely agitated and perspired profusely. "Now," he whispered, "the child commands the seven pure spirits. What do you want him to see?"

The Marshal hesitated. He did not wish the little fellow to be frightened with something out of the ordinary. Any homely test would serve the purpose.

"Can he tell us what his sister is doing?"

The sorcerer muttered an incantation then addressed the *pupille* in a low tone. "Can you see your sister?" he said.

"Yes, I can see her."

"What is she doing?"

"She is seated by the window in her room. She places her hand to her breast."

"Is she in love?"

"No, she is in pain. I see the door open. My brother enters. She embraces him."

"But that is impossible," cried the Marshal. "My elder son is many leagues away."

Joseph (Cagliostro) breathed upon the *pupille's* face and wakened him. "The vision can be verified," he said coldly.

The Marshal sent a messenger immediately to his house. The messenger returned soon and informed him that his son, whom he had thought so far away, had returned unexpectedly and that shortly before her brother's arrival, the daughter had had an attack of heart palpitations.

It is interesting that at the end of his life (he was imprisoned in a vertical tube cut into the solid rock at San Leo in Italy by the Inquisition), he wrote his own epitaph. "Much nonsense and many lies have been written about me *for no one knows the truth.*"

E. J. Harrison[14] relates a number of instances of verifiable clairvoyance performed by Zen initiates. The Sufis assert that Zen is a local development – to some extent deteriorated – of their own tradition and was implanted in Japan by Sufis from Afghanistan.

The following instances cover phenomena which the team witnessed in a Sufi circle in England.

Harrison recounts the story of a Japanese *sennin* ("yogi") called Tomekichi who found himself in the company of a foreign missionary in Tokyo. Neither spoke the other's lan-

---

[14] *The Fighting Spirit of Japan*, Foulsham, London, 1976.

guage and pantomime having failed to convey much abstract conversation, the *sennin* closed his eyes for a moment then proceeded to expound his viewpoint in fluent English. The missionary was dumbfounded and, it appeared, so was the *sennin*, for he was totally ignorant of English and "on coming out of his temporary trance could not speak or understand a word. Nor had he any memory of the speech he had just made."

The parallel between this account and the story of Tudor Pole in the presence of Abdul Baha is remarkable.[15]

Harrison describes an educated modern Japanese called Kaneda who earns his living as a schoolteacher and is in the habit of acting as interpreter at scientific conferences where papers have been submitted by foreign scientists in their own language. Though quite ignorant of the language involved, Kaneda gives an immediate translation of the content. He has also demonstrated that if a person writes an imaginary letter with an imaginary pen on a blank sheet of paper, he can call out the contents which have in fact never been committed to writing at all.

A Dervish teaching-story relating to the Sufi Master Bahauddin Naqshband tells how a would-be pupil approached Bahauddin. He had read the master's writings and wanted to enrol as a pupil.

> Bahauddin told the youngest member of his circle, a sixteen-year-old boy, to stand up.
> "How long have you been with us?" asked the Sheikh.
> "Three weeks, O Murshid."
> "Have I taught you anything?"
> "I do not know."
> "Do you think so?"
> "I do not think so."
> The Sheikh then said to him: "In this newcomer's satchel you will find a book of poems. Take it in your hand and recite the entire contents without mistake and without even opening it."
> The boy held the book unopened and then said, "I fear it is in Turki."
> Bahauddin said: "Recite it."
> The boy proceeded to do as he was told, reading a closed book in

---

[15] W. Tudor Pole, *Writing on the Ground*, Spearman, London, 1968.

a language he did not know. The stranger then fell on his knees and begged to be enrolled as a pupil.

Bahauddin said: "It is this kind of phenomenon which attracts you. While it still does, you cannot really benefit from it. That is why, even if you have read my *Risalat*, you have not really read it. Come back when you have read it as this beardless boy has read it. It was only such study that gave him the power to recite from a book which he had not opened and at the same time prevented him from grovelling in wonderment at the event.[16]

Power of Will Projection

In relation to powers under this category, the team encountered the most serious strictures on secrecy. Virtually no details of training or methods were freed for publication and the team was obliged to offer the following illustrations only, without comment.

An example of will projection is given in a Sufic treatise *Drops from the Fountain of Life* by Ali b. Husain Kashifi, a Sufi in the Khwajagan ("Masters") tradition.

It dates from about AD 1503.

In my youth I was ever with our Lord our Master Saiduddin of Kashgar at Herat. It happened that we, one day, walked out together, and fell in with an assembly of the inhabitants of the place who were engaged in wrestling. To try our powers, we agreed to aid with our "powers of the will" one of the wrestlers, so that the other should be overcome by him; and after doing so, to change our design in favour of the discomfited individual. So we stopped, and turning towards the parties, gave the full influence of our united wills to one, and immediately he was able to subdue his opponent. As the person we chose, each in turn, conquered the other, whichever we willed to prevail became the most powerful of the two, and the power of our wills was thus clearly manifested.

On another occasion, two other persons, possessed of these same powers, fell in with an assembly of people, at a place occupied by prize-fighters. To prevent any of the crowd from passing between and separating us, we joined our hands together. Two persons were engaged in fighting; one was a powerful man, whilst the other was a spare and weak person. The former readily overcame the latter; and seeing this, I proposed to my companion to aid the weak one by the power of our wills. So he bade me aid him in the project, whilst he concentrated his powers upon the weaker person. Immediately,

---

[16] Idries Shah, *Wisdom of the Idiots*, Octagon Press, London, 1969, p. 60.

a wonderful occurrence took place; the thin, spare man seized upon his giant-like opponent, and threw him upon the ground with surprising force. The crowd cried out with astonishment, as he turned him over on his back, and held him down with apparent ease. No one present, except ourselves, knew the cause. Seeing that my companion's eyes were much affected by the effort which he had made, I bade him remark how perfectly successful we had been, and adding that there was no longer any necessity for our remaining there, we walked away.

Harrison, in his *Fighting Spirit of Japan*, already quoted, gives examples of an oral tradition about the powers of the Zen masters. Some of these were related to him by present-day Japanese.

A real master of fence in feudal days . . . could exercise a species of mesmeric force at will to such good purpose that he himself would instantly become invisible to his antagonist, whose gaze would be helplessly fascinated by the point of the expert's sword, which in turn might be multiplied to seem like half a dozen points all equally real . . . .

In the second place, the expert could arrest the movement of his adversary's weapon in the very act of striking. . . . Paralysed into immobility at such a juncture, the victim would be left with his entire body exposed to the expert's attack.

In the third place, if the expert wished to avoid unnecessary exertion or to spare the life of his foe, he could, in a few minutes, convert the latter's bloodthirsty rage into fatuous good humour. I have been assured . . . that the conversion of an enemy's anger into laughter is by far the most difficult.

On a par with these astonishing performances is a manifestation of magnetic influence by experts whereby birds can be made to fall to the ground from a tree, apparently lifeless and again instantaneously revived and put to flight.

All this belongs to an oral tradition recounted to Harrison by present-day judo students and experts, but he was able to find some examples of similar powers still exercised in modern Japan.

He became friendly with an elderly Japanese Nobuyuki Kunishige, who told him:

A man who has thoroughly acquired the art of *Aiki-no-jutsu* verges on the divine. The clairvoyance so much talked about nowadays is nothing but a part of Aiki.

The old masters of my school have sayings to the effect that with full knowledge of Aiki one can see in the dark, bring walking men to a stop, or break a sword brandished to slay. These words can be accepted as true. I draw this conclusion from my own experience in stopping bleeding.... I believe men can enter the divine realm through constant culture of their mental and physical faculties.

Kunishige, then a man of over sixty, gave Harrison a display of an extraordinary power. He squatted down in approved Japanese fashion and invited Harrison to squat opposite him. Harrison, a six-footer, and very much more powerful than the elderly Japanese, was told to put both hands on Kunishige's chest and push him over. No judo holds or twists were employed, it was simply a question of a six-foot man trying to push over an old man squatting opposite him. Harrison almost had a seizure trying to do it and failed completely. Kunishige then took his little finger, placed it lightly on Harrison's chest and sent him flying.

Kunishige then tied the ends of a kimono sash together and put the loop round his neck. He then invited two of his students to pull him over. The utmost efforts failed to move him by as much as an inch. Kunishige then calmly went for a stroll round the gymnasium, taking the two men with him in spite of their combined efforts to hold their ground.

An interesting reference to the state (*hal*) in which powers of the will may be exercised is given in *Magic and Mysticism in Turkey* by Lucy Garnett, who collected first-hand information about various Sufi groups in Turkey.[17]

> There appear to be two different kinds of *hal* induced by methods of a totally different character. (1) An abnormal state of agitation by contagious emulation. It is possible in this state to endure physical injury without loss of blood, "mysteriously and speedily healed". (2) Appears to be permanent or assumable at will, due to the fourth or highest degree. Sheikhs and Dervishes of superior grade ... are equally credited with ability to acquire this degree of sanctity and on attaining it they become endowed with various spiritual and superhuman powers. Among these may be named what is termed: "The Power of the Will."

Also relevant to the earlier passages quoted is another remark by Lucy Garnett:

[17] L. M. J. Garnett, *Magic and Mysticism in Turkey*, Pitman, London, 1912.

Not individuals only, however, but crowds have been known to be affected in this way by eminent Dervishes; and according to Moslem legend, even opposing armies have been caused to desist from hostilities, completely subdued by the pacificatory spell thrown over them by some "Man of Peace" who has compelled their leaders to sign treaties drawn up by himself.[18]

Direct Perception

What is called direct perception is one of the possible powers of developed man, but, unlike, for example, clairvoyance and telepathy, it is not known in the West in the form practised by Sufis and the literature of Western occultism does not offer a convenient label.

It involves making mental contact with another "whole", material or otherwise, and "reading" it so as to obtain knowledge of its nature, past, present or future. This knowledge is called "direction" by the Sufis and is "read" in a form that accords with the cultural images and idiom of the percipient, not the subject.

The team saw several impressive examples. They also saw exercises by which the faculty was developed. This involves a technique known as "imprisoning the gaze". The pupil is taught directly by the Sheikh and is shown how to concentrate his mental force on one object before deflecting it upon another from which he is to "lift" information. The technique cannot be learned without a teacher, though a false form of it can be otherwise acquired. The teacher not only contributes knowledge, but also a specific energy without which the process cannot be powered.

One major use of the procedure is to verify the truth and relevance of traditional Sufic teaching material so that the process of Sufic influence on man is kept continuously renewed, active and effective.

Direct perception, it is claimed, cannot be significantly developed in a pupil below a certain level of capacity and cannot be developed in an individual who has aspects of his nature which make him unworthy to serve humanity.

A false form of direct perception may be acquired outside the conditions mentioned, but the result is distorted and the action becomes destructive of the operator.

An example of direct perception, exercised in a non-material field, is given in an account by Muhiyuddin Ibn el-

---

[18] ibid., p. 150.

Arabi "the teacher of Andalusia". It is quoted in *The Darvishes* by J. P. Brown.[19]

> Once when I was in the vicinity of the holy and reverend Kaaba (in Mecca), it happened that, absorbed in mental reflections on the four great jurisconsults of Islamism, I beheld a person who continuously made the Tawaf or circuit of that holy building. His height was quite as elevated as the Kaaba itself. Two other individuals were engaged in the same occupation, and whenever these were near to each other, the power would pass between them, without, however, separating them. From this I concluded that the individuals must belong to spiritual bodies only. As he continued his circuits, he recited the following: "Truly, we have been, for many long years, engaged in walking round this holy house, but you are doing it only now."
>
> On hearing these words, I formed a desire to know who he was, and to what tribe he belonged. So I fixed him with my eyes, after the manner called *habs-i-nazar* (imprisoning the gaze), and when he had ended his circuit, and desired to depart, he was unable to do so. Finally, he came to my side, and feeling that I was the cause of his detention, begged me to allow him to depart. I answered him with the words *Bismillah ar-Rahman ar-Rahim*, "In the name of God, the merciful and the clement", and added: "I will allow you to go only after you have let me know what kind of a being you are, and to what tribe or people you belong." He replied, "I am of mankind." I next asked him how long it was since he left this world. He replied, "It is now more than forty thousand years." Surprised, I added, "You say it is so long, whilst it is only six thousand years since Adam's time, and yet you state that you are of mankind." He answered, "The Adam you speak of was the father of the human race, though since his time only six thousand years have elapsed, thirty other worlds preceded him."

Theory of Attraction

Subtending the various para-psychological energies which the Sufis employ, the team thought it could catch a glimpse of a unifying principle. The form in which this principle is enunciated at the present time is not available for publication, and is in any case of such a subtle and elusive nature as would make it very difficult for the team to summarize.

---

[19] Edited by E. Rose, reprinted O.U.P., London, 1968.

The idea is, however, contained in a classical passage of Sufi poetry which is quoted by Sir William Jones.[20]

The most wonderful passage on the theory of attraction occurs in the charming allegorical poem *Shirin and Farhad, or the Divine Spirit and a Human Soul disinterestedly pious*, a work which from the first verse to the last is a blaze of religious and poetical fire. The whole passage appears to me so curious that I make no apology for giving you a faithful translation of it:

There is a strong propensity which dances through every atom, and attracts the minutest particle to some peculiar object; search this universe from its base to its summit, from fire to air, from water to earth, from all below the moon to all above the celestial spheres, and thou wilt not find a corpuscle destitute of that natural attractability; the very point of the first thread in this apparently tangled skein is no other than such a principle of attraction, and all principles beside are void of a real basis; from such a propensity arises every motion perceived in heavenly or in terrestrial bodies; it is a disposition to be attracted which taught hard steel to rush from its place and rivet itself on the magnet; it is the same disposition which impels the light straw to attach itself firmly to amber; it is this quality which gives every substance in nature a tendency toward another, and an inclination forcibly directed to a determinate point."

[20] Jones, *On the Philosophy of the Asiatics*, cited by J. P. Brown, in *The Darvishes*.

CHAPTER ELEVEN

SUFI DISCOURSES, RITUALS, INITIATION

The team's experience led them to look at published Western opinions about Sufis and Sufism in a critical light. The conclusions of Western investigators suffered, almost without exception, from prior assumption.

It seemed that those with a religious orientation found data to prove that the Sufis are a religious group within Islam. Those with a bias to occultism found plenty to support their view that the Sufis were primarily occultists. Anthropologists found interesting relics of primitive ceremonial.

The same process could even be observed within finer gradations. Christians found activity among Sufis which they regarded as essentially Christian. Occultists with a bias towards one or other form of magic found the Sufis clearly engaged in their own speciality.

To investigators working "from outside", the Sufis appeared to offer a sort of magic mirror in which all could see what they had decided in advance was there to be seen.

Thus Communists, on the rare occasions when they have deigned to look outside their own canon, can discover that Sufism is a sort of precursor of the enlightenment that Marx was to bring.

"The social aspect of Sufism attracted the poor, especially those in towns from whose midst many of the early Sufis had sprung. It also evoked certain sympathies among feudal intellectuals who were growing increasingly aware of their humiliating, subordinate role at the feudal courts. The philosophical aspect of Sufism, in its turn, aroused the partisanship of many men of culture, since in some measure it freed human reason from the stifling clasp of dogmatism."[1]

---

[1] Michael I. Zand, *Six Centuries of Glory*, Moscow, USSR Academy of Sciences, 1967, pp. 115–116.

Professor Rom Landau, who investigated many "fringe" religions in books like his *God is My Adventure*,[2] was attracted to the study of the Sufi teacher Ibn el Arabi and sees in him an important influence in European literature.

In China, Dr. Li Soong, whose mind reaches out to overall concepts, has analysed the teachings of the Naqshbandi Dervish school and suggests that the activities of this Order, in the Gobi and China proper, represent "the maintenance and sustaining of the most ancient human developmental teachings which we would do well to investigate if we are to arrive at a higher destination of humankind".

In India, the President of the Republic has edited a book in which Sufism is seen in terms of morality and the attainment of bliss.

"Sufism teaches how to purify one's self, improve one's morals and build up one's inner and outer life in order to attain perpetual bliss. Its subject matter is the purification of the soul, and its end or aim is the attainment of eternal felicity and blessedness."[3]

The team began to realize that the paradoxes which the Sufis habitually use when asked about the nature of their activities were less paradoxical than they seemed. Sayings like: "Sufism is other than any other cult"; "Sufism looks like religion, it is not religion" suggest "something in the round" which the team sensed very strongly when in close contact with Sufis, but which they could not pin down in any familiar category.

The team concluded that no single hypothesis, religious, psychological, magical or social, would account for the whole of Sufic manifestation. They were driven to accept that the phrase: "He who tastes, knows", far from being a piece of double talk, gratuitously irritating, was in fact an irreducible formula for suggesting what, by its very nature, could not be stated explicitly.

One member of the team suggested a possible explanation of the centuries-old difficulty of describing the nature of Sufic activity. If, as the Sufis assert, their system reaches areas of the human mind untouched by all other religious or psychological

---

[2] Nicholson and Watson, London, 1935.

[3] Sheikh-el-Islam Zakaria Ansari, *History of Philosophy*, London, 1953 and 1957, Vol. 2, p. 171.

systems, it would follow that all attempts to describe it would necessarily be defective for this reason alone.

However difficult it may be to elucidate Sufi activity there is no lack of people prepared to make an attempt.

The *Index Islamicus* (Supplement edited by J. D. Pearson, Cambridge, 1962), lists over 80 learned publications on Sufism (mostly by specialists) in the four years ending 1960 and this list is by no means complete. If full-length works are added to this list, the contributions of Orientalists to the subject of Sufism are in the order of one every fortnight from 1956 to 1960. If reprints and works in Eastern languages are included, Sufism is seen to be attracting attention at the rate of one book or monograph every seven days!

It would seem that an unprecedented preoccupation with an "occult" subject is to be seen all over the world and may offer evidence for the view already advanced here: that the Sufis, for reasons connected with the present state of world affairs, are "coming into the open", probably by the technique of arousing interest directly.

Even from its brief experience of Sufi activity, the team realized that no account of what-it-is-all-about is possible in direct terms and they realized that certain incidents to which they had not attached any significance were examples of indirect teaching. An example of this from published material is to be found in Garnett's *Magic and Mysticism in Turkey* already mentioned. Lucy Garnett is quoting from *The Mesnevi*:

"When on a visit to a fellow Sheikh of great repute, he was asked by a Dervish: 'What is poverty?' Jalaluddin Rumi did not answer. The question was repeated thrice. When Rumi left, the Sheikh reprimanded the Dervish for his insolent intrusion which was 'the more inexcusable as he (Rumi) fully answered thy question the first time thou didst put it'. The Dervish, surprised, asked what the answer had been. 'A poor man', replied the Prior, 'is one who, having known Allah, hath his tongue tied'."

The team decided that it would be pointless to attempt any summary of Sufic activity on analytical lines. They agreed that three pieces of material, one ancient and two modern, probably represented the best attempt they could make at suggesting indirectly the nature of the Sufic activity they had glimpsed.

The first is some twenty sentences of comment or instruction to his pupils by Jalaluddin Rumi (1207–73). The second is an interview with a Sufic teacher in England. The third is a tape-recorded conversation with a Naqshbandi Sheikh in Afghanistan.

From Rumi

1. Do not imagine that similar appearances must have similar causes.
2. People learn indirectly as effectively (sometimes more so) than directly.
3. If you want to study something, you must undergo the whole course of study. If you are prejudiced about it, you may not be able to study any part at all.
4. You are shocked not by right and wrong, but by the conventional conception of right and wrong.
5. People are affected by things in accordance with their mental and emotional set.
6. People expect things to turn out in a manner laid down by them. Sometimes at least it is just as well for them that they do not have the say in the end.
7. People try to teach, for instance, when what they have to do is to learn.
8. Adopt the superficialities, the parrot-cries (even if you think that they are serious) and you will lose.
9. Try to judge with inadequate tools and you will get nowhere, and even harm others.
10. People are unaware of the real hidden relationship which Sufis have.
11. Things which appear harmless, even desirable, even one's own property, can be extremely dangerous.
12. Neither blind imitation is right, nor blind obedience.
13. Things are repeated again and again in the Teaching because people hear but do not listen.
14. The way in which you may approach what you want may be too long a way to suffice you before you are too late.
15. Things which have to be tackled have to be done at the right time. That time is generally soon.
16. You may think that you understand something, but the

slightest experience of it may cause you to lose all your understanding.
17. The teacher helps you when you think he is hindering you.
18. What you think helps you may more than hinder you.
19. Divisive weakness will destroy any unity.
20. The "high-minded" attitude towards something can go too far.

Interview with a Sufi Teacher in England

Q.: We know Sufism mainly by its ancient and classical literature. What is the value of this material?
A.: This literature is of intellectual and cultural value only, just like any other literature, unless interpreted by a Sufi in a Sufi circle, for the particular membership which he is teaching.
Q.: What is the Sufi teaching entity or unit?
A.: The Halka – "Ring" – a group chosen by a teacher. He may teach it direct, or may appoint a Khalifa – "Deputy". The chief teacher's Halka is the head one. A number of Halkas make up the Tarika – "Path" – which is the word for the current School.
Q.: Why are there so many ways of putting the Sufi study methods: the three circles, the arc of ascent and descent, the meditation, concentration, contemplation, and so on?
A.: These are not different ways. They are fragments of the total number of elements in a Sufi School: like you might say in an ordinary school there is the class for French, English, Geometry and so on. Each one is a part of the education being offered. The confusion has arisen through people trying to simplify and choosing an attractive series of words for their studies.
Q.: Can Sufism be studied academically? Can one be an "intellectual" Sufi?
A.: Many outward manifestations of Sufism can be studied outwardly. People study and try to practise Sufi exercises, music, literature and so on. This is not, however, the study of Sufism, which is a matter of participation.
Q.: Do you have to use the term "Sufism", which is associated in many minds with Moslem enthusiasts or Western imitators?
A.: Most of our activities do not use the word at all. But when

there is a reason for using the word, there is no word whose employment will not be challenged by somebody or other.

Q.: Are Sufis more "scientific" than religionists in their attitudes and activities?

A.: They are, because they are practical as well as being experientialists. They know which parts of human experience are useful tools, which are methods and ways, and which are truly higher, spiritual, and so on.

Q.: Do Sufis proselytize? If so, how?

A.: Sufis select people with certain capacities. This they cannot do by propaganda, because propaganda conditions people to certain extremes in belief which they would only have to abandon in due course.

Q.: Why do Sufis reject so many people who go to them? Surely Sufism should be for all?

A.: They do not reject anyone who is worthy. But the condition of the man who wants to become a Sufi, and what he thinks his condition really is, may be two different things. People may be capable of becoming Sufis at one point; then lose the capability. Time may have to pass before they can apply again. Enthusiasm for Sufism or for "secrets" is no basis for approaching the study.

Q.: Despite the efforts of students, clerics and orientalists, it has not yet been decided exactly what Sufism is. Can you say whether it is a religion, or whether it is mainly derived from Christianity, say, or whether it is a psychology?

A.: Sufism cannot be described because it is unique, of its own kind. When a religionist studies it, he may regard it as a religion. He then labels it according to his own scale of religions. "A donkey can judge thistles, but he cannot judge melons."

Q.: How can one judge whether a certain Sufi school or teacher is genuinely representative of Sufism?

A.: You cannot, unless you are a Sufi. But if the school or individual resembles a recognizable form of "esoteric training" or "religious organization", and so on, it is less likely to be sufficiently Sufic to develop the individual correctly.

Q.: By what signs in oneself can one tell whether a teaching is the right one "for me"?

A.: By sensations and reactions which differ completely from customary ones. Indications which one does not experience through the contact with anything else. In contacting Sufism, you are coming into a relationship with a completely new experience. Its sensation is correspondingly different from established "religious" or other experiences.

Q.: Do your answers hold good for all enquirers, and would you answer in the same way if you were approached by an Oriental?

A.: Answers are, broadly speaking, for a certain time and a certain society. All would depend upon the time and the cultural situation of the enquirer. This is the best way of presenting something of Sufism to a Westerner who has been interested in what he calls "higher knowledge", in these days.

Tape-recorded Conversation with a Sufi Sheikh in Afghanistan

Q.: In your field work, in distant countries such as the Western ones, do you encounter difficulties which you do not anticipate?

A.: None.

Q.: Do you have to work through difficulties just as if you had not anticipated them? If so, why?

A.: Yes. And because it is in the working-through the difficulties that the development of man takes place.

Q.: Is there a value in adopting a psychological system, as we use them in the West, to explain the past, to work with the present, to solve one's problems, to make possible living on a higher level?

A.: By itself, no. You must have certain special exercises and practices, held by one of our delegates.

Q.: Such of your representatives as we have met have not always encouraged us. This is why we have come to you.

A.: You have come to us because we have permitted it. You cannot go over the heads of representatives, like meeting the managing director when the manager does not give satisfaction. Our delegates know what to do, when to "blow hot" and when to "blow cold".

Q.: Do the meanings of studies which we make from time to time become known to us later?

A.: Yes.

Q.: Do you use objects and concepts for teaching that are unknown to us?

A.: Objects and concepts which you do not link with "higher teaching" as you know it, yes.

Q.: Is there an extra-sensory link between you and your delegates, between them and us, and between people past and future?

A.: There is.

Q.: Are you concerned with arts and practices which are used by non-religious groups?

A.: Yes. Because the use of a thing is not known to you, do not suppose that it has no use. Because a thing has fallen into the wrong hands, do not suppose that there are not hands which know how to work with it, without its adverse associations.

Q.: How can so many sincere people all be following different faiths, all find something of value in them, and yet have beliefs and opinions which are sometimes diametrically opposed to one another?

A.: This cannot happen if we discover real sincerity. The kind of sincerity which these people are using is not connected with faith, but with a personal indulgence: they like it, so it is true. They find something which they want, they call it something of value. It is of no spiritual value or importance. It is of social value. When they discover that they would be as well satisfied with any "faith", as they call it, just like the other "sincere" people, they will start to look for real faith and real religion, beyond the childish game.

Q.: Why do people follow teachers and teachings with great intensity and still fail to find truth?

A.: Such people are not looking for truth. They are looking for teachers and teachings. If they knew what truth was, so that they could pursue it, we would find them, as we do indeed find people. It is the people in between: the people with capacity for sincerity who are not taught it, because organized groups and religions make use of the people's insincerity. The chief way in which they do that is to offer emotional rewards and status rewards, which the people accept.

Q.: Why do you use so many different terms for the Sufi Path?

A.: Sometimes, where "Sufi" has an honorific value, we shun it, partly to avoid self-indulgence, partly to leave the field clear for imitators, who present unsufic organizations under this name. Where the word Sufi is unpopular and represents in the minds of, for example, Hindus and some Westerners, "Mohammedan fanatic", we may use it to demonstrate that we are not what we are labelled. Sometimes again, we use a wide variety of other names, because of the convenience or otherwise of working. Many of our organizations have no "spiritual" aspect as far as the outward man can see, and these work the best, unhampered. But I cannot talk about those to a person who already deals in the "spiritual" cloak of things.

Q.: Do you believe in merit from deeds, in punishment, in secret knowledge?

A.: There is merit in deeds only if you can disconnect yourself from anticipation of merit. There is punishment if you fear punishment, because if you act in fear you should be punished, even if you have done what you think is "good". There is secret knowledge, which will never be perceived by anyone who is thinking about Secret Knowledge, because its form and communication are invisible to such people.

Q.: What is the major difference between your treatment of students and that of other schools?

A.: There are many. To single out the one which fewest people can understand: we work to contact people at a level deeper than working on their emotions. All other systems concentrate upon conversion, giving people attention, giving them things to do, tests to perform and so on. Our major test is to leave people alone, until they find out whether or not they can feel anything true about us. We have discovered, you see, that the system which is supposedly testing people by means of trials is in fact maintaining their attention in contact with itself. The result is that people are trained (conditioned, you call it today) to concentrate upon the school or system: they have become brainwashed, though they call it faith. If they reject, not becoming trained, all the better for the system in question, for it is spared the problem of a recalcitrant in its ranks thereafter. With us, it is different: we cannot survive with "conditioned" people in our ranks. We reach something deeper in them.

Q.: Do the Sufis concede that there are other valid systems transmitted from the past?

A.: A few years ago a Russian mission examined many practitioners of Yoga, attempting to deduce from their practices the original system upon which it was built.

They learned, of course, certain things: such as the fact that many Yogic postures and breathings have an auto-hypnotic effect.

But, since these people did not know the possible effects of posture, breathing and so on, they were not in a position to deduce the effects.

When we study one of the "traditional" systems, like Christian prayer recitals, or Yogic postures, we are able to know what they were originally intended for: just as you as a Westerner would know what the accoutrements of a soldier were originally for if you saw one, after you had served in the Army of the period when such apparatus was used.

Unless you grasp this point there is little use for further discussion.

One particular type of Sufic teacher has consistently baffled observers – and not only Western observers – whether he has been recognized as a Sufic figure or not. This is the "crazed saint", perhaps the ultimate exemplar of indirect teaching, achieving his results by oblique action. His students suspect the nature of this activity in proportion to their degree, but the activity of the "crazed saint" remains incomprehensible to outsiders.

One member of the team obtained an interview with a pupil (already aged) of such a teacher. The interview took place in Kafiristan and appropriately enough under a mulberry tree.

The old gentleman, who must have been about seventy, was known as Sheikh Hindki. He had come originally from India.

> In my home town there used to be a strange man. People all liked him, and they used to ask his advice on many subjects. He came from Central Asia somewhere, and we called him Bokhari Saheb.
>
> He had a small carpet shop in one of the bazaars. He used to have tempers, which nobody could account for: sometimes he got angry about the slightest things. Sometimes he seemed to be unjust or ridiculous.
>
> I used to go to sit with him from the age of about sixteen years, observing what he said and did. After three or four years, I realized that it was not what he said or how he said it: it was the effect which he caused. For instance, when a man wanted to get a job with the local municipality, Bokhari Saheb went to the Town Clerk and told him that there was something wrong with the man. So he didn't get the job. But the man who did – he died suddenly

when the roof of his office collapsed. There were hundreds of incidents like that, spread over many years. I began to realize that Bokhari was an agent for something or someone who knew something and could protect people, no matter how it was done. It was usually done in the last way in which you would expect it.

Eventually I asked him about it, and he said: "If you want to learn, join me, and work with me. Familiarity, companionship, and asking no questions will harmonize you with it, so that much of your future time will be saved."

I used to act as an assistant to him, whenever he wanted something done, or said, and so on. I still could not learn what was the source of this wisdom which was disguised by peculiarities.

I stayed with him for forty years. One day he said: "I shall die in a fortnight or less. Go to Beluristan and become the servant of the Namuss." In ten days he was dead. After seeing to his funeral I came here, after quite a long journey and many difficulties finding the place. Now I play my part, and I am on the Way.

A fair amount of Sufic literature exists on the activities of teachers in the "crazed saint" pattern. The following is an attempt to summarize his qualities.

1. Supernatural powers.
2. Healing.
3. Physical indulgences.
4. Takes money.
5. Redistributes money, gifts, etc.
6. Never withholds action because of lack of money.
7. Exercises are an alteration of harmony and opposition, of piety and apparent impiety.
8. Goes against the norms of the society in which he lives and works.
9. Is never understood, because people who support him seek to conceal his "excesses" as quirks and not as an essential part of his operations; also because people do not recognize that some of his actions are illustrative, miming the weaknesses of others.
10. Is opposed by the orthodox authorities, civil and religious.
11. Attracts many people who follow only the lure of the strange, who are thought to be his disciples, creating an incorrect outer impression of his activities and associates.
12. Has dance, music, or other physical movements, exer-

cises thought to be religious by the converts, to be improper by the orthodox.
13. Has spent a great deal of time in mortification and also in indulgence. The twin operation of these, their polarity, releases in him a strange power. He attempts to release it in those with whom he is in touch as well.
14. Usually only a small ("acceptable") part of what he says and does is reported, and this becomes respectable, may even become a sub-cult. Or he may even come to be absorbed, after his death, as a saint by the orthodox church.
15. May be from far away, a barbaric figure, rough, foreigner, etc.

* * *

In the matter of recruitment to Sufi groups and the ritual of initiation, the team found three references in *The Darvishes* by Brown, already quoted, which covered their limited experience.

These are given for interest.

"Whenever anyone desires to enter this Tariqa (Path) and feels an affection for the Sheikh of a *Takia* (Dervish establishment), he seeks for a *Murid* (disciple) already belonging to it and expresses his wish to become a disciple of the Sheikh. In reply the Murid enjoins upon him to continue frequenting the *Takia* and to wait upon its members and visitors. The service required of him is of a domestic character and must be performed by the pupil, whatever may be his social or official position. It lasts for several months, or a year, and serves to increase his love for the order of the Sheikh and prevents him falling off, or joining any other *Takia*. He is not, however, under any obligation to continue it, and may leave and join another if he chooses."

The initiation of a probationer may not take place for some considerable time.

"The Bai'at or election of the *Murid* (disciple) by placing of hands on his head, or the hand of the Sheikh in his hand, in some cases only takes place several years after his original admission to the Order.

"The period much depends upon the will of the Sheikh, and the degree of knowledge and spiritual acquirements of the *Murid*.

"The Sheikh – or the *Murid* – is held to see a vision either of the Prophet, Ali, or the Pir (chief) of the Order; and this ceremonial is the only one of which the secret, if indeed one exists, has not been divulged to me. The *Murid*, at that time, takes an oath never to divulge it, and not to commit certain ordinary sins."

At the actual admission (in the case reported by Brown to the Qadiri Order) the Sheikh takes the hand of the aspirant and says:

"This hand is the hand of the Sheikh (Abd-el-Qadir) and the Director of the true path is in your hand.

"I am the Sheikh of Abd-el-Qadir: I accepted this hand from him and now with it I accept of you as one of his disciples."

Aspirant: "And I also accept of you as such."

Sheikh: "I therefore do now admit you."

Chapter Twelve

SCIENCE FICTION AND THE ANCIENT TRADITION

We began at the present time, then plunged back to the conjectured beginnings of the world. We have since flicked through the pages of the human story at random and have arrived back again at our own time.

Does the life–process seem like the result of random forces? Or does it suggest the unfolding of a vast and solemn plan? The verdict, in the last resort, must be an emotional one. No mustering of selected historical incidents, no suggested sequence, no inter-relatedness can prove the existence of a noumenal level. At best we can see flecks of foam on the surface and suspect the existence of a wave-system underneath. Of its very nature this must be invisible.

But if there is some great plan for man and the world, with solar and cosmic goals set against millions of years: and if our present state is one stage in such a plan, then certain considerations arise which must be squarely faced.

We are accustomed to regard the democratic forms of the 20th century as advances on earlier social forms – though Plato would not have agreed. If we do, we have to admit that they were bought at a price.

Modern democracies were born out of the French Revolution. This and the so far unstabilized upheavals to which it gave rise, manifestly involved fear, suffering and death for millions. Does the end justify the means? Can an Intelligence which employs such means be "good" in any sense we can entertain?

Concurrently, the developing skills of science have freed millions from a grim survival-level existence and provided material rewards on a prodigious scale for millions more. But with its gifts, science has presented a bill. We must pay for our toys with stress and fear and the surrender of ancient and revered human values.

If this has been "arranged", can the Intelligence which arranged it be benign? It seems that any theory of Intervention must stand accused by human standards. We feel that suffering is regrettable enough when it is the consequence of chance and hazard. If it is purposive and deliberate, we can only regard it as intolerable.

The answer, if there is one, must lie in the idea of scale.

Let us assume that we, as humans, have some ordinary aim to achieve this day. By any standards we are able to apply, this aim is "right" and "good". To discharge it, we must, let us say, catch a certain bus. The bus is starting away and is already accelerating and only by a strenuous sprint can we hope to catch it.

Our decision to make the effort triggers off a whole sequence of bodily events. Extra adrenalin pours into our blood. Our muscles contract in exceptional effort. By our deliberate action we destroy millions of body cells. Each of these cells is a little life. They die – in a real sense they are sacrificed – to our aim.

Do we feel compassion? Can we truly say that we experience remorse for their destruction from an action we took?

Here there is a factor of scale which is all-important. Everything in the universe may be significant: but everything is not equally significant. Whether such a concept squares with our subjective ideas of "good" and "higher" is immaterial. *This is how things are.* Like Carlyle's correspondent, we have to accept the universe.

We seldom notice that our capacity for compassion is a gradient. We can have no more than theoretical concern for the fate of the yeast we use to bake bread. Yet it is life. We feel minimal responsibility for cold-blooded life, increasing concern for warm-blooded life and maximum concern for human life. For cellular life we cannot feel at all. The gulf of scale is too great. It is beyond our limit.

This limitation of scale is connected with time: with the maximum and minimum of the "present moment" which our consciousness is able to span.

A time-scale gap closer to everyday experience may illustrate. Suppose a young child has a thorn deeply embedded in a finger. The mother sees the situation in terms of a present moment vastly greater than the child's. She sees her baby's life as a whole, its well-being, growth, maturity. She takes a needle, digs it under the thorn and removes it.

The child's present moment is restricted to the three or four seconds during which a needle is piercing its flesh. In terms of the child's present moment the mother is committing an incomprehensible act of cruelty, a deliberate infliction of needless suffering. The child does not understand, and cannot, that the mother's action arises from concern for its own ultimate good.

To appreciate this, the child would need access to a present moment which it does not possess and, at its stage of development, cannot possess.

Also, the thorn must be the consequence of some action by the child itself – however helpless it may have been to avoid it.

By analogy, the Reign of Terror and two world wars may represent no more than instantaneous needle-jabs within a consciousness whose present moment is ten thousand years.

If the whole of humanity is an organism on another time-scale, its ultimate good may require action by an Intelligence possessing an enormously greater present moment. To the individual man, whose present moment at maximum is his own lifetime, such action can suggest only indifference at best and at worst deliberate cruelty. If his present moment could be greatly extended and if, from this viewpoint, he could see some sort of Ego-continuity outside a single life, his relationship to "fate" would be wholly transformed.

But such considerations seem remote and impersonal. Pressures on elementary life-forms to produce mankind: even, vastly more recently, the manipulation of religious or cult impulses to create environmental opportunities for vast populations – such things are remote from our immediate experience. If influences to coax or restrain human development along preordained lines play on human life, they should be detectable in some shadowy form in our own day and experience.

The team which made contact with a number of Sufi sources concluded that telepathy was employed not only as an inter-Sufi communication system but as a means of "influencing people and things".

If such an influence exists, it clears many "coincidences" which prove intractable to ordinary explanation.

There are many examples of inventions, individually improbable, being arrived at simultaneously by different people.

Writers sometimes find themselves impelled to write extraordinary fantasy which is later found to be prophetic.

Dante, in the *Divine Comedy*, gives an exact description of the Southern Cross, a constellation which is invisible in the Northern hemisphere and which no traveller in those days could ever have seen.[1]

Swift, in *The Journey to Laputa*, gives the distances and periods of rotation of the two satellites of Mars, unknown at that time. When the American astronomer, Asaph Hall, discovered them in 1877 and noticed that his calculations corresponded to Swift's indications, he was seized with a sort of panic and named them *Phobos* and *Deimos*: Fear and Terror.[2]

In 1896, an English author, M. P. Shiel, published a short story in which we read of a band of monstrous criminals ravaging Europe, slaughtering families which they considered were impeding the progress of humanity, and burning their corpses. The story was entitled: *The S.S.*[3]

On November 21, 1959, Sydney Jordan, the author of the script of the "Jeff Hawke" science fiction cartoon strip in the London *Daily Express* had his "Sci-fi" characters land on the moon and plant a plaque to mark man's conquest of a new planet. The date engraved on the plaque was "August 4, 1969".

Jordan thus "predicted" the actual event to within a fortnight, *ten years in advance*.

A London editor dealing with fictional manuscripts is often astonished to find that writers, sometimes on opposite sides of the world, seem for some unexplained reason to hit on identical plots for their stories at the same time. In one week in 1969 he reported reading nine stories with virtually the same plot. This plot had not previously turned up in his editing experience.

If, as suggested, telepathy is one means by which human activity is incited or inhibited, it is conceivable that "spin-off"

---

[1] L. Pauwels and J. Bergier, *The Dawn of Magic*, Gibbs and Phillips, London, 1963, p. 136. The extensive Sufi literary influences on Dante were exhaustively researched by Asín in 1926. See M. Asín Palacios, *Islam and the Divine Comedy*, London, 1968 edition (tr. H. Sutherland).
[2] ibid.
[3] ibid.

from such energies may cause trends of thinking of this sort at mundane level.

It may also be that coming events are deliberately foreshadowed to prepare a mental climate for the event that lies on a line of probable actualization.

There are reasons to suppose that almost the whole of science fiction belongs to this category.

Space travel and atomic energy came as only minimal surprises to world populations which were barely emerging from the steam age. Verne and Wells and a whole host of later writers like Asimov and Clarke envisaged coming developments of science so concretely that they were able to present their "fantasies" as virtual realities. Thus the ideas became acceptable mental currency *in advance of their actualization*.

The idea of altering human behaviour by the deliberate manipulation of environment is one with no apparent ancestry. Barely discernible traces of it are to be found in esoteric literature. Suddenly, from nowhere, it becomes a familiar everyday idea. It would be hard to imagine a subject less likely to appeal to a mass television audience, yet Patrick McGoohan's *The Prisoner* was built on this idea – and with the suggestion that a level existed, above which people were immune to this manipulation.

T. S. Eliot's *Cocktail Party* and *Cards of Identity* by Nigel Denis elaborate the same theme.

Why did a most detailed extension of the same arcane idea occur to John Fowles, whose *Magus* captured popular interest to an extent unprecedented in any comparably "difficult" field?

In *The Magus*,[4] quite explicit, was the idea of a group of people possessing *a different kind of knowledge* which enabled them – and apparently entitled them – to manipulate the psychology of selected ordinary men and women. Those so affected felt themselves to be the victims of some intolerable persecution which, however, held for them an irresistible seduction and nostalgia. Only after they had been "processed" through suffering to rebellion and then to resignation did they begin to glimpse the catharsis through which they had been steered and the new level of life to which their experience entitled them.

[4] John Fowles, *The Magus*, Cape, London, 1966, and Pan Books, 1968.

At the present time dolphins have suddenly become of world-wide interest. Scientists are investigating their intelligence. Documentary films are made about them. Factual and fictional writings about them appear almost every week. The idea that dolphins are in some way "special" seems to have been written into mythology thousands of years ago. Dolphins have been available for study ever since. There have been many cultures capable of studying them; yet only in the late 1960s do dolphins suddenly, unaccountably, become important.

Suppose man's future is to involve him in meeting, somewhere in the universe, with life of approximately his own level but in unfamiliar forms. Such an encounter could be rehearsed exactly in the experience of those who at present are trying to communicate with dolphins.

Did Rossum's *Universal Robots* and *Metropolis* prepare the last generation for our own generation's encounter with the computer?

Seen from the present moment of the generation born before 1920, today's Permissive Society and the LSD and Marijuana "scene" appear to be only deterioration, a fall from higher standards already reached. But just as the wrestling of democracy from authoritarian kingship, a process seemingly entropic at the time, may have been the minimal basis on which a present and future situation could be based, so the actual experience that extra-sensory states exist may be the foundation for a future which contains extra-sensory experience as a widespread attribute.

Any attempt to assess the "Permissive Scene" may also be complicated by a factor which is quite unsuspected: the suggestion of the deliberate creation of degeneracy in the youth of the West as the aim of a magical operation of revenge, set in motion around 1920 and only now being executed.

But if the future reaches back to the past to prepare us, it may also use the same means to warn.

An example of this may be a recent science fiction story by Walter M. Miller, *A Canticle for Leibovitz*.[5]

Here the concepts show such remarkable insight into actual mechanisms that it is to be conjectured either that the author is

[5] W. M. Miller, *A Canticle for Leibovitz*, Weidenfeld and Nicolson, London, 1960; Corgi, London, 1963.

a remarkably sensitive "receiver" or else has structured his insights on the basis of knowledge from a genuine source.

Nuclear warfare has destroyed civilization: but an electronics engineer called Leibovitz who foresaw the disaster had founded a monastery – with Church permission – in a remote desert in America.

During the immediate post-war period, the masses had slaughtered such of the surviving scientists as had not gained sanctuary in the Church. In the Dark Ages that follow, the real events of recent history become distorted and turned into myths. The nuclear disaster, the cause of which is no longer remembered, is called the Flame Deluge. Mutants resulting from the fallout – two-headed monsters – are called the children of Fallout, Fallout being the demon who caused the holocaust.

At Leibovitz Monastery the monks preserve records of the Golden Age that preceded the Demon Fallout. These are manuals of technology and bits of old blue-prints which no longer mean anything but are held to be holy relics. The monks learn them by heart, make copies of them and sell them to other monasteries.

The Church is riddled with superstition. The Flame Deluge has been written into Scripture and the Cardinals at New Rome wrangle endlessly over the niceties of the Immaculate Conception. Church ritual is meaningless – old bits of electronic equipment are strung together as holy necklaces – but nevertheless this ritual serves to prevent knowledge from the past from going completely into oblivion.

One day a monk, on solitary vigil in the desert, is surprised by a ribald old tramp who shows him the entrance to a previously undiscovered fallout shelter. There, among the skeletons, the monk finds some charred paper including a blue-print of a design signed by Leibovitz and another relic from the Golden Age, a manuscript entitled Racing Form.

When he gets back to the monastery, the monks elaborate this story until the old wanderer becomes a reincarnation of The Blessed Leibovitz himself, complete with halo – although the old tramp had in fact thrown stones at the monk for refusing to accept some of his bread and cheese.

These priceless discoveries are sent to New Rome and two Papal Commissions investigate the miracle of their survival and rediscovery and the entitlement of The Blessed Leibovitz to be sanctified. After spending fifteen years making an illuminated copy of the blue-print, the monk who found it takes the original to the Pope, who kisses it and canonizes the long-dead electronics engineer – having received guidance from above for this step.

On his return journey to his monastery the monk is waylaid and eaten by two of the cannibal Children of Fallout. The old wanderer appears again on the scene and buries what remains of the poor monk.

Six hundred years pass. Mankind is still in a state of barbarism and there are rumours of a major war. All the same, literacy is on the increase and there is renewed interest in science and philosophy.

Leibovitz Monastery still retains some of the ancient texts, but others have been destroyed in the forays of nomads and ignorant Crusaders. The current Abbot realizes that the old texts are incapable, of themselves, of reviving civilization, but he feels that they could assist emergent science. He allows them to be inspected by a team of "scientists" sent by one of the ruling princes.

The Abbot has misgivings, however. He knows that the ancient civilization had been destroyed by materialism. He fears that the new scientists will use any knowledge they get, to destroy the Church which preserved it. Then, free of the restraints which the Church might have provided, they will proceed once again to destroy civilization.

Science always washes its hands of blood. Yet knowledge of science cannot be withheld till man is wise, or he would never merit it. Neither infinite power nor infinite wisdom is sufficient to bestow Godhead on man. There must be infinite love as well.

One of the monks, working from the old manuscripts, actually produces electric light in the monastery from a crude, hand-operated dynamo. The visiting scientific commission is amazed – because it was simply not possible to construct the device *directly* from the books. How did the monk's jump from theory to practice come about? Was this a miracle?

Staying at the Abbey is a "Poet Fool" who is irreverent about everything. He sees through science and religion alike. He writes scurrilous verse and has an artificial eye with which he claims he can "see". After performing a self-sacrificing act he is killed by a soldier. Is it possible that wisdom may reside in someone who is neither of church nor science?

The old wanderer appears again. He claims to be the Wandering Jew, born before Christ.

He tells the Abbot that he feels and accepts the burden of the whole Jewish race. Could the Abbot take upon himself the whole burden of Christendom? The burden of Man is on every man – though a Christian was relieved of most of it by Christ. The Abbot has a sudden recollection of the Poet Fool. *He* had not regarded it as a burden but as ancestral glory which he had inherited and which he held as his birthright. The Jew is still looking for the Messiah, but as he searches the faces of the scientists he knows that He is not there.

Another six centuries pass and a Generation of Light succeeds the Dark Ages. Man has now colonized space and another nuclear war is beginning. By this time St. Leibovitz has become the patron saint of electricians and some men revere St. Poet of The Mysterious Eyeball.

Still intact, the Abbey is by now completely modernized. But the change is only in externals. Its old activities are still slavishly and meaninglessly continued. The Abbot, working with a translation machine, muses that souls were first vegetative, then animal, then rational, then instead of souls becoming angels they became machines.

The Old Jew appears again, still looking for the Messiah. The Abbot feels there is no hope of Heaven for Man. The human species has been born insane.

The Papacy is now planning to send a party of monks and bishops to colonize another planet. With them they will take all the Church's historic Memorabilia and from their base in space they will try to evangelize other worlds. On Earth, the Church has ceased to pray for peace. It pins its hopes on its Message surviving elsewhere.

Meanwhile, the radiation-count is rising. Refugees pour into Leibovitz Monastery. Voluntary euthanasia is administered to the fatally irradiated by a secular medical unit. This so outrages the Abbot that he breaks his vow of non-violence and has an unseemly brawl with a doctor in order to prevent the euthanasia of a mother and child.

For the doctor, pain is the only evil and society is the only lawful arbiter of right and wrong. To the Abbot, the doctor is a murderer, depriving the woman of what she could gain by suffering, and breaking God's laws.

There is an explosion, the Abbey is wrecked and the Abbot finds himself half-crushed in the ruins. He now tries to prove for himself in practice that pain is not the evil, but fear of suffering is. Society he sees, tries to increase security and minimize suffering. The result is minimal security and maximum suffering. The Abbot tries to take on himself the suffering of others.

A two-headed woman struggles up to the Abbot. She wants him to administer baptism for her second head which, till now, has been asleep.

As it slowly awakes, the face reveals the features of infancy and innocence – the face of a being which is born free.

Suddenly the woman speaks with a new voice and refuses the Abbot's baptism. Instead she administers the sacrament to him. She acts with authority, as though under direct instruction "sensing the Presence under the veils". In her eyes the Abbot sees the promise of resurrection.

Has God, through all the ages, he wonders, manifested Himself not in Science, not in Church but in wholly unexpected places?

In this astonishing story are contained insights into processes not normally suspected.

Miller's points might be summarized thus:

> Established religion, in any age, perpetuates outworn dogmas, no longer understood and no longer having any developmental value. Even this fossilized ritual can, nevertheless, be the vehicle through which knowledge is saved from oblivion.
>
> The devotees of religion are conditioned by both fears and promises of reward to carrying out the religion's moral precepts and to accepting personal suffering. This can lead people to goodness, to self-sacrifice and to humility but it cannot take them to the Kingdom of Heaven.
>
> During the dark ages which sometimes follow wars, learning is preserved in a Church though it may not be understood. Eventually this knowledge leaks back to the outside world and science is thereby enabled to begin again. Science, however, always develops in conflict with religion and is then used by temporal powers for materialistic ends.

Since neither Church nor Science can change man's nature, the result must always be the destruction, with the aid of scientific knowledge, of the civilization that gained it.

During this recurring and self-perpetuating process, the spirit of God never deserts mankind. But it does not truly manifest either in the followers of religion or the followers of science. It is manifested in and transmitted by certain rare individuals whom the world considers least worthy.

If fiction like "Leibovitz" and the message it contains is "spin-off" from a deliberately arranged contact with a possible future, the warning is very clear. If it were possible to see similar contact with a remote past and find a similar warning the message would be doubly underscored.

It will be remembered that Muhiyuddin, the Teacher of Andalusia, obtained information by direct perception from a discarnate entity beside the Black Stone at Mecca. It stated that although Adam was the father of the human race, "thirty other worlds preceded him".

The appearance of both the Wandering Jew and the Poet Fool in fiction written today and located in the future suggests the endurance and vitality of the ideas which these figures embody.

The Wandering Jew legend appears superficially to be an essentially Christian idea but it can be found, in some of its many forms, antedating the Christian era by many centuries. Even in its Christian form, the Jew is not always a Jew. In some legends he is a Roman. He appears also as Malchus, who lost his ear to Simon Peter's sword. He has also been Judas, Athanasius, Melmoth and Theudas. He is Zerib Bar Elia (Elijah) and Michob Ader (the identity used by O. Henry in his famous tale). One of his names is Lakedion or Laquedem which looks very like *L'kodem* the "ancient one", i.e., humanity.[6]

The Wandering Jew was a well-known idea in the East at the end of the first Christian millennium, throughout Europe in the Middle Ages and through the agency of Goethe, Shelley, Hans Christian Andersen and modern writers like Viereck and Eldridge has been appearing all over the world ever since.

[6] Joseph Gaer, *The Legend of the Wandering Jew*, New American Library, New York, 1961.

Even in some conjectured Dark Age of the future he is to be seen pursuing his hopeless search in Leibovitz Abbey.

If the activities of a "School" involve the implanting of certain concepts at selected times and places, always in a form acceptable to the time, we may suspect that the Wandering Jew is one such concept.

Joseph Gaer in his *Legend of the Wandering Jew* draws the elements of the legend together from many sources.

Scriptural references led the Christians of the first millenium to believe that one of the signs of the Second Coming of Christ would be the appearance of "the Anti-Christ". As AD 1000 approached, a number of irreverent opportunists appeared in Palestine and elsewhere "denying the Father and the Son" and claiming to be the Anti-Christ. They were generously prepared to accept from Christians the personal property they wanted to unload against the Day of Judgment. When AD 1000 came and went without the world ending, these various Anti-Christs in the Near East became blurred into a composite memory. The Anti-Christ passed into the collective memory in the symbol of a man who could be tall, short, fat, lean, wealthy, poor, apostate and devout all at the same time.

When the First Crusade reached Jerusalem the Anti-Christ had become the Wandering Jew and was chiefly identified with Malchus. The Crusaders returned home with a Wandering Jew corpus, the common denominator of which was a man who did not die but who was doomed to wander till Judgment Day.

Two hundred years later the idea was greatly authenticated during an ecclesiastical conference in St. Albans Abbey. One of the delegates was the Archbishop of Armenia whose talent as a spinner of yarns captivated the delegates. He claimed to have seen Noah's Ark perched on an Armenian mountain, and to have met Joseph Cartaphilus, the Wandering Jew.

Joseph, who had been a porter in the hall of Pilate, had then been wandering for twelve centuries. He had spitefully chided Jesus to hurry on to his crucifixion. For this action he had been cursed to wander the earth, tormented by remorse ever since. "Joseph", the Bishop told the St. Albans conference, "places his hope of salvation on the fact that *he sinned through ignorance*."

This story was preserved in the records of St. Albans and a surviving manuscript dates from 1250.[7]

The legend spread back from Britain to the Continent, but the "Beloved of God", Cartaphilus, now came to be known as Buttadeus ("Smiter of God"), a remarkable example of a fundamental idea being represented by the play of opposites.

The "Smiter of God" suggests that the Jew is now identified with one of Pilate's officers (John 18:22, 23) who struck Jesus for not being sufficiently servile to Pilate during the interrogation.

The story gets a new impetus three hundred years later. About 1510, a poor weaver in Bohemia called Kokot, finds a frail old man at his door late at night. He gives him shelter and learns that the old man, "his eyes pools of sorrow", is the Wandering Jew.

The old man reveals that he had once before called at this same house and had been received with similar hospitality by Kokot's grandfather. He mentions a legend in Kokot's family about treasure and reveals that it was he, the Wandering Jew, who helped Kokot's grandfather to bury it. He shows Kokot where to find it and the latter, wild with excitement, runs up and down the street showing all his neighbours his new-found gold. But when he gets back to the cottage, Joseph has disappeared.

The story in this form has many significant elements reminiscent of Sufi teaching material.

About 1550 the Wandering Jew turns up in the presence of Cornelius Agrippa who is himself a figure representative of a secret tradition. Agrippa of Nettesheim is deeply religious, but is also reputed to be a magician. He has access to legendary treasures but dies (1535) in abject poverty. He has spent his life (like Paracelsus and the Wandering Jew himself) in wandering. In a patriarchal society he is a feminist.

Joseph persuades Agrippa to exercise clairvoyance and show him, in a magic mirror, scenes from his boyhood. The sight of a Rabbi's daughter whom Joseph had loved fifteen hundred years ago is too much for him and the old Jew runs from Agrippa's house in renewed torment of soul.

Still in the 16th century, the Wandering Jew appears to a Moslem General, Fadilah, who is offering a prayer of thanks-

[7] Gaer, op. cit.

giving in his tent after the Battle of Elvan. Fadilah describes Joseph as "looking like a very old Dervish". The legend was collected a century ago by Sabine Baring Gould.

The Wandering Jew tells Fadilah that he is really the Prophet Elijah (Zerib bar Elia) and gives Fadilah an account of the external conditions which will immediately precede the Second Coming of Christ.

Here the Jew is linked to a long pre-Christian Hebraic legend of the immortal prophet Elijah who, like Arthur in our own era, "was taken to be in the body till the end".

In Mohammedan legend Elijah is the same as Khidr, the mysterious "Green One" who appears in the flesh at critical moments to guide and safeguard the worthy.

In English chivalry, the Garter Order is believed to have sprung from the Khidr Order in the East. The Khidr is also identified in some European traditions with the Count of Saint-Germain – who is also immortal. 16th-century German versions of the Wandering Jew legend say that the Old One eats and drinks practically nothing, a circumstance noted over and over again in European appearances of Saint-Germain.

Thus an ancient Hebraic tradition, Mohammedan lore, the Arthurian idea, English chivalry and the occultist father-figure Germain, appear to be variations and mutations of a single archetype.

According to Fariduddin Attar, the Khidr or Khizr is the "guardian of the source of the waters of immortality" and Sir Richard Burton (who was an initiated Sufi) says Khidr represents the completed Sufi.

The Wandering Jew legend in Slavonic countries has a peculiar element. There the Jew's wanderings involve him in a mission to preach and exemplify the brotherhood of man. He appears only to people at the point of greatest despair, or at the point of suicide. He convinces them of the need to live out their fate, whatever the cost.

A very close affinity is to be seen between this aspect of the Wandering Jew and Sufic teaching material about the Khidr. Here is one example. It is taken from a compilation of legendary Sufic teaching stories.[8]

---

[8] Idries Shah, *The Way of the Sufi*, Cape, London, 1968, pp. 161–162.

Khidr is the "unseen guide" of the Sufis, and it is he who is believed to be the anonymous Guide to Moses in the Koran. This "Green One" is often referred to as "the Jew" and he has been equated in legend with such figures as St. George and Elijah. This tale – or report – is characteristic of the super-normal functions attributed to Khidr, both in folklore and among the dervish teachers.

"Once, while standing on the banks of the Oxus river, I saw a man fall in. Another man, in the clothes of a dervish, came running to help him, only to be dragged into the water himself. Suddenly I saw a third man, dressed in a robe of shimmering, luminous green, hurl himself into the river. But as he struck the surface, his form seemed to change; he was no longer a man, but a log. The other two men managed to cling to this, and together they worked it towards the bank.

"Hardly able to believe what I was seeing, I followed at a distance, using the bushes that grew there as cover. The men drew themselves panting on the bank; the log floated away. I watched it until, out of sight of the others, it drifted to the side, and the green-robed man, soaked and sodden, dragged himself ashore. The water began to stream from him; before I reached him he was almost dry.

"I threw myself on the ground in front of him, crying: 'You must be the Presence Khidr, the Green One, Master of the Saints. Bless me, for I would attain.' I was afraid to touch his robe, because it seemed to be of green fire.

"He said: 'You have seen too much. Understand that I come from another world and am, without their knowing it, protecting those who have service to perform. You may have been a disciple of Sayed Imdadullah, but you are not mature enough to know what we are doing for the sake of God.'

"When I looked up, he was gone, and all I could hear was a rushing sound in the air.

"After coming back from Khotan, I saw the same man. He was lying on a straw mattress in a rest-house near Peshawar. I said to myself: 'If I was too raw the last time, this time I'll be mature.'

"I took hold of his robe, which was a very common one – though under it I thought I saw something glow green.

"'You may be Khidr,' I said to him, 'but I have to know how an apparently ordinary man like you performs these wonders ... and why. Explain your craft to me, so that I can practise it too.'

"He laughed. 'You're impetuous, my friend! The last time you were too headstrong – and now you're still to headstrong. Go on, tell everyone you meet that you've seen Khidr Elias; they'll put you in the madhouse, and the more you protest you're right, the more heavily they'll chain you.'

"Then he took out a small stone. I stared at it – and found myself paralysed, turned to stone, until he had picked up his saddle-bags and walked away.

"When I tell this story, people either laugh or, thinking me a story-teller, give me presents."

The Wandering Jew and Khidr may be regarded as opposite sides of the same coin. Both have prototype origins in early race-memories.

On one side of the coin is Cain, who was cursed for his sin and obliged to wander forever. Strangely enough, some medieval legends say the Wandering Jew carries a curse-mark on his forehead. Cain/Cartaphilus is the composite symbol of man condemned to a certain kind of immortality connected with recurrence. *His fate is the consequence of his sin.*

On the other side of the coin is Enoch/Elijah/Khidr. This is the composite symbol of the man who has won true immortality. *His fate is the reward for his merits.*

In Rabbinical tradition, Enoch's arrival in heaven is associated with a cosmic storm. Elijah, who "did not taste of death", "went up by a whirlwind to heaven".

In medieval Europe, the appearance of the Wandering Jew was accompanied by terrifying storms.

Rabbinical traditions assert that after his translation in the flesh to heavenly state, Elijah remains in touch with the earth and visits those in extremity of distress to comfort them. Here there would seem to be a clear overlap with Khidr legends. The *Jewish Encyclopedia* is quite explicit. "Elijah the Prophet became the prototype of the Wandering Jew."

Rabbinical tradition does not, however, have only one Wandering Jew. It has thirty-six and these thirty-six are only the earthly counterparts of a heavenly band of the same number. Yet the thirty-six figures of Rabbinical legend are never seen separately but appear on earth as a single figure. This would seem to be a variation of the Moslem concept of the Abdals already mentioned.

The astonishing vitality of the Wandering Jew idea is shown by the fact that it has found a new vehicle within the last century and a half – the Mormon religion.

According to Mormon ideas, a righteous man named Lehi emigrated with his family from the Middle East to South

America around 600 BC. Some of his descendents, the Lamanites, were the ancestors of the Red Indians. Others, the Nephites, gave rise to the righteous white races.

After the crucifixion, Jesus appeared in South America to the Nephites, three of whom were chosen to receive special spiritual gifts with the words: "And ye shall never endure the pain of death: but when I come in my glory ye shall be changed in the twinkling of an eye from mortality to immortality."

Like the Wandering Jew, the Three Nephites have been reported all through American history ever since. Also, like the Rabbinical legend of the Wandering Jew, the Three Nephites never appear separately, but always as a single individual.

This individual is an old white-haired man dressed in ancient clothes! Joseph Smith, to whom, Mormons believe, the *Book of Mormon* was revealed, may have known of the Wandering Jew legend. Certainly many of his German and English converts at Utah must have done.

* * *

We have looked at many strange figures and some even stranger stories. Some appear to refer to the same idea; others to an entirely opposite idea. Could they be obverse and reverse of a single concept? Could this have been implanted deliberately in the human subconscious?

It seems that when cultures rise and fall, their arts and their literatures do likewise. But there is something which has a higher factor of survival. Fables outlive fact. Legends penetrate where logic perishes. Folklore, myth and legend transcend the fluctuations of the historical process. It is as though a myth carries such a penetrating energy that it can leap the gap between cultures – a carrier-wave that unites the ceaseless and separate generations.

If there are those whose psychology is superhuman and whose present moment spans many generations of men, it seems likely that they will employ a medium with a comparable time-scale. Perhaps they use myth to make the mankind-child *feel* what he does not yet understand – or to recall what he once knew.

The Jew/Khidr/Enoch/Elijah composite, for all its seeming diversification, carries an integral subconscious content.

Myth personifies abstract ideas. The Wandering Jew is the personification of mankind. Once upon a time he sinned. Though he sinned in ignorance he sinned wilfully. As a result he is "cursed". He is condemned to make repeated appearances on the temporal scene, searching for a means to undo the past.

The Jew is not one man but many. He is thin, fat, short, tall, devout and irreverent. He is mankind. In this corporate sense he is immortal.

The Messiah personifies the concept of redemption. The Wandering Jew is searching for the Messiah, for redemption which is a means of altering the past. He does not understand that while he searches for it on his own terms he can never find it.

Enoch/Elijah/Khidr/Germain personify the man who has found what the Wandering Jew is looking for. He is not condemned to immortality against his will. He has been rewarded with the immortality he has earned and he uses it to help the evolutionary process on the earth. Yet in a sense his immortality, too, is corporate for he, also, is one-in-many. Yet the many – the Rabbinical Thirty-Six, the Mohammedan Abdals and the multiple Nephites – *appear and act as one*.

The monks of Leibovitz Monastery superstitiously preserve documents they do not understand because of some subconscious imperative. One day, miraculously, they produce light.

Humanity cherishes the myths it does not understand. One day perhaps . . .

CHAPTER THIRTEEN

THE EXECUTIVE OF THE PEOPLE OF THE SECRET

The time has come to sum up.

To those who claim logic as the highest principle, the material we have collected will be wholly unconvincing. It will appear no more than special pleading and proof by selected instances.

Yet logic at its limits can demonstrate no more than the consistency or otherwise of a closed system. Plato's firelit cave is a closed system and its prisoners find logic adequate to explain all that they experience. No logic can trigger off the intuitive leap which would suggest to them the existence of a reality greater than their world of flickering shadows. And shadows may be thrown by neon lights no less than by cave fires.

To those predisposed to occultism, all that we have tried to bring forward will probably confirm existing subjective preferences. It may also, most regrettably, provide material for developing others.

But there may be readers less decisively committed; readers prepared to try and extrapolate from logic.

They may feel that the material collected here suggests a wholly unsuspected viewpoint; a framework within which the scientist and the priest may sit in peace together: a universe in which freewill and determinism can coexist.

With rashness both unpardonable and unavoidable we suggest the following tentative conclusions.

History is not the equilibrant of chance and hazard. It does not just happen. The script for the long human story was written by intelligences much greater than man's own.

Certain gains and goals for mankind – and for the biosphere of Earth – must be attained within certain intervals of Earth time. These gains are essential for the balance and growth of the solar system of which the Earth is a part. The solar system may itself be subject to a similar pressure in the interest of the galaxy of which it is a part.

The direction, speed and end of this process is "the Will of God".

The Will of God is the aspiration of Divinity that the universal process shall proceed in a certain way to a certain end while leaving open the possibility that it may elect to proceed quite otherwise to quite else.

Very high intelligences direct the evolution of the universe in an attempt to ensure that the Divine aspiration shall be realized.

These intelligences are coercive in proportion as their material is unconscious. They are persuasive in proportion as their material is conscious.

The universe is a gradient of consciousness and on this gradient the earth occupies a low level. Its highest raw material is mankind. Mankind is collectively unconscious of the evolutionary process of which he is a part and he is subject therefore to determinism approaching a hundred per cent.

Even so, the direction imposed on mankind is only relatively coercive. Because of the high energies which are potential in him, man may not be compulsively directed. Means have to be employed which do not outrage the integrity of his potential nature.

This is achieved by arranging a bias in favour of those situations which contain developmental possibilities and by limiting man's *opportunities* for making involutionary choices.

About this line there may be marginal interplay of determinism and free will.

On the "present moment" of a man or a generation of men these pressures may appear both random and hostile.

Responsibility for this process on Earth lies with an Intelligence which has been called The Hidden Directorate. This may correspond to the level symbolized in occult legend as an Individual (e.g., "The Regent" or "The Ancient of Days", etc.). It is to be equated either with Demi-Urgic level or with the level immediately below.

No grounds exist for an opinion as to whether this Intelligence is, in any sense, comprehensible to man, a single or a composite Intelligence, or whether it is discarnate or corporeal.

Below this level, certain members of ordinary humanity, in whom qualitative changes have taken place, are in touch with the Directorate and may at intervals share its consciousness.

This group of advanced human individuals is what has been referred to as the Hidden Executive. It is the reality behind all legends of "masters" and "initiates" from earliest historical times to the present.

There may be several Centres on earth from which the Executive operates, corresponding to the division of responsibility for humanity assigned before the Withdrawal of 12,000 years ago.

One such Centre is – or was – in Afghanistan and corresponds to the legend of the Markaz ("Powerhouse"). There may be other Centres corresponding to various ethnic groups.

The Executive works to implement the overall plan of the Directorate. This activity is at extra-sensory level.

The Executive also operates at the level of ordinary life through a descending order of initiated subordinates. These take part in the ordinary life of nations and are almost wholly, but not quite, unsuspected. *These are the Secret People.*

Those active within ordinary life have been known by many names at various periods of history – and pre-history. Those under a chain of command from the Afghanistan Centre have been known as Sufis.

Side by side with action on humanity-in-the-mass, the Executive and its subordinates are concerned with local attempts to raise the conscious level of individual men exceptionally.

Such specially selected ordinary individuals may aspire to qualify for participation in the work of the Executive. The process by which they may so qualify is the Magnum Opus – the "Great Work". This is equivalent to a vertical ascent to a higher level as opposed to a gradual rise with the evolutionary tide.

Opportunities through which ordinary men who have "begun to suspect" may qualify to enlist in The Great Work are never wholly absent at any time in history, but in terms of the

Earth's time-scale, they occur irregularly. Such occasions are related to extra-terrestrial events and these events are not at the discretion even of the Directorate.

When "the solar wind blows", a major operation of soul-making is begun by the Directorate. As a result, a relatively large number of human individuals may complete a significant part of The Great Work in a single generation. A small number may reach completion. Both categories will serve the evolutionary process of mankind thereafter, but their post-mortem situations may be different.

Knowledge of such matters has never at any time in history been absent, but it has always been available in the form of allegory, never explicitly. Many of the Greek myths are allegorical descriptions of sequences in the Magnum Opus. In recent historical times, corresponding to the development of intellect, suggestions have become increasingly explicit. They have probably never been more explicit that at the present time. This may suggest that the end of a major era is envisaged.

There are indications that an "Occasion" is currently developing and that its possibilities are being focused chiefly in the West. It is not possible to conjecture whether this is a major or a relatively minor event. It seems safe to assert that it exists.

If this is so, and if it is true that information about these matters is now explicit, it may be objected that it is hardly explicit enough to indicate a line of action to those who might be ready to respond.

It may be that matters will never be more explicit than they are and that a successful search for a Source is – and always has been – the minimum price of admission.

Appendix A

SOME IMPORTANT FIGURES IN THE SUFI TRADITION

Seventh Century

MOHAMMED (567–632) and some of his companions, including his father-in-law ABU BAKR and his son-in-law ALI.

SALMAN THE PERSIAN originally a Zoroastrian sought the faith and practice of the Hanifs. Attached himself to Christian teachers, one of whom when dying told him to journey south. After being captured and sold into slavery, Salman finally joined Mohammed's companions at Mecca.

Mohammed died in 632. In the same year forty-five individuals from Mecca and an equal number from Medina took an oath of fraternity and fidelity and chose the name *Sufi*. Mohammed's successor, Abu Bakr, and Ali founded special assemblies at which Sufi exercises were held.

UWAYS EL QARNI (d.657) Sufi master living in Arabia at the time of Mohammed, but never met the Prophet. Founded first austere Sufi order.

Eighth Century

JAFAR SADIQ (700–765) Sufi teacher, considered by Fatimites as Sixth Imam.

JABIR IBN-HAYYAN known in the West as GEBER (721–776) pupil of Jafar Sadiq. Was link between ancient alchemists of Egypt and Greece and those of the Middle Ages.

ABU HANIFA founder of one of the great Islamic schools of law.

DAVID OF TAI (d. 781) studied under Abu Hanifa.

MAARUF KARKHI (d. 815) pupil of David of Tai, thus "son" of David. The Freemason's "Solomon the King, Son of David" has been equated with him. Founded Sufi fraternity called The Builders. Original builders were Abd al-Malik's architects who built the Dome of the Rock in Jerusalem at end of 7th century.

ABU EL-ATAHIYYA (748–826) a potter in Baghdad at the time of the Caliph Haroun al-Rashid. Was a contemplative and left a collection of mystical verse. Belonged to Aniza tribe, whose badge was a goat.

After his death, his disciples, called the Wise Ones, adopted torch between goat's horns as symbol of illumination. Cult of the Revellers can be traced to el-Atahiyya. Group from his school later migrated to Spain.

RABIA EL-ADAWIA (d. 802) Famous woman Sufi.

Ninth Century

THUBAN ABULFAIZ DHU'L NUN (d. 860) the Egyptian, called "King or Lord of the Fish". Thought to have been a black Nubian. "Black" also used for Egyptian (from colour of the soil) and for "Knowledge" (from *fehm* which means "black" and "knowledge"). Was third in teaching succession after Daud of Tai and Maaruf Karkhi. The Masonic Pillar of the Temple "Boaz" may be "Albuazz" a form of Dhu'l Nun's name Abulfaiz. Founded the Malamati order of Sufis, which has similarities with Freemasony.

HUSSEIN IBN MANSUR EL-HALLAJ (858–922) "the Wool Carder" spoke the Sufi secret "I am the Truth" and was dismembered as a heretic by the inquisition of Caliph el-Muqtadir. Prayed for mercy for his murderers just before he died. Had emphasised the importance of Jesus as a Sufi teacher. Hallaj the "murdered man" of Freemasonry.

BAYAZID EL-BISTAMI (d. 875) a classical Sufi Master. Sufi circle called the *fehmia* (The Perceivers) traces its philosophical pedigree to him.

JUNAID OF BAGHDAD (d. 910) one of the first classical Sufi authors.

Tenth Century

ABU-ISHAK CHISTI the Syrian. A descendant of Mohammed, of the Hashemite family. At Chist in Khorasan founded the Chisti Order, an offshoot of the line of the Masters. Specialized in the use of music and exercise. His followers used to enter a town and play a tune with flute and drum to gather people before reciting a legend or tale. This was the origin of the Western jester.

AL-FARABI known to the West as ALFARABIUS. A Sufi philosopher and Neo-Platonist, forerunner of Avicenna.

IBN MASARRAH OF CÓRDOBA (883–931) founded the Córdoba illuminist school, which had a profound influence on the West. From him the love theme came into western literature.

IKWAN EL SAFA (*Brethren of Sincerity*) a secret group, whose object was to make known the whole body of knowledge of the time. Published fifty-two treatises at Basra in 980.

Eleventh Century

EL-GHAZALI known in the West as ALGAZEL (1058–1111) "the

Spinner". Was a Persian of Meshed, orphaned at an early age and brought up by Sufis. Reconciled the Koran with rationalist philosophy and was called the "Proof of Islam". Wrote *The Destruction of the Philosophers*, *The Alchemy of Happiness* and *The Niche for Lights*.

ALI EL-HUJWIRI (d. 1063) born in Ghazna (Afghanistan), settled in India. His task was to establish the claim that Sufism was consistent with the principles of Islam. Was known in India as Data Ganj Baksh. Wrote *The Revelation of the Veiled*, the first book in Persian on Sufism.

NIZAMI Vizier of Baghdad. Founded the great college of Baghdad, where Omar Khayyam was taught. Wrote *The Treasury of Mysteries* and *The Story of Alexander*.

OMAR KHAYYAM Astronomer and poet. Wrote the Rubaiyat. Was a friend of Nizami, said to have "been to school" with the Great Assassin. Lived at Nishapur.

EL-TUGHRAI a writer at the time of Omar Khayyam.

IBN-SINA THE BOKHARAN (980–1037) known in the West as AVICENNA. Persian philosopher, physician and scientist. Wrote a *Canon of Medicine*, first translated in the 12th century by Gerard of Cremona and used as a text book in European universities for centuries. Wrote the *Ash-Shifa* (the Recovery, i.e. of the Soul, from Error) containing books on logic, metaphysics and natural sciences, including meteorology, zoology, psychology and physics, which was translated into Latin in the 12th and 13th centuries. His *Book of Equitable Judgment*, in which he distinguished his philosophy from that of the Christian philosophers of Baghdad, was lost during the pillage of Isfahan in 1034.

SOLOMON BEN GABIROL (1021–1058) known in the West as AVICEBRON. Was a Jewish Sufic sage of the Córdoba school, founded by Ibn Masarrah. Wrote in Arabic *The Fount of Life*. The Franciscans accepted his teaching from a Latin translation a century later. Explained the Cabbala to philosophers after its appearance in Europe.

EL MAJRITI (d. 1066) astronomer, who brought the Encyclopaedia of the Brethren of Sincerity to Spain.

EL KARMANI of Córdoba. Disciple of El Majriti.

Twelfth century

ZIYAUDDIN NAJIB SUHRAWARDI (d. 1167) follower of Junaid. Founded the Suhrawardi order. Wrote *The Observances of the Disciples*.

HAKIM SANAI OF AFGHANISTAN the earliest Afghan teacher to use the love motif in Sufism. Rumi acknowledged him as one of his inspirations. Wrote Dervish songs and *The Walled Garden of Truth*.

ABU BAKR IBN TUFAIL known in the West as ABUBACER. Physician, philosopher and finally Vizier at the court of Granada. Wrote *Hayy ibn-Yaqzan*, the prototype of Robinson Crusoe, based on a story by Avicenna.

ABDUL-QADIR GILANI (1077–1166) born at Nif, South of the Caspian. Used terminology similar to that of the later European Rosicrucians. Was called the "Rose of Baghdad". Founded the Qadiri Order, which was formed around the idea of the Rose, *ward*, standing for *wird* (dervish exercise). Specialized in the "Science of States".

FARIDUDDIN ATTAR THE CHEMIST (1150–1229) illuminate and Sufi author. Born near Nishapur. Studied under Sheikh Ruknuddin, then left him and wandered to Mecca and elsewhere. Wrote *The Memoirs of Friends*, a collection of the lives of historical Sufis and the *Mantiq ut-Tair* (Parliament of the Birds) which influenced the Roman de la Rose and Chaucer. He had an initiatory order with which the Order of the Garter, founded a hundred years later, showed parallels. Was killed by the Mongols.

IBN EL-ARABI (b. 1164) the Murcian. His father was in touch with Abdul-Qadir Jilani. Studied law and Islamic theology at Lisbon, the Koran at Seville and jurisprudence under Sheikh el-Sharrat at Córdoba. Spent his free time with the Sufis and wrote poetry. His mission to create Sufi literature and cause it to be studied, so that people might enter into the spirit of Sufism. Used the 'scatter' method. Author of *The Bezels of Wisdom* and *The Interpreter of Desires*.

IBN-RUSHD OF CÓRDOBA (1126–1198) known as AVERROËS. Philosopher and writer on Arabic law, philosophy, astronomy and medicine. Author of a monograph on music, which shows influence of the Brethren of Sincerity. In *The Incoherence of the Incoherence*, defended Neoplatonic and Aristotelian philosophy against el-Ghazali's *Incoherence of the Philosphers*. El-Ghazali and Averroës together constitute a double Sufic current (action and reaction). As Rumi said, "It is necessary to note that opposite things work together, even though nominally opposed." Averroës' chief work: commentaries on Aristotle. Also wrote a handbook of medicine, translated into Latin in 1255 and a commentary on Avicenna's poem on medicine, translated 1280. A large number of his philosophical works translated into Latin, mainly by Michael Scot between 1217 and 1230. Accepted as a commentator on Aristotle at Paris and Oxford from about 1230. Albertus Magnus, Adam of Buckfastleigh and Thomas Aquinas regularly consulted his commentaries. Was a pupil of Ibn Tufail. Anticipated Jung in expounding a theory of the collective unconscious.

SUHRAWARDI THE MURDERED (1154–1191) Easterner, domiciled in Aleppo. Was killed by order of the Orthodox, whose pressure Saladin's nephew was unable to resist. Wrote *The Wisdom of*

Illumination stating that Illuminism was the science of Light and was identical with the inner teaching of all the ancients, Greeks, Egyptians and Persians.

Thirteenth Century

FARIDUDDIN SHAKARGANJ (Father Farid of the Sweet Treasure) (d. 1265) nobleman of Afghanistan of the Chisti school. Died in India, where his tomb is revered by people of all faiths. His functions were healing and music.

SHEIKH SHAHABUDIN MOHAMMED SUHRAWARDI (1145–1235) nephew and disciple of Ziyauddin Najib Suhrawardi, the founder of the Suhrawardi Order. Chief Sufi teacher in Baghdad. Author of *The Gifts of Deep Knowledge*.

SAYED NURUDIN OF GHAZNA (Afghanistan) disciple of Shahabudin Suhrawardi. Took the Suhrawardi teaching to India, where King Altamash made him the highest ecclesiastical dignitary of the state.

NAJMUDDIN KUBRA (d. 1221) called the 'Pillar of the Age'. Also a disciple of Suhrawardi. Founded the Kubravi Order. Worked miracles and had an uncanny influence over animals by means of thought projection. Probably a connection between him and St. Francis of Assisi. Members of his Order called the Greater Brothers. Was killed on the battlefield by the Mongols.

SAADI OF SHIRAZ (1184–1291) educated in Baghdad under Shahabudin Suhrawardi. Friend of Najmuddin Kubra. Author of the *Gulistan* (Rose Garden) and the *Bustan* (Orchard). Writings of his group provided subjects for the *Gesta Romanorum*. Translations of his works from 17th century on influenced German literature. Affiliate of the order of the Masters.

SAYID KHIDR RUMI KHAPRADARI (The Cupbearer) associate of the father of Jalaluddin Rumi, of Shahabudin Suhrawardi, Fariduddin Shakarganj and Shah Madar.

SHAH MADAR taught the essential unity of all religions, especially the esoteric way of Christianity and Islam.

NAJMUDDIN GWATH-ED-DAHAR QALANDAR studied under Nizamuddin Alia of Delhi, who sent him about 1232 to study under Khidr Rumi. Made a teaching journey to England.

JALALUDDIN RUMI (1207–1273) born in Bactria at Balkh, fled with his father from the Mongols to Baghdad and finally to Rum. Founded the Mevlevi Order of Whirling Dervishes. Author of the *Mathnavi-i-Manavi*, *Fihi ma fihi* and *The Diwan of Shams of Tabriz*. Considerable influence on the West, greater in recent years, when most of his works have been translated from Persian into western languages.

Fourteenth Century

MAHMUD SHABISTARI Persian sage. Author of *The Secret Garden* (1319).
NAJMUDDIN BABA son or successor of Najmuddin Gwath-ed-Dahar Qalandar. "Followed his father's footsteps" from India to China and England in 1338.
HAJI BEKTASH blessed the Janissaries, the militia raised in 1326 by Sultan Orchan and recruited from Christians. Cut the sleeve of his fur mantle and gave it to the captain, who put it on his head. This was the origin of the fur cap worn by the Janissaries.
KHOJA SHAMSUDDIN HAFIZ (d. 1389) Persian poet, who wrote of love, wine, nightingales and flowers. Author of *The Interpreter of the Secrets, The Speech of the Invisible* and a collection of poems called *The Divan*. A translation of the latter by von Hammer-Purgstall influenced Goethe.
BAHAUDDIN NAQSHBAND (d. 1389) great teacher of the Dervish school called *Khwajagan* (the Masters) in Central Asia, which influenced the development of the Indian and Turkish empires. After his time it became known as the Naqshbandi Chain, the "Designers" or "Masters of the Design". Bahauddin spent seven years as a courtier, seven looking after animals and seven in road-building. Is credited with having returned to the original principles and practices of Sufism.

Fifteenth Century

HAKIM JAMI (1414–1492) disciple of Sadedin Kashgai, head of the Naqshbandis, whom he succeeded as the director of the Herat area of Afghanistan. In his *Alexandrian Book of Wisdom* he showed that the Sufi esoteric transmission link of the Khwajagan (Masters) was the same as that used by western mystical writers. Named as teachers in the Sufi transmission, Plato, Hippocrates, Pythagoras and Hermes Trismegistos. Author of *The Abode of Spring, The Romance of Salaman and Absal* and *The Epic of Joseph and Zuleika*, which had an influence on the West.
SHEIKH ABDULLAH SHATTAR Sufi teacher. Visited India, wandering from one monastery to another, making known the Shattari method (the Rapidness) derived from Bahauddin Naqshband.

Appendix B

The Khwajagan

Tradition asserts that there is an inner circle within the Sufic membership which preserves the most vital secrets of the techniques of inner development and also the secrets of the most effective methods of manipulating environment for development purposes. This tradition is called the Khwajagan (Persian: "Masters").

The succession of individual leaders within this tradition is known and had been included in a paper by a Turkish writer, Hasan L. Shushud. The paper was translated in 1969 by J. G. Bennett and published in the journal *Systematics*, Vol. 6, No. 4.

A summary of this is now given with permission.

The Khwajagan

Tradition asserts that for thousands of years there has been an "Inner Circle of Humanity" capable of thinking in terms of millennia and possessing knowledge and powers of a high order. Its members intervene from time to time in human affairs. They do this, not as leaders or teachers of mankind, but unobtrusively by introducing certain ideas and techniques. This intervention works in such a way as to rectify deviations from the predestined course of human history. This inner circle, it is claimed, concentrates its activities in those areas and at those times when the situation is critical for mankind.

The period AD 950–1450 is said to have been one such time. Then hordes from Central Asia poured into the decaying empires of China, India, Baghdad, Byzantium and Rome. At the centre of this disturbance an organization appeared called the Khwajagan. Its members were mostly Turks or Persians and their main centres were in Bokhara, Samarkand, Balkh, Herat and the Hindu Kush region.

This area had a long prior history of spiritual activity, Zoroaster (600 BC) spent most of his life in Balkh, and Salman the Persian, one of the earliest converts from the Magian religion who became a Companion of Mohammed, was from the same area. Arithmetic was probably founded in this region. El-Harmezi (AD 844) made significant advances in algebra and Abu-Masher of Balkh (died 866) influenced the development of astronomy in the West (through translations by Adelard of Bath).

The first head of the Khwajagan was *Yusuf Hamadani* (1048–1140) who was known as the Kutb ul Evliyya or "Axis of the Saints".

As a boy he had studied at Baghdad under *Abu Ishak Farih*, a follower of the *Imam Abu Hanifa*. He then travelled for a time studying under various learned men, but then rejected all study and devoted himself to prayer, asceticism and the inner struggle with his own nature. This period over, he placed himself under the direction of the Sheikh *Abu Ali Farmidi*. Farmidi was the teacher of *El-Ghazali* and was in the direct line of spiritual descent from *Bayazid Bistami, Imam Riza* and other early Sufi saints.

Before he was thirty, Yusuf Hamadani was reputed to be a master of spiritual science. He then gathered round him a few selected pupils and it was these who became the founder members of the Khwajagan.

Hamadani, from his own insights, introduced techniques new to Sufi practice – techniques which were not to become generally available, if at all, until the Mongol invasion had partly expended its force in the second half of the 13th century. These techniques included the Halka or group and the use of the Sohbat or "conversation" as vehicles for the transmission of the spiritual force of *baraka*. Hamadani instructed a special group of eleven men in these techniques and also perfected a method of communicating without words.

Hamadani's first successor was *Abdullah Berki of Khwarizm* (d. 1160) a mystic with extraordinary spiritual powers who passed his own secrets to his followers in turn. The second successor was *Hasan Andaki*, one of the original eleven initiated by Hamadani.

Andaki's successor was *Ahmed Yasavi* (1042–1166?) from Yasi in Eastern Turkestan (now Sinkiang). He had studied alchemy there under *Baba Arslan* who, when he was dying, told Yasavi to go to Bokhara, a thousand miles to the west and there enter the service of Hamadani. Later Yasavi was to succeed Hasan Andaki and become fourth leader of the Khwajagan.

Yasavi did not hold the office for long. He received an inner indication that he should return to Turkestan and he made over his charge to *Abdul Khaliq Gujduvani*. On his return to Eastern Turkestan Yasavi founded the Yasiwiyya Dervish Order.

It is said that Order survives to the present day, operating in the Gobi Desert area to transmit the spiritual science of the Khwajagan.

The Yasiwiyya Order makes use of ritual movements and dances accompanied by music called the *Salna*. This, if rightly understood, enables the student to submit his mind to the Supreme Intelligence and to attain mastery of his own body.

Gujduvani was thus the fourth successor of Yusuf Hamadani, founder of the Khwajagan, but legends assert that he was independently initiated by the Khidr himself. It is said that he learned the technique known as The Prayer of the Heart (Zikr-i-Qalbi) directly from Khidr. There may, however, have been a parallel transmission of this technique through the mantras practised by the Buddhist monks of the Hindu Kush.

Gujduvani formulated the precepts of the Khwajagan in eight succinct rules (Essence of the Teaching of the Masters) and was also the author of Precepts for Living.

Gujduvani died in 1190 and was succeeded by *Ahmed Sadik of Bokhara* who took over at a time of greatest danger for the Sufic mission. When Jenghis Khan was proclaimed Grand Khan of all the Mongols in 1206, Sadik proceeded to transfer the Inner Circle of the Master to Bokhara where it remained for centuries. Three lines of defence were prepared against the interruption of Sufic activity which would result from the Mongol invasions.

1. Some Sufis emigrated.
2. Some remained and deliberately allowed themselves to be of assistance to the new régime.
3. Some remained and preserved their activity by disguising its outward form.

Among those who emigrated was the father of *Jalaluddin Rumi*. He was a theologian and mystic of the "Western School", a follower of *Ibn el-Arabi*. Rumi senior, in face of the Mongol peril, left his home in Balkh and fled with his son to Baghdad, then to Damascus and finally to Konya. Another emigrant of the same school was *Nijemeddin Daya*, who also reached Konya which was to become a centre of spiritual activity till the 20th century.

Among the Sufis who remained, some succeeded in becoming the trusted advisers of Jenghis Khan and were behind the successful administration by which Khan governed his conquered lands. These included *Mahmud Yalavaj* and his son *Mas'ud Yalavaji*.

In the convulsions of the next two centuries the Khwajagan continued without interruption their task of teaching the way of accelerated spiritual development and of preparing an élite through whom this influence was carried through Asia, Europe and North Africa.

The "underground" group may have withdrawn into the mountain passes of the Syr Darya River where the great cave systems would allow the unsuspected existence of a spiritual community completely withdrawn from the world.

During the actual Mongol invasion the Khwajagan was led by *Khwaja Arif Rivgerevi*, fourth successor of Gujduvani. He was followed by *Mahmud Fagnavi* and then by *Azizan Ali*. By the time he succeeded to the leadership in the middle of the 13th century, the Mongol Empire had reached its maximum expansion and it was safe for the Khwajagan to reappear openly. The spiritual techniques which they brought with them from their half century of withdrawal came as a surprise to many Sufi orders who had remained "in the world".

Orthodox Sufi orders had no previous knowledge of some of these techniques which included the Halka or group, the Sohbat or conversation between teacher and disciple, the Zikr or spiritual exercise and the Mujaheda, constant vigilance with one's own weaknesses. They also used methods of "awakening" by means of shocks and surprises. They also promoted practical enterprises in ordinary life.

Azizan Ali is credited with great spiritual powers. He could communicate with his fellow Masters and with disciples at a distance. He could read the thoughts of disciples and was known as a healer using hypnotism.

Azizan Ali was succeeded by his son *Ibrahim* and later by *Mohammed Baba of Semas*. His fourth successor was the *Sayed Emir Kulal Naqshband* founder of the Naqshbandi order which has spread throughout the world.

Kulal as a youth was taking part in a wrestling match when Baba Semasi caught his eye. He immediately stopped wrestling and became his disciple. Later he was to become the instructor of *Sayed Bahauddin Naqshband* whose birth had been foretold by Samasi.

Bahauddin Naqshband had marks of saintliness from his childhood and at his Halka, as a mere boy, he saw Abdul-Malik Gujduvani seated on a throne with his successors around him. Bahauddin is said to have inherited the *baraka* of Gujduvani.

Bahauddin left the circle of Emir Kulal and joined the Halka of *Mewlana Arif of Dikkeran* with whom he travelled in search of a group known as the Ahl-i-Hakk (The People of the Truth). When Mevlana Arif died, Bahauddin spent a short time with a Turkish Sheikh called *Kasim* at Bokhara and then served for twelve years under another Turkish Sufi, *Halil Ata*, who was counsellor to the Sultan. Bahauddin accompanied him to court, but had no wish to inherit court appointment. Many of his own pupils, however, were to become teachers and counsellors to princes and rulers of many nations.

Bahauddin's place in the tradition of the Masters is not that of one who founded a new order, but of one who by dint of many years' search synthesized the individual techniques of many teachers and passed the composite techniques to his own followers.

The Naqshbandi Order claim that they are the successors of the Khwajagan and have inherited their *baraka* and their knowledge.